FROM RUSTY

2002

Forthcoming Books by Karla McLaren

Further into the Garden: *Discovering Your Chakras**
Your Aura and Your Chakras: *The Owner's Manual*
Emotional Genius: *How Your Emotions Can Save Your Life*
Healing for Healers: *How to Give Without Giving it All Away*

*see back page for ordering information

REBUILDING THE GARDEN

HEALING THE SPIRITUAL WOUNDS
OF CHILDHOOD SEXUAL ASSAULT

KARLA McLAREN

Laughing Tree
Press

COLUMBIA, CALIFORNIA

Original cover painting by Ann Koziol.
Cover design by Kath Christensen Graphic Design.

This book presents powerful healing techniques for survivors of childhood sexual trauma. If you intend to use the information in this book, you must take this work seriously and with clear intent, or confusion may result; therefore, the author and publisher cannot assume liability or responsibility for actions inspired by information in this book. Since you are prescribing for yourself, use your own best discernment, or consult a holistic psychotherapist, medical expert, or trained healer for specific applications to your individual situation. Please, approach this work with due caution, spiritual intelligence, and a deep sense of personal responsibility.

First Printing 1997
Library of Congress Catalog Card Number: 96-95404
ISBN 0-9656583-0-9

This book is printed on recycled paper.

To the courageous people whose souls I studied:
you were never my students; you were my teachers...
you are my friends.

CONTENTS

PREFACE

People who were not molested in childhood, God bless them, rarely understand why so many sexual assault survivors stay so sick for so long. Looked at from a rational and somewhat shallow viewpoint, it must seem odd that we sexual assault survivors don't manage very well. We are probably the most analyzed, workshopped, re-birthed, twelve-stepped, and pandered-to group on the planet, yet most of us battle ever onward with depression, panic disorders, addictions, weight and eating problems, sexual dysfunction, reproductive illness, multiple personalities, or schizophrenia.

Even high-functioning survivors, though we aren't outwardly ill, often find ourselves trapped in loveless relationships, belittling jobs, or other spirit-engulfing situations. Most of us, after a while, give up on the idea of a happy life, and settle instead for quiet desperation, seasoned with a reasonable number of suicidal episodes.

Though most of us have had a ton of therapy, I think very few survivors of molestation and incest have grasped the spiritual essence of childhood sexual assault: in one confusing, stomach-churning moment, our childhoods ended, and our initiation into a kind of warrior's life began. This powerful event, so often belittled in our spiritually and sexually ignorant society, placed us directly in the center of the opposites: of good and evil; of love and hatred; of wisdom and stupidity; of mercy and vengeance; of consciousness and unconsciousness; of victim and perpetrator; of light and dark. There was no turning back—no forgetting— no getting on with life. In that moment, we aged a thousand years, as our spirits entered into the eons-old battle between viciousness and love. All of us have played our parts in the warrior mode, as victims, as emancipators, and as perpetrators against ourselves or others.

Any current book (and there are many) about healing for survivors of molestation will contain a laundry list of the myriad social, emotional, and physical effects of childhood sexual assault. *Rebuilding the Garden* contains concrete (if somewhat unusual) centering, separating, and healing techniques to address the core of all molest-centered issues, which is that the energy and the intention of the molestation is still lodged inside each of our bodies, making life nearly uninhabitable.

Sexuality is an act of procreation, certainly; but it is also an act of bonding on an energetic level. Sexual contact connects our bodies, our emotions, and our energy patterns to those of our partner. As adults, we can easily recall the attitudes, emotions, and bodily sensations engendered by lovers long since gone. In most cases, we can still see the changes in lifestyle and personality structure that the relationship fostered.

The same is true for molested children, but our little bodies and untested personalities were essentially torn asunder and programmed for destruction by tragically inappropriate sexual contact. We too remember the attitudes, emotions, and bodily sensations of our first sexual relationship. We've experienced changes in lifestyle and personality structure in response to it—changes that have haunted and tormented us throughout our lives. *Rebuilding the Garden* addresses these destructive changes immediately, then moves swiftly towards real separation, real therapy, and real health.

When the separation process taught in *Rebuilding the Garden* is mastered, many of the psycho-social and behavioral markers that typify molest survivors lessen in intensity, or disappear altogether. In essence, the use of spiritual healing tools can heal that which decades of mind-and-emotion-centered therapy cannot. With energy work, the restoration of the central being, and the removal of the damaging foreign energy of sexual trauma, is entirely possible.

We are spirits *in* bodies, not one thing or the other. As we near the end of the century, it is high time to rescue spiritual healing from the ridiculous fringe markets and bring it to bear on real problems. *Rebuilding the Garden* does just that.

An important note: this book is non-sexist in intent, which has made referring to *the molester* very important. At times, I refer to molesters as him or her, but I have tried to even out the male references with the female. It is vital for each of us to understand that human evil lives equally in both genders. Accusing and bashing men or women in toto is not only idiotic, it is damaging to each and every one of our souls. Sexual assault is not about issues of sexuality or gender—it is a twisted and ultimately self-immolating grasp for power over others. Weak people of both genders are deeply susceptible to the notion that they can control others; men *and* women molest children.

ENTERING THE GARDEN

Though I would soon enter a closed group of women who were victims of incest, whose emotional experience was closer to mine, my molest-healing journey began in a drop-in group at a rape crisis center. In those early days, hearing other women's assault stories helped me to uncover my own rage and nausea about my long-ago, long-buried assault. After a few weeks, though, the stories became too immediate and frightening. It became difficult for me to deal with all the pain in that room, especially when the women speaking had fresh, visible cuts and bruises.

One night, when the newest woman began to tell us about the assault she had lived through the previous evening, I panicked. I drew my legs up to me, hugged them tight and folded up. I needed to get away. Though I was breaking therapy etiquette, I stopped listening and essentially left the room. Her story went on right across from me, but inside my head I began to hear another: a story, strangely enough, about a garden.

In my mind, I stood outside an intricately carved wooden gate and saw a lovely, long-haired woman tending to a beautiful and vibrant walled rose garden. The woman saw me, smiled, and suddenly I was inside the garden and safe in her arms. I know I was as tall as she, but she smoothed my forehead and kissed me as if I were a child. She showed me to a marble bench and went to tend her plants.

As I watched, her loved ones came and enjoyed the garden: they sat and read in a quiet spot, they admired all the flowers (but did not take any; they were hers) and they played in the streams that coursed through her garden like laughter. Through it all, this woman was in control of the people and the growing things, but it was a form of control I had never seen before, and couldn't understand. Her garden was safe and private, but not at all exclusionary; it was sacred, but not mysterious, and it was completely inviting without being completely open. I sat and tried to breathe her alien world into me.

I closed my eyes and looked inside my own life for such a garden, for some private space of my own, but found nothing—no light, no sound; nothing. When I looked up to get my bearings again, the beautiful woman and her garden were gone, and I was utterly alone in a dark and barren place. Not knowing what else to do (and not wanting to go back and hear that rape story), I stayed in the dark and waited quietly for something—anything else to happen.

After a while I heard a sound, a quiet, rusty creak. I became quite still, breathing as softly as I could, eyes and ears intently focused on the silent darkness. Another creak, and I pinpointed the sound. I got up and inched towards the sound, and as if in encouragement, the creak became louder until I was able to make out the faint silhouette of a small doorway in a large rock wall. I could now see that the creak was coming from a battered hinge in the doorway, where the splintered remnants of a door hung, swinging slowly from side to side. Though I couldn't see anything beyond this doorway, I knew that it led to a garden.

I stooped to enter, and suddenly there was light enough to see, at least those things nearby. I saw utter destruction: filth, uprooted plants, statues smashed to bits, and puddles of foul and brackish water. There was no sun, no sound but the creaking of the hinge, no water flowing—no life. I knew this place, immediately and without a doubt of any kind. This murdered place was my garden. This was the center of my soul.

A small look was all I could bear. I had no urge to stay. As I fled to safety, I noticed for the first time that the place I called my center was a makeshift, ill-defined area outside all of the darkness. My center was completely separate from my garden. In essence, the center I knew and used sat somewhere outside and to the left of my soul.

I immediately saw the connection between my ruined garden and my ruined childhood. The doorway in my rock wall was only big enough for a small child, and the statues, though broken, were clearly representations of characters in my favorite bedtime stories. My garden had been destroyed during my childhood, and it had stood there waiting, untouched and unhealed, until this very night. This garden was not a lively, growing sanctuary; it was the place in which I had stored my experience of molestation.

It became clear as never before that sexual assault is a form of emotional and spiritual breaking and entering: sheer reckless vandalism. There was no sexuality, no gender-fight in my garden—there was only an ugly stench of brutality. I saw that sexual assault is simply a destroyed person's attack on an unprotected person—nothing more, nothing less.

My childlike inner beauty, my burgeoning sense of separateness and control—these were things my molester couldn't allow me, or anyone around him, to have (he brutalized his own family and molested other neighborhood children as well). His seductive offer of forbidden sex, his avowed deep longing for me, his "adult" secrets, all were his way to weasel into my garden—into my soul. Sexual assault was the weapon he used to destroy it.

I had been deeply wounded in an essential and private place, wounded in the very center of my spirit, but because I did not know of my spirit, I was unable to find the wound. Even when I began a course of intensive psychic study at the age of ten, this wound went unexplored. Even now, in this day of the trendy and over-commercialized New Age, our culture has no vocabulary and no context to explore or celebrate or even discuss the spirit.

Since the lasting wound of sexual assault occurs in a quiet spiritual center that no one ever mentions, it is very hard for assault survivors to understand why they don't get better. Even after psychotherapy, body work, twelve-step programs, fasts, vision quests, primal screaming, re-birthing, or meditation—they don't get better. The wound remains open and unhealed, in the sense that a private door was kicked in, an inner life was violated, and a garden was uprooted and defiled.

Sexual assault ejected me from the center of my own life. Because I am human, I found a way to survive and go forward without any real connection to myself, and without ever healing. My suicidal, over- or asexual victim's stance, decades past the actual molestation, stemmed from the buried, unspeakable knowledge that I had no real center—no self to protect or honor.

In my garden, it was all I could do to balance on the twisted leg of an overturned bench, wrap rotted vines around my beauty, and try to shield myself behind a shattered door. Though I soon exited and created a separate,makeshift center, I saw myself as that garden: defiled, dead, worthless. It took twenty-three years of this sadness before I realized that the true center of my spirit was a wild, untended disaster area.

Entering group therapy was a life saver, but it was also a horror, because it forced me to re-live the anguish that had brought my life, so many years after the molest, to a dead stop. That night, the anguish was too real, and hearing this other woman's rape story—rape after rape after rape—was unbearable. There was no protection left in me. Her rape, her wound, was mine, but not mine. When I finally lifted my head and saw my group-mate wondering, focusing on me, I told her of a garden that was hers, but not hers.

As I spoke, though, I saw something inside the woman whose story I did not want to hear. Although her garden had been vandalized, it wasn't dead or dark like mine, and she was not destroyed. She was standing just outside of her garden, confused but well, and she was here in therapy, getting support and information about her right to safety, privacy, and respect. She could find her way back to wholeness. She could rebuild because *she was not her ruined garden*. She was the gardener!

She owns the seed and channels the water. She has the mortar and hinge and rosewood. She creates the statues, she builds the gates, and she designs the walkways. She can repair all the damage, because she is not that ravaged garden. She is the gardener, and so am I! And so are we all.

That night, I knew: I could go forward from there into wellness. The psychic and spiritual healing skills I had worked with since the age of ten would build the foundation for a new life. I also saw that I could help others along their way, and keep them safe and sane while they went back and re-created their inner lives, or their gardens. I suddenly thought: my God, all the pain wasn't pointless. I might have an answer, not just for me, but for other molested people as well.

I began to teach a class called Rebuilding the Garden, and the results were astounding. People were actually able to move onward, to rebuild and begin to live again. With each class I gave, I moved onward as well. I learned what to expect, what not to do, and how to make each skill and exercise safer. Most importantly, I learned how to maintain a sense of spiritual ethics when working with the suicidal urges, rages, and furies that all assault survivors must address. I even found a way to work with less intense emotions so their surprisingly useful messages could be deciphered more easily.

Now, I know that my Garden class is a powerful tool for moving onward from the horrid aftermath of childhood sexual trauma. Writing this book and offering this information on a wider scale is the next step in my healing. I hope reading it can be a healthy next step for you as well.

There is much to be designed and repaired, built and planted, but it can all be done. The skills, tools, and energy are within each of us. All we need to do is learn a little about the world of spirit; about seemingly new but very old concepts like grounding, centering, separating from others, and about communicating as spirits.

Childhood sexual assault has been a life sentence for so many of us, but it doesn't need to be any longer. Internal peace, love, laughter, and safety are our birthright, and absolutely no one and no experience can take them away. We have survived a situation that no sane person would wish on their worst enemy, and we made it through. Now, we can step out of the world of constant survival and re-create a garden of rich, constant, healing growth that will live at the center of each of our souls. The healing home we have sought for so long has been, as Dorothy of Kansas found, within each of us all along.

This book is set up in three parts. The first section is a beginning meditation and healing class which will give you the skills you most likely lost during your molestation. The second section contains a series of cleansing, separating, and healing processes which will allow you to move forward in life and consciousness—to move on to a new place with yourself and others. The third section offers a more advanced set of skills, and a Troubleshooting Guide to help you live your life a bit more comfortably after you have separated from your molest experience.

Before you actually start, skim through the book and look at the illustrations. Get a feeling for what we will be doing. I've made these processes as simple and fun as I can, but they do require you to change your usual way of relating to people and situations. Clearly, I think I've found a wonderful healing method (or I wouldn't have taken ten years to write this book), but it may not be your method. Do not consider this to be a lack of spirituality on your part. If this way is not your way, you'll know.

The spiritual, psychic focus of this book may be uncomfortable for you. This I can understand. Remember, *you* perform the healing miracles in your life. This book doesn't need to have any part in your healing. You have everything you need to be well. If you just can't understand or work with this particular method, you're not a failure. This is not the only answer. This book shares just one of many ways to recover.

GETTING REAL

Aren't metaphorical stories lovely? And don't they make you want to scream when you're trying to work through an intense personal difficulty that just won't translate into the metaphor? Heroic journeys are great adventures, and at certain mystical points in our lives, we can all make the precise shifts outlined in these beautiful, mythical tales. But how can we translate the story of the Garden into our everyday struggles with trust, boundaries, rage, addictions, and sexuality?

How do we create a Garden in the middle of going to work, doing our laundry, and balancing our checkbook? Where does the Garden fit in at, say, the muffler shop, or a family reunion, or when we're out of control and bellowing at our loved ones—or curling into the fetal position and dreaming of never-ending sleep? What does it look like, what does it feel like, how do people *act* when their Gardens are alive and growing?

If I could point to one marker that defines a survivor of childhood molestation, it would have to be the sense of alienation—of watching "normal" people and feeling consistently and inexplicably shameful and out-of-place—of being completely separate, completely outside the regular world. Using the Garden metaphor helps place that alienation in an understandable context. If a person has been kicked out of his own center, then of course he will feel alienated, in nearly every place and in nearly every relationship he encounters. Molest survivors *don't* fit in! Forget about the exterior world of family and job and relationships-- molest survivors don't fit inside their own hearts and souls!

Therapy, psychiatry, body-work, and heroic journeys can help to move molest survivors away from the terror of their inner lives. Sexual victimization, however, especially in childhood, creates a wound in such a deep and integral place that it does not always respond to emotional, intellectual, or physical release.

Sexual assault has been called the Murder of the Soul, which is beautifully dramatic, but far too dark. Through my work as a psychic healer, I've seen first-hand that the soul does not die; however, it does become severed, dissociated, and seriously wounded. A wounded soul will respond only partially to therapies that do not recognize or address its place in the often silent center of the psyche and the personality.

The message of the Garden is this: a wounded spirit needs a spiritual healing, a rebuilding of the central foundation of the self, which I call the Garden. In addition, a severed, alienated individual needs to be re-attached, to be taken out of the darkness, and placed once again in the center of a healthy, growing, knowable inner self. When that shift has been made, many of the markers of the survival mode (emotional volatility, addictions and compulsions, suicidal tendencies, weight problems, anorexia, impossible relationships, asexuality, hyper-sexuality, disease) will become unnecessary and unappealing.

The way we get back to the Garden may seem unusual at first, because we have to start over as children, spiritually speaking. When we were children, our burgeoning spirits received a terrible blow. When "normal" kids were learning to speak, to fit into their families, to ride their bikes and to scam cookies from their moms, we were learning about terror, perversion, and the lurid power of sexuality. Many of us were also learning how to leave our bodies and our realities during the assaults—to dissociate and survive.

Spiritual healing for us has to start at the very beginning, at getting us to own our bodies: to stay in them, to like them, to protect them, and to be proud of them. By now, many of us have learned emotional, intellectual, and even physical protection techniques, but very few of us know how to protect our spiritual territory. That territory originates in our bodies, so our first job will be to get ourselves back inside of them.

Don't groan at the thought of spending years on this process. As you will soon learn, spiritual healing can occur in a split second. You know how long it can take to heal emotions, and bodies can be in an absolute time warp when you're trying to lose weight, but the spirit—wow! Once you get comfortable with skills like grounding and centering, destroying images, and burning contracts, you'll be hopping along in a most expert and superior way! Of course you have to keep at it once you start, because even a perfect Garden will look horrid if it's neglected, but I think you'll have fun.

This work is very simple. We'll be learning the basics of self-communication and spiritual safety. There is no need to throw out your religion or belief system in order to understand and use these techniques. This work will help you clarify your life by clearing your assault's mental, emotional, physical, and spiritual residue from your present-day behavior. It shouldn't require you to disavow any teaching of any kind.

Much of this book deals with skills anyone can use, and there are many sections where references to molestation cannot be found for pages and pages. This is very important to me. I don't need to brand you and bring you back with the constant reminder that you are a survivor of molestation. If you picked up this book, you already know that.

I'd like to see us move beyond our traumas, so I won't tell you scary stories about the terrible abuses that I and some of my students experienced. I'll also try not to dwell on how hard it is for molest survivors to function. It can be very healing to finally stand up and identify ourselves as victims of childhood trauma, but a lengthy over-identification with such pain can cause more separation and difficulty, not less.

This book is about identifying and then moving beyond those old difficulties, about moving away from victim consciousness and out of survivalistic psychological functioning. This book is about healing the spirit of what happened so that you can rediscover your own true spirit, and your own limitless healing energy.

Before you were molested, you were a normal human being, which means *you still are*. Underneath your survival techniques, defensive postures, flashbacks, and trauma, you are still the complete, brilliant, creative, intrinsically meaningful spirit God sent here. You have the right to read this book as a grand and beautiful, normal human being, and not as a collection of symptoms, quirks, and neuroses.

We don't need to live in the shadow of molestation, constantly defining ourselves by how well we are forgetting, minimizing, forgiving, or resisting our memories or our molester. We must create an inner foundation that does not rely on any outside experience. We must create a Garden—a sanctuary inside our own bodies—where we can experience peace, security, and revitalization, *no matter what is going on in our lives*.

Through working with energy and spiritual communication, we can restore what has been taken and repair what has been smashed. We can remove ourselves from the category of victims or survivors. We can step into a world of freedom, simply by stepping through that splintered gate with the knowledge that we have everything we need to rebuild and re-fortify the Garden we will soon call home. We can embrace our world with all its beauty and all its horror. We can balance light with dark.

Rebuilding our inner sanctuaries can be the most exhilarating, powerful, and joyous time imaginable. That we are using psychic as well as psychological tools, that we are edging into the goofy, nutty fruitcake, karma-covered New Age territory—none of that matters. What matters is that we become well again, and that we live in peace and safety in this crazy world. We can get there from here.

AND NOW, THE WARNING: Change is wonderful and change is vital, but most living systems will resist change. This resistance, this *stasis*, is also wonderful and vital. Both are needed in a healthy body, a healthy family, a healthy community, and a healthy society. However, because we are trained to look at one thing or another, and very seldom both, we objectify change and stasis as good or bad depending on our situation.

We love it that our bodies utilize stasis and continue to run and maintain their weight when we forget to eat, sleep, and care for ourselves, but we hate it when they utilize stasis and won't drop weight just because we want to get into summer clothes. Conversely, we love changes when they benefit us, and hate them when they don't. We aren't trained to take the long view and see change and stasis as equal parts in a perfect and healthy continuum.

This book will change your life, which means that your life and the people in it will attempt to utilize stasis in order to keep you from changing. Though your people may drive you out of your mind, and their "stay as you are" tactics may actually feel unsafe and unsettling, stasis just *is*. When people slow you down and question you and threaten you and get in the way of your change, it means they consider you a part of their universe. By stifling you, these people are protecting you, their universe, and the status quo. This pull for stasis is a sign of a working (though not necessarily healthy) system that is being shaken up by your steps toward consciousness.

I don't want to sugar-coat this stasis stuff. My early attempts at healing got me hit and yelled at and thrown out of my marriage. I see now that my husband was grasping for stasis and trying to protect me from the pain of change, but that his relating skills were stunted and inadequate. By the same token, my stunted relating skills led me to choose that marriage. My efforts at healing and change did not create the lack of kindness which permeated our marriage; my healing efforts just brought that lack to the surface, where I could finally look at it, and then choose otherwise.

My point is this: you may at this moment be living in a molesting, degrading environment where safety is not readily available. This is often true for people who were molested as children, because, in many ways, chaos and fearful situations feel normal; they feel like home. Nothing will change this fact unless you change your idea of home. When you change, stasis must awaken and call to you.

Depending on your environment, stasis may come at you in the form of concern, interruptions and increased attention from others, criticism and derision to bring your self-worth back to a manageable low, or physical violence to keep you fearful and under control. All interference needs to be addressed verbally, through separation techniques included in this book (such as destroying images and burning contracts), or legally, but you must understand that interfering people are only trying to help you live up to the relationships you have agreed upon together.

When we enter into relationships of any kind, we make psychic contracts stating which behaviors are acceptable, who does what to whom, how we will all look and react, and on into infinity. In many cases, molested people create and nurture relationships that require them never, ever to change. In this way, chaotic and abusive relationships actually help molest survivors to ignore their dreadful memories. They can pretend that their unhappiness lives in the present—a present that keeps them so busy surviving that they don't have energy to look under the surface of their current pain. This uncomfortable stasis in the external world helps to protect molest survivors from the terror of their inner lives.

This is not just a condition of molest survivors, though. Even in healthy relationships, the freedom to make sudden change is rarely a part of unconscious contracts. When one makes changes, contractual partners may feel a right to re-examine those unconscious contracts and force compliance in whatever way they can. This is not a bad thing in itself. It just *is*. Often, people who won't allow change are simply trying to protect a position and a relationship that was agreed upon over time—whether the parties were conscious of it or not. It is immeasurably helpful to remember this fact when working through this book.

In this work, we have a very large number of separation and safety tools to help us make our vital changes without pulling a huge blob of stasis down onto our lives, but it is important to realize that stasis is a vital, irreplaceable aspect of nature.

Once our healing tools are a part of us, and our lives and bodies have accepted new ideas like grounding and centering and healing our auras, they will become a part of our new stasis, and we won't have to consciously ground and heal ourselves every day. These changes will become a part of us, and they won't be considered foreign or threatening. Soon, any threats to our new-found healing abilities will pull a blob of protective stasis over our auras and our grounding, and we'll know we've moved on to a new place in consciousness. We will have forged a new contract.

As we move on in consciousness, we will most likely move on in our relationships as well. This can feel lonely and frightening if we don't realize what's happening. As I made my changes, I became disconnected from my entire nuclear family, but now have a series of friends and relations who are my spiritual family. Stasis helped me realize that I was losing something that had importance, but change helped me to know I was moving on to something closer to my real self. Both change and stasis are necessary in any real forward movement, and both will alternately challenge and support you throughout your life.

As you move onward, your old ways of living will call to you. Sometimes, they will scream. If you can know the calls as stasis and thank them for protecting you, you will move on more gracefully. If calls for stasis come from the people in your life, no matter how painfully loud the calls are, you can see them as love offerings and safety messages of one kind or another. If you can see the concern behind the calls, and address your people from that knowledge (instead of from an ignorant peevishness), you will not only move on more gracefully, but you will bring light into the lives of those around you.

It's important to note, as you make the changes to come, how people react, and how they attempt to maintain the status quo. You may be very surprised, in the weeks and months ahead, at who supports you with concern and attention, and who hinders you with violence and shame. Your circle of friends may change in startling ways as your energy changes, but soon, you will reach a new stasis, and create a new contractual foundation for your life and relationships. The key here is to remove yourself from people who try to maintain stasis at the cost of your health and sanity.

If you are not currently able to remove yourself from an abusive environment, please skip ahead and read the chapter in Part II called *Burning Contracts*, and keep yourself safe until you can get away. If you want to stay in an abusive relationship (to people, work or living arrangements, or drugs), I would ask you to put this book down and stop right here.

This work exists to navigate you out of the inevitable downward spiral abusive habits or environments provide. You will begin to break away from old patterns. You will shake up your world. If you're ready to move on, this shake-up is excellent. If you want to stay where you are, and you are being abused or abusing yourself, this work will create terrible upheavals. When these shake-ups happen, your lack of resolve will turn them into full-scale, inescapable dramas--instead of interesting detours in your journey home.

The real warning is this: don't go any further if you want to stay where you are. It is a very dangerous thing to undertake a spiritual journey if you have no intention of ever getting anywhere. Please, if you want to stay where you are, accept my regards and *put this book down*. There are many paths to wellness besides this one. You have the time to honor stasis in your own present-day world. Your change may need to come later.

However, if you're ready to go, turn the page and let's get started.

PART I

BEGINNING MEDITATION & HEALING

Your body is your country
and there are many points of entry.
You should put immigration officers everywhere.

Sri Swami Satchidananda

BEGINNING MEDITATION & HEALING

A ROOM OF YOUR OWN

I began my metaphysical training at the age of ten when my female family members joined a group that studied with a trance-medium, or channeller. Channelling was not then the cottage industry it is today; we were just a bunch of folks listening to the life and health information of an interesting spirit. The experience wasn't inherently dangerous, yet it turned out to be damaging, because all of us in the group began to depend on the trance-medium for answers we should have been learning to give ourselves. By the time I left at seventeen (okay, they threw me out for consorting with outsiders), the group was filled with bright and dedicated, but mostly lost people.

Real, useful spiritual knowledge came from a loony, contentious psychic study center in northern California. On my first shy-but-cocky visit there, I was told, "You're not in your head! Get in your body and get grounded!" Huh? What? I thought the center members would pay homage to my studious and precocious spirituality, but instead they treated me as a pest, because energetically, I was truly chaotic.

For the next few years, on and off, I took classes, gave healings, and learned how to use my intuition in real and useful ways. I learned energy techniques like grounding, spirit communication, psychic healing, and yes, how to get in my body and stay there. Though the center was filled with turmoil, I learned to be a safe and responsible psychic instead of a chaos-filled, vision-besotted crazy person (though to some, the distinction is quite vague).

When I left the center, (actually, *they* threw me out for asking too many uncomfortable questions about their fees), I began rather sheepishly to offer healings and classes. Soon, I found my own way, my own gifts and information, and my own abilities. My work changed and unwound from the center's psychic-power-and-control ideas to include a great deal of the information I had learned from that original trance-medium (whose spiritual, love-and-responsibility-centered information was frowned upon at the center).

Within all the fun and wacky stuff I picked up at the center, the most important thing was that the concept of being out of the body was not psychic mumbo-jumbo. It is a very real state of being, especially for people who have experienced sexual or physical assault at an early age. In the world of psychology, the state of being out of the body and ungrounded is called *dissociation*.

In the broadest explanation, dissociation is an alteration in consciousness that occurs in response to extreme physical or emotional stimuli. It is thought of as a protective mechanism, and ranges from the simple act of fainting in response to sudden or overwhelming sensations, to the complete splitting seen in people with multiple personality disorders (who, it is interesting to note, are almost exclusively survivors of childhood sexual trauma). Dissociation at this level is purely unconscious—it is a reaction that may help to insure survival in the face of uncertainty. Dissociation, though, can become a learned response, especially if unbearable physical and emotional stimuli are repeated.

Survivors of repeated childhood sexual assaults are often masters at dissociation, and in this they resemble, strangely enough, prisoners of war and kidnap-torture victims. The symptoms all three types of survivors experience are remarkably similar. These can include night terrors and flash-backs, phobias and delayed stress reactions, suicidal depressions, weight, drug, and eating problems, and an uncanny ability to traipse headlong into dangerous situations and relationships.

Here's my theory: during childhood sexual trauma—when any real sense of safety and "self-ness" disappears, when Gardens are defiled—the conscious minds of molested children simply leave the world as we know it. This leaves the unconscious to deal with and record the trauma. Coming back into their bodies afterwards, these children soon find that the somewhat simple world they once knew is no longer available. From that moment on, they learn to survive as best they can, without an anchor, without a net, without a childhood, and without a center. Their center, or their Garden, becomes the unconscious storehouse for their trauma.

Because they have no "home" to go back to, these survivors usually learn to use dissociation as a matter of course—as an all-purpose protective device. In their after-event lives, molest survivors will often unconsciously seek traumatic relationships and situations that help them to trigger their dissociative abilities. This after-event dissociation acts as a stress-relieving tool that keeps their attention off of their inner selves and helps them to maintain a safe distance from their remembered trauma. Getting close to their center, and focusing attention back on their bodies, is usually too scary and intense. For many survivors of deep trauma, the process of dissociating actually relieves their pain and tension.

Dissociation is a very powerful and life-altering event, one that can insure survival in the face of danger and suffering, but without conscious awareness of their ability to dissociate, survivors of trauma may set up a post-assault life which approximates their trauma. If they do, they can utilize the wonderfully powerful escape-hatch of dissociation over and over again. People stuck in this kind of endless, uncontrolled loop don't even realize that they are not living in the present, or in their bodies.

The present—where the sun is shining and doors are unlocked and hands do not grasp at them—has very little impact on dissociated people. Because they have split off and abandoned part of themselves to their nightmare, they cannot move away from their life-altering trauma.

No matter how much forgetting they try to do, or how much "getting on with it" they attempt, split and dissociated people cannot get away from the terror. They cannot get back to their ruined Gardens, and cannot find their way back to sunlight. These people are stuck in a raw, unconscious survival mode. The unconscious cannot possibly forget what happened, but the conscious self refuses to remember, and probably seeks dissociation on a daily basis.

From a psychic viewpoint, split people are fascinating to watch. Their bodies walk around just like anyone else's, but their conscious awareness sort of hovers nearby. What I like to see is a spirit planted firmly inside the body, with focused energy and awareness behind the eyes--split people can't manage this. The best description I've heard of this constant out-of-body state came from another psychic who said, "Hey, your spirit's got its toes hooked into your eye sockets!" Bet you can't guess who she was talking to.

This splitting is the only way many trauma survivors can function; they live beside their pain, outside of their trampled Gardens, and away from their fearful memories. The part of them that experienced the trauma in its entirety is left utterly alone and utterly unhealed while they float above and apart and play at being normal. This normalcy, though, does not last for very long, because the unconscious must and will throw the stored energies forward. The symptoms (flashbacks, panic attacks, suicidal depressions, the inability to create a non-traumatic life) which trauma victims abhor as unpleasant and even insanity-producing are, in my experience, signs of incredible health and activity.

Follow me on this one. Recent research has proved something people have long guessed: that people in altered states such as anesthesia or coma are still recording everything that goes on around them. Many surgery patients, when put into a hypnotic state, have been able to recite verbatim the conversations they heard while they were completely sedated. Add to that the fact that coma patients, when revived, can sometimes recall the dates and times loved ones visited, and you've got a rather good case for a much larger definition of consciousness than we generally allow.

When we dissociated and left our bodies, or floated above the room in our minds, or went to a fairy-tale world, we still experienced our assault. The part of us that holds the memories (and, as you will find, many, many other parts of us) needs our help—just like it helped us when we needed it, by letting us split off and leave the pain behind.

The flashbacks, the day and night terrors, the constant replay of assault memories, and the surprisingly assault-like jobs and relationships we find ourselves in—these are not signs of chaos and insanity! These are the articulate and inarticulate pleas of the part of us that recorded every moment of our assault. These are calls for help, for healing, and for wholeness, but unfortunately, they tend to drive our consciousness even further out of our bodies.

If I constantly leave my body (which in non-trauma situations means that I am emotionally unavailable and essentially unreachable), my view of the world is that there is only fear, threat, pain and loss, against which I must constantly defend. I may let some love and tenderness through, but still I remain poised, armed against some dreadful future event. I stay separate from most people, because I am protecting myself (or them) from my chaos. I wait and watch, constantly reliving (or trying to eradicate) my painful past, or dreaming of a brilliant future where I find the perfect love and the perfect career, become fabulously rich, and cure all disease. I do not have time for the meaningless boredom of the present. I am very well defended, but I am not alive.

If I do by chance enter my life, I see that I am going nowhere and am in unbearable pain. I am desperately lonely, ugly, inherently flawed, unable to relate... so I leave again and dream of the future, but make no real, in-the-body plans to get to that future. Sometimes I will institute an amazing flurry of positive changes, followed by an equally amazing and inventive series of sabotaging actions and counter-moves. I may even choose a relationship where my struggles toward health threaten my equally ill partner. My life is in a constant limbo.

But, if I try to live in my world, it hurts too much. I remember my assault in bits and pieces, and I see in living technicolor that there is no protection—no avenging God who rescues tiny children from evil. Leaving doesn't work, staying doesn't work, living doesn't work, and the assault never, ever goes away.

Listen: sexual assault memories *don't* go away because they *shouldn't* go away—not until there is something to replace them, some way to heal them, and some way to understand them. The replay, the memories, the physical shadows of touch; none will go away until they have your attention and your help. The psyche, which includes and oversees your conscious and unconscious selves, constantly strives for balance and wholeness. It will replay the moment balance and wholeness were lost until it has answers.

Your psyche will allow you to dissociate for only so long, and then it must re-create wholeness, re-attach your spirit, and find workable answers. When it has answers, your psyche will go on to other issues, but the only way it can get its answers is if you get your consciousness back into your body, listen to yourself, and stop the constant, numbing replay of your trauma.

Creating a satisfying end to flashbacks and replays will make it easier to remain in your body, especially if you have the support of our first energy tool in the Garden class: a meditation center and sanctuary called *the room in your head*.

Many therapies and meditation systems help people create mental sanctuaries, but we'll go one step further, and create this sanctuary within your body, within the present time, and within your actual life.

The room in your head is a private and unreachable place that does not depend on others or on physical surroundings for its peacefulness. It doesn't even require quiet or large blocks of time. It is a place where privacy is always available, and it is inside your body. The room in your head can help to anchor your consciousness in your body by giving you a focal place in which to center your attention.

CREATING THE ROOM IN YOUR HEAD

Here's how to make your room: draw an imaginary line straight backwards from the top of your nose to the back of your head. Now draw another line from the top of your right ear (by that depression behind your cheekbone) to the top of your left ear (see illustration). The point where these two lines intersect will be the center of your room. Make sure that the floor of your room is centered low in your head, at about the middle of your nose, and not any higher. If it's any higher, you could experience dizziness (see the Troubleshooting Guide for an explanation). Create four walls, a floor, and a ceiling—all inside your head. In the front part of this room, there will be two windows (your eyes) with a door between them. Hang a *Do Not Disturb* sign outside this door while you work.

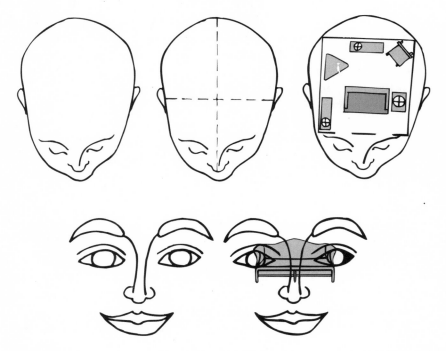

Now comes the fun part: decorate this room in any style you like, but remember that this is your sanctuary. Don't fill it with noise and bustle, or make it inviting to anyone else. Other people are absolutely not allowed in this room. Bring in art and pillows, a hot tub or a fireplace; turn your room into an Egyptian temple, a crystal cave, an old English castle library, or a Mesopotamian pavilion. Do not recreate a room that exists in your life already; instead, make this room your fantasy destination.

Create a luxurious, comfortable seat for yourself right in front of the windows of your eyes, and have them look out on your very favorite nature scene. If they do, you can have a sense of peace and a connection to nature that won't depend on your surroundings. Even in the middle of a traffic jam, you can be looking out on a garden or a forest, or upon the desert at moonrise.

When your room is ready, take your seat in it and practice looking out from behind your eyes. Try staying in your room for a minute or so, but don't worry if you can't just yet. It can take a little practice to actually stay in your body. I've had my room for almost twenty years now, and sometimes I stay out for days or weeks at a time. When I notice this, I don't smack myself, I just get back in; however, I'm always reminded that I never do my best work during these completely out-of-body times.

One very easy way to tell if you're not in your room is to bring your hand towards your face and press the bridge of your nose with your fingers. If you feel your attention being moved back into your head, you probably weren't there to begin with. Another quick way to check in is to notice whether you can see your nose and your eyelashes without focusing on them. If your awareness is centered behind your eyes, your nose and your lashes will always be within your field of view.

Keep working at staying behind your eyes and in your room. If you don't want to be there at all, change the decor or the configuration until you are comfortable. Check in with yourself throughout the day to see how your room or your feelings about it have changed. Don't hesitate to redecorate, and remember that this room can be as opulent or fantastical as you like. It won't cost you anything!

Most people have heard that it is best to Be Here Now, but many assault survivors couldn't *get* here now to save their lives! I had heard over and over again that the only real power lives in the present—that the past is a memory and the future a dream. None of it clicked for me until I got into my body. The room in my head anchored me to the real world because it gave me a place, for the first time that I could consciously remember, to be alone, in control, and at peace. The description that comes up in class about this room is "the control center." I agree with that. Being in your room feels like being in the cockpit of an airplane, in a lookout tower, or on a throne. There's a lot of quiet power inside our bodies.

As for the Be Here Now theory? Each of us lives in a vessel that can only be here now. Our bodies cannot live in the past; they cannot travel to the future; they can only exist in each moment. If we climb into our bodies and sit behind our eyes, we will live in the moment. It's as simple as that.

Since all power exists in the present moment, living in our bodies will give us the power we need to live and grow and heal. Living outside of our bodies and traipsing through past and future has taught us to survive, but not to live. If we are to move through our molest experience and its aftermath, and truly come into the present, we'll need to learn to depend on our bodies--to trust them and ourselves--to support them with our conscious attention. It's the most important thing we can do if we're serious about moving on, because with this in-the-body support, we will finally have the strength to deal with the reality we've been hiding from. We will finally have the strength to deal with the memories.

In every Garden class and at every assault survivor's group I've ever encountered, there comes a point where memories of abuse will spring forth, uninvited and in appalling detail. It always happens, and if the group leader isn't ready for it, the process can be very damaging for the group members involved. People, even the bravest people, would really rather not remember trauma; without competent help, they fight the process and create a grand drama.

Without help, people will leave therapy at this pivotal juncture, go back to battering relationships, and leave their once-proud sobriety behind. This is such a shame, because the painful flow of memories is a sign of a vibrant psychological shift that could be the foundation for finally mending the spirit of the trauma, and breaking out of the prison of repeated dissociation.

When the stored memories begin to emerge, it means that a new level of strength has been reached, or that a suitable support system exists. Suddenly, physical and emotional memories—unexamined for years and even decades—can come forward. Just as suddenly, their challenge can be met by a new, older, wiser, and entirely different person than the child who endured the assault with very little comprehension.

People at this spiritual junction can move away from the need to unconsciously create chaos and pain in the present so that they can dissociate in response (and continue in their once-protective pattern of running from their memories by filling their present lives with chaos).

People at this junction can finally begin to address the actual moment of their split and wounding, and bring it to the surface. With the help of the room in the head and some simple spiritual healing techniques, this surfacing work becomes easy.

When we can get into our bodies and focus our attention on ourselves, we can see ourselves as separate from the world around us. When we know how to create separations, we can begin to separate ourselves from our trauma. Instead of flying off and dissociating, we can calm ourselves down and simply observe, from behind our own eyes.

Suddenly, the burden that had been carried for so long in shadowy memories and flashbacks can be lifted up into the light. With these flashbacks, the psyche is signalling that it is ready to examine the reality of what happened to us. From behind our own eyes in the present moment, we may be surprised to find that we have a remarkable ability to deal with our traumatic memories. We may even find that we can come to our own rescue.

A few weeks after I told the Garden story to the women at the rape crisis group, six of us were spun off into a smaller, childhood trauma-only group. It was such a relief to be away from all the instant, visceral pain of recent rapes, and in with a group of women who knew what it was like to grow up as I did. I felt so at home.

The first night, our group leader had us envision a house. Without my conscious choice, my house became my molester's, and the adult me stood outside the front window watching the toddler me being molested. The horror I felt was indescribable. I wanted to run, but the toddler turned towards the window, begging me with her eyes to do something. I couldn't. No one had stopped my molester—no one had rescued me, so I couldn't rescue her. I shrugged in helplessness, and she screamed at me in fury until her face turned purple and the scene went black. I gasped for air as I came back into group, but was too frightened and ashamed of myself to tell anyone there what had happened.

That night and the rest of the week were absolute hell. I was so suicidal that I scared myself (thoughts of suicide having provided a perverse, at-least-I-can-get-out-of-here comfort up until that point), and I would burst out in tears in public and have to hide. It was so awful that I almost didn't go back to group, but when I did, I had the leader help me to meditate again. The scene reappeared. Without waiting to be asked for help, I broke the glass of that front window with my fists.

This time it was me screaming until my face turned purple. I yelled, I threatened, I stormed, and I frightened my molester away. I brought in helicopters with huge pincher-claws that lifted my molester up and away, and I called in big police dogs and mountain lions to scare him and protect me. I rescued myself in the way I always hoped someone would rescue me. After all the hoopla died down, the toddler and I giggled at each other as only we could, and I got her dressed and carried her out of that house forever.

It did not matter at all (as I had previously and erroneously thought) that the toddler me did not get rescued in the real world. All that mattered was that she was rescued now and could leave that house in the arms of someone who understood what she had gone through. All that mattered was that my psyche had some answers, and a new, more satisfying way to complete the story that had taken up so much of my time and energy. I was able, with that rescue, to create a link between that distrustful child and myself. After the rescue, I created a resting place for her, right beside my comfortable chair in the room in my head.

It was strange at first to think of myself as two separate people, but now it all makes sense. Until I rescued myself from that house and that whole remembered situation, I lived with a gnawing feeling of incompleteness; I knew that something was missing inside me. This feeling more than any other created my sense of alienation. I knew that normal people had something I didn't. Everyone I knew assured me, throughout my life, that I was whole and well, but I didn't feel whole in any sense. I knew instinctively that a part of me was missing.

When I collected the three-year old me from that house, I collected a lot of other things as well. The part of me she represented held not only pain and memories, but a childish sense of optimism; my love for animals and nature; my love of words and writing; my ability to identify dangerous people, and so very much more. My world was simply un-tethered without the support of that strong, angry, intuitive three-year old. In my need to survive, I had shut her away and fragmented; my consciousness left the scene of the crime. It was an elegant and necessary adaptation at the time, but it harmed both of us as our lives went on.

My post-trauma life was frenetically active. One of my unstated duties was to assure my numbed family that I was okay, which I did by becoming very tough. Another duty was to toughen up my little sister, who was also molested by the same man. Another was to try to make it through public school, which for an intuitive, hyperactive little girl with no filters or boundaries whatsoever, was years and years of unrelenting pain.

By the time I left school, I was a 300-year old 16-year old who described herself as, "A thousand layers of memories and experiences gingerly draped over a large bubble filled with nothing." That was a perfect description of a person living without a useable center. My post-trauma life was simply a hodgepodge of memories and opinions with nothing to anchor them, because I had left my center behind, encased in pain and confusion.

After the rescue and after I made a safe nest behind my eyes for my assaulted self, I began to see my life and the people in it in an entirely new way. I became uncomfortable with some people, and much closer to others as my little girl told me (from inside my head, not through crazy unconscious acts) what she wanted in relationships.

I changed my clothing and hairstyle, I changed my eating habits, and I began to see that my life wasn't supporting me in the way I needed it to, or in the way she needed it to. It's funny, because while I was protecting her and creating a safer room and body for her to live in, she was teaching me how to protect myself and live in the way I meant to live before all the carnage descended upon me. Give a rescue, get a rescue, I always say.

What the rescue does is this: it takes the split, assaulted part of your being, the part that has been trying to get your attention in its chaotic and unconnected way, and removes it from the constant trauma of its own memories. When rescued and safe, this split being will be able to begin to move with you through the healing process instead of moving against you. As you shield and protect this aspect of yourself that has gone for too long without love or support or safety, you will both be able to enjoy a much-needed and long-deserved rest.

PERFORMING YOUR OWN RESCUE

After you feel comfortable with the room in your head, (which means you can stay in it for more than a few minutes, and that it is still there waiting for you when you leave and come back to it), try a rescue. Don't be afraid. The assault is not happening to the present-day you. The assault is just a vivid memory in your mind; from within your room, you are all-powerful. You get to say what happens from inside your head.

Can you remember your assault? Mine happened so early in my life that I could only remember flashes: how the room looked, parts of my molester's body, the smells from the kitchen two rooms away. Whenever a memory came up, no matter how small, I or my little girl (if she could) stopped what was going on, and I always ended the scene by forcing the molester away, taking my little girl in my arms, and placing her in a safe nest in the room in my head. However, wherever, or whenever your memories begin, you can create a powerful end to them.

You may want to rush right in with Twirling Machetes of Death, but be cautious. You don't want to scare the wits out of your already-frightened assaulted self. Get in your control seat, let an assault memory come forward, and rescue yourself in a way that feels powerful (the Machetes may work for you—just remember that your assaulted self may not trust anyone, even you, so be observant).

If you can let rationality rest and give full permission to childish thoughts, you'll come very close to what your little one wanted to have happen in a perfect world. Create that perfect world and get your child-self out of there!

Help your little one up, clean them, clothe them, and take them to the room in your head. Create a safe area for them in a secluded part of your room. This area can be in front of a fireplace, in a hammock, in a big claw-foot bathtub, in a nest of pillows and blankets, in a canopy bed, or even in a small cave behind a waterfall.

Whatever your child wants is what they need. They may even want to sit with you in your control chair for a while. That's fine too. This is their room as much as it is yours. Make sure to provide comfort food, toys, quiet games, art supplies, animals, and so on. Make sure your room is home to a convalescing child. Give your child what they want; when you do, you will be surprised to find that it's what you want as well.

For some, this portion of the book will be the biggest stumbling block, because many assault survivors cope by minimizing their experience. They don't or won't rescue themselves because the assault wasn't a very big deal, or it happened to a lot of people, or they can't remember it all that well, or whatever.

A very common minimization is, "Well, I was never penetrated (or the molester was another child), so it wasn't *that* damaging." Minimizers are masters at what I call shallow intellectual healing; they talk a good life, but they don't live it. Minimizers appear healthier than chaotic people whose memories flood their daily lives, but both kinds of survivors are precisely as imbalanced and in need of some form of intervention.

Though they assure everyone that they are fine and really "done with" their molestation, minimizers will often inexplicably find themselves in relationships or situations that resemble the emotional atmosphere of their assault.

Minimizers will have oppressive jobs, marriages without boundaries, long-standing struggles with trust, health, weight, compulsive behavior and more—and it will be the twisted genius of their health-and-wholeness seeking psyches that creates these patterns for them.

When a person refuses to remember a trauma, they will find themselves—again and again—in traumatic situations that force them either to remember, or to dissociate further. Minimizers invariably choose the latter. Minimizers are staunchly defended, but completely unprotected.

Minimizers are often overachievers, or "runaway" healers (people who can fix anyone or anything but themselves) who appear to be extremely capable and together until you get too close to them. Inside, a constant battle rages between the hyper-rational conscious adult and the out-of-control, unconscious molested self. The constant splitting and dissociation these people function within can be absolutely overwhelming.

Minimizers often feel cavernously empty and disconnected; they live in constant fear of being found out as frauds. Though they are often wildly successful out in the world, their inner lives are unbearably noisy. Minimizers spend a great deal of time and energy not listening to the quiet (and ear-piercing) inner voices that cry out for their healing. Often, minimizers become progressively isolated as they age—since they don't listen to themselves, it becomes very difficult for them to hear others.

Minimizers, *hear this*: if you had the most gorgeous body in the world and you walked down Main Street in a shimmery see-through body stocking, and you had on a flashing neon hat that said, "I WANT TO MAKE LOVE!" it would still never, ever be okay for anyone to touch you, let alone have sex with you, without asking!

Your body belongs to you and it always has belonged to you. It doesn't matter where you were or what you wore or what you thought. No one had the right to touch you if you didn't want to be touched, and no one has the right to engage children in sexual relations. Period.

Forget all the qualifying statements and excuses and arguments. Sexual assault is WRONG. Sexual assault is damaging and it affected you. Sexual assault continues to affect you, and it won't go away simply because you refuse to look at it. Trust me on this one!

It is very painful to recall abuse, but in many twelve-step groups it is said that "The pain I may feel by remembering can't be worse than the pain of knowing and not remembering." Yes, it is frightening to get back in touch with your life and accept that unmanageable pain and anguish were your reality, but you can only rescue yourself and begin to heal if you realize that something damaging occurred and that you are dealing with it every single day—whether you want to or not.

You don't have to become a walking testament to helplessness, but the reality of your victimization and the split you experienced (and are still experiencing) must be allowed to come forward. The body remembers; the emotions remember; the spirit remembers; and real healing will only come about when these memories are validated.

Find the words that work for you in this stage, or simply say, "I was confused and frightened and made to be a part of things that felt queasy and awful. I was hurt, and nothing else matters when I get hurt, so I will not pretend to be okay. I never asked to be hurt. I didn't do anything wrong, and I didn't deserve to be assaulted. I couldn't control what happened, and what happened was wrong. I want safety. I want freedom. I want out."

Keep saying this or something like it until you believe yourself. You'll be surprised at how quickly you will respond. Don't close back down when the tears or the emotions come up, and don't run from the memories springing from that little person you once were. These things are not happening in the present. You have power in your own mind and you have safety within your room. Use them and try a rescue.

Even if all you can do is imagine an assault like yours at first, just do it. Create rescue fantasies as often as you can, and soon your ignored and tucked-away younger self will begin to trust and open up once again. You'll need the support and the memories of this little person in order to go further, but they'll need your help to move away from their constant pain and fear. Keep rescuing yourself from imaginary situations, and soon you'll begin to remember what really happened. By then, you'll be a spiritual rescue pro.

After your first rescue, you may find more assault replays coming forward, and even replays of embarrassing situations in your childhood totally unrelated to your assault. This is great! Once your unconscious sees you clearing out, it will pull forward all sorts of things it's been wrestling with. Keep rescuing, amending, learning, and growing. Let the past come forward, meet it with your present day abilities, and let it go.

Don't allow painful memories to dog you and shame you. Meet them from behind your eyes, rescue the person who lived through their trauma, and go forward. Become a master at giving yourself the things you needed in the past. From within your room, you can say the things you should have said, do the things you should have done, and then watch as your present life becomes more peaceful.

Your ability to heal and release your past self from remembered trauma will translate directly into a new ability to care for yourself in the present. When your tremendous backlog of unexamined and unhealed issues begins to be relieved, you will become much more aware of your present needs and discomforts. You will, through rescuing yourself from past messes and discomforts, be able to use your new protective abilities in the present. Releasing energy from your past frees up energy in your present, and since the present is where all power and healing reside, your life will become more workable and livable.

But remember, we are not trying to make the assault disappear—hey presto! That is the kind of thinking which led to our dissociation in the first place. The assault happened, it's over with, and we can't change the facts. What we can do is heal our reaction to the assault; what we can do is heal the split that haunts our present-day lives.

In many situations, what we remember about our assaults may not even be true in the literal world. We may have entwined our real memories with scenes from nightmares and stories, or we may have erased parts of our memories and replaced them with symbolic images. The psyche is filled with powerful stories and scenes, many of which don't translate into the logical, everyday world. Nevertheless, the stories themselves still have deep meaning.

By now, your assault memories will have changed from the merely factual to the deeply personal. Your memories may even have taken on a grandly mythological or archetypal flavor. This is a wonderful shift, as long as you don't take it all at face value and go to the police with your memories.

The tragedy of the false memory syndrome is that, because we don't think mythologically, we can't as a society process the material that is coming out of the collective psyche. When we first heard of the recovered memory arrests, and the devilish child-molesting cults, something awakened in all of us. An awareness of child sacrifice and the endangered world of childhood brought many of us to a new level of understanding about our lives, and about the state of our society. In the years since, when most of these memories were found to be highly suspect, and often untrue, most people, in response, also abandoned the thoughts and awarenesses that the original stories occasioned. It was as if we were all betrayed, and made to look foolish, because we believed those stories.

This new backlash against recovered memories, though it may seem more rational than our previous unthinking acceptance of them, is not an imaginative solution. In both instances, we're missing entirely the mythological content of the stories.

Though the children and adults who are bringing forth recovered memories at this time may not be recounting the literal and legal truth, they are bringing forth a spiritual truth that should not be ignored. Our need to have photographic evidence and concrete, corroborating details has, tragically, ignored the collective psyche's fevered account of our society's daily sacrifice of children.

The collective psyche works in paradox, extremes, undercurrents, and tall tales. If we can interpret psychic messages like recovered memories through a mythological or archetypal framework, we can understand what the collective psyche is trying to say. The essence of the communication is not about dog and cat murders, or ritualized child molestations which turn out to be fabrications. The essence is that the psyche is recounting the child killing and spiritual cannibalism that go on in our world as a matter of course.

In our under-educated, TV-drunk culture, we are fed ideas about ourselves and our world that are not only untrue, but insane. Westerners are lulled into a sense of capitalist peace-and-plenty, where every gosh-darned person can grow up to be president, though almost no one will.

Our self-centered, money-driven culture touts its independence, yet relies completely (and parasitically) on the labor and resources of the rapidly deteriorating third world. We are leaving our children in the care of others to scrabble after money—to make them secure—yet the world we are creating in our unconsciousness nearly ensures our children's peril. We're eating our planet from the inside out, yet we continue to expend our energy on silly externals.

I don't consciously recall a time as deeply disturbed as ours, but I do recall that in historical times of deep strife, myths and stories would pop up to explain and elucidate the situations ancient peoples faced. Often, similar versions of myths would spring forth on different continents at the same time. Though the myths were peopled with giants and dragons, talking stones, and three-headed beasts, their messages were honored and passed onward. People understood that the taller the tale, the truer it was in the deep places of the collective psyche.

Recovered memories often take on mythological proportion. Children and adults report ritual sacrifices, devil-worship, shape-shifting, parents turning into terrifying beings, and large, organized, faceless groups of offenders. Without any mythological, spiritual, or intellectual training, we as a culture made a grave mistake. We took all these stories at face value, and then, when they proved untrue, or only partially true, we rejected them lock, stock, and barrel.

We didn't understand that *something* had happened to the story-tellers, that *something* has happened to our culture, even if that something can't be recounted in ways the police and the courts can process. We missed the entire boat on this one, but this process of rescuing ourselves can help bring that boat back to dock.

With the rescue, we're not pretending we were saved in the past; we're saving ourselves now from the looming shadows of old, unhealed wounds. We're fighting our dragons, we're re-forming our myths, and we're re-engaging our stories in a ritual manner. We're stopping the molest-scenario replays so we can get on with our lives—so we can integrate our molested selves once again.

As we move forward in healing, we need to have conscious access to the little person who experienced the trauma and still lives there, completely aware of just how frightening and wrong the situation was. If we learn the language and dances of the inner world, and maintain contact with that inner person, we won't fall into the minimizer's trap. We'll know exactly how we felt and still feel, and we'll be on guard when assault-like experiences lumber into our present-day lives. We'll protect ourselves by understanding our wounds, and by honoring them.

As adults, we tend to rationalize our pain and pretend that the past didn't affect us. In essence, we make the pain unimportant. When we do this, we make the entire reality of the split self who lived through and lives in unbearable pain completely unimportant.

When we minimize, we don't protect our child-self; we protect our molester by excusing the attack in a whorl of psychobabble. When we pretend to be fine, we protect the family members who failed to help or continued to hurt us; and when we make the excuse that life is just hard, we protect reality itself.

I say this: let reality and all the people in our lives hire their own protection. We need to rescue ourselves from the monsters we fear, heal our unrepeatable reality, and stop de-personalizing our own private experience of hell. We need to rescue ourselves and create safety by knowing that we experienced pain that was as real and true as life itself.

Not going anywhere in life, not living in peace, not truly knowing how to behave around people, relying on relationships for inner peace: these are just some of the characteristics of people who have lost parts of themselves to trauma. These are the people who come to me for classes, and when I see them, they are often at the end of their ropes. People usually don't come to psychic healers *first*.

Nothing they've tried has ever worked, and they begin to consider their quiet despair as normal and unchangeable. They talk or exercise or meditate or drug themselves out of their pain, but it always comes back anew. They get therapy and get on with it until they can't go on anymore. Soon, they begin to think that for some reason, out of all the beings in the universe, they were placed on the planet without all the requisite stuff they need to thrive. Often, they wonder if God has forgotten them, since magic and peace and joy seem consistently to pass them by.

I will tell you what I tell them: as a psychic healer, I've had the chance to see hundreds of spirits with thousands of complaints, and I have never, ever seen an incomplete soul. I do not as a healer have access to a Chock Full O' Chakras or Auras R Us. All spirits are complete. We all have everything we need, and complete access to all information. What we choose to do with what we have is up to us.

When we dissociate and split off, we lose conscious contact with a part of ourselves. Because we sense that something is missing, we begin to live as if we are not whole. We stop our forward movement, and cannot rely on that which is "left over," because of the failure inherent in our sense of loss. We feel abandoned by the world of light and happiness, and unwelcome there. When our lives get too out-of-control, we hit a center of darkness that is unlivable; we have no place left to go. Or so it seems.

Here's what this moment looks like in a spiritual healing, even in the most severe psychic emergencies and suicidal episodes: the person before me sits in a very dark space (their temporary, makeshift Garden), which they have made even darker by squeezing their eyes shut. Right next to them is a vibrant, lit-up, totally impatient version of themselves (usually the little person who lived through the trauma), who absolutely exudes excitement about going forward and taking the next step, scary as it may be. The conscious adult personality, eyes still shut, sits in grief and terror, knowing that such lightness and energy are never to be theirs (because they lost it, then ignored it, and now run from it whenever possible).

Back when I did healings, these were my favorite people to heal. People who were finally in that deep, dark, unconscious place—even when they were wrestling with chaos, suicidal emergencies, and psychotic episodes—were as ready for real change as anyone ever gets. The darkness they experienced was in direct relationship to the light blasting at them from all sides.

When I went in and started to heal such people, their split-self would talk my ear off. I looked like an excellently evolved and powerful psychic, because intense healing information came through, but basically, I just acted as an interpreter for these people's own limitless healing ability.

Or I used to, anyway. See, I never really found a way to make it clear to people that I wasn't doing anything amazing. After the healing, they'd tend to become awe-struck, believing the healing was all about my abilities, and not theirs. This was counter-productive, because they'd give the power of the healing to me almost immediately. Soon, they'd close their spirit eyes again and start the old trouble brewing. That's not healing for anyone.

Now, I simply teach people about the room in their heads and the rescue, and try to stay out of their process as much as possible. When they can get their split-self into their room and into their conscious awareness, that same amazing psychic healing ability becomes available to them, and belongs to them in a way my healing never could. This is much better. If you can get yourself into your body, you'll see what I mean.

If creating your room or completing a rescue are difficult, it is perfectly acceptable to just pretend to do so. Creating the room in your head may be the first conscious contact you've had with your body for a very long time. Your body will usually have a great deal to say to you about this pain here and that person there and these emotions and so on.

This chatter will fade, and the technique called *grounding* in the next chapter will help your body to calm down and pay attention. For now, it is fine to simply establish the space behind your eyes, fill it with things you adore, make yourself a comfortable chair, and look out on your favorite nature scene for as long as you can manage at this point.

I must stress that being in the center of your head should not feel natural to you if you have been dissociated. The focal point of your consciousness could be anywhere. If you're a good athlete or mathematician, your consciousness may hover above and in front of your head, but it could also be behind you, or beside your shoulder. It is natural and healthy for your consciousness to move in its own way. It should drift whenever it likes, but you should have an aware connection with it, and be able to call it to attention whenever you need to.

Your consciousness has had many years of practice in popping into certain areas as you have gone through various life and learning situations. You already have a reading and writing focus, an art or music focus, a cooking and eating focus, a driving or sports focus, a just-before-bed focus, and so on. You may also have a very distant dissociation focus, and a closer-to-the-body, everyday focus to go along with it. Your consciousness already knows how to move, and how to stand still. This exercise of creating a meditative focus can be simplified if you realize that you are merely creating a new center for your consciousness to visit.

You should not try to force your consciousness to stay in the center of your head at all times. This would not only be unnatural and unhealthy, it would be impossible. Your consciousness must be allowed to move as it wishes until you need to center yourself for meditation. Then, it should be able to gather itself behind your eyes as you work.

As an aid, you can simply press your fingers on the top of your nose and usher your awareness back into your room. It's not cheating; I do it all the time. Then, when I'm done with my meditation, I let my conscious focus go wherever it likes. It knows what it's doing.

Remember: we are trying to deal with the past, but we can only do that from the present—from a safe, sane, and centered present. Creating the room in your head is one way to begin to live in the present. The room in your head links you to your body, and offers a sanctuary for both your present-day self and the part of you that lived through the terror of the past. With the techniques ahead, we'll be able to rebuild and heal and process more information, but we've got to have a work-space first.

Take your time and create your room (cave, grotto, throne room, turret, tent, or whatever), even if you can't get into your head at all. If you have difficulties like headaches or visions or strong emotions, don't worry. Just check the Troubleshooting Guide in the back of the book, and you should find some relief. Create a foundation and keep reading. It gets easier.

BEGINNING MEDITATION & HEALING

GETTING GROUNDED

If we've spent a lot of time outside of our lives and our bodies, they may feel very unsafe and disconnected from us. We echo this bodily sense of insecurity in a number of ways: we may feel constantly out of place in social situations; we may over-connect to people or groups in a futile attempt to belong; we may shrink from touch or open displays of emotion; or we may become hermits. Creating the room in the head is a gentle way to say hello to our bodies and begin the process of re-connecting, but our bodies need more than a greeting from us if they are to live in peace. Grounding and connecting to the earth are the next steps.

People can connect with their bodies and the earth in many ways: through touch and body work, through eating, through being out in nature or in water, through contact with animals, or through healthy sex. I call the process of getting into the body and connecting to the present and the earth *grounding*. It is a very simple process that most people do naturally on a regular basis.

If you've ever been lightheaded from not eating and then felt the sigh of contentment as you fed your body the perfect meal, you've experienced grounding. If you've ever melted into the back rub you got from a trusted person at the end of a stress-filled week, you've experienced grounding. Anything that brings you back to the present and back to a sense of pleasure and release is grounding.

People who are not grounded tend to be unfocused, unsettled, stress-filled-and-filling, and heavily invested in controlling everything around them. People who are naturally grounded are usually earthy, centered, and at home in their bodies. The act of grounding tends to center and focus people because it calms their body down, making it a warm and peaceful place in which to live. Controlling others or splitting off become unnecessary, because grounding gives the body a way to control itself, release pent-up energy and emotions, and cleanse itself at all times.

Grounding is an especially important tool for people who have learned to dissociate and leave their bodies in response to stressors. Grounding helps to keep split people centered and in the present, regardless of the chaos going on around them. It is also an excellent aid in creating and maintaining the room in the head, because grounding can help to drain all the crazy-making chatter out of the mind. Grounding can also help in the process of moving assault memories out of the body, which makes living there a much easier proposition.

CREATING YOUR FIRST GROUNDING CORD

Here's how to ground yourself: sit upright in a straight-backed chair with your arms and legs uncrossed and your feet flat on the floor. Get into the room in your head if you can. Place your right hand just above your pubic bone, and your left hand behind you at the base of your tail bone.

Stay centered, and envision a circular energy center inside your pelvis, right between your hands (if you know about the *chakra* system, you'll recognize this center as your first *chakra*. See illustration). This center is usually envisioned as a disk of three to five inches in diameter. This disk faces forward, with colored energy visibly swirling inside it (the color should be red).

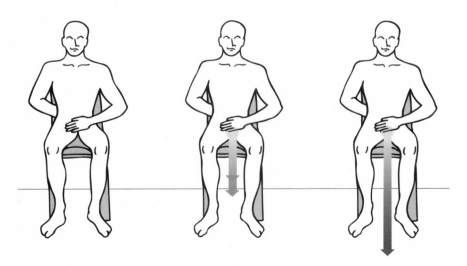

This firmly anchored disk of energy resides within your body at all times. This energy center has been there since before you were born; it has a constant and unlimited supply of energy, and its primary function is to protect and serve you.

Now, stay in your head and envision the energy swirling inside this *chakra*, and see a cord or a tube of this same energy moving straight downwards. The cord can be the same diameter as your *chakra*, or slightly smaller. It may help to envision a brightly colored, plumbing-pipe-sized grounding tube. Visualize your *chakra* as being firmly anchored inside your body, and see your cord moving downwards, out of your genitals, through your chair, and into the floor beneath you.

Know that there is an unlimited amount of energy available to create your cord. You are not draining your first *chakra*, but simply redirecting some of its inexhaustible energy down towards the center of the planet. Keep breathing, stay inside your head, and relax.

See your grounding cord moving further downward, through the foundation of the building you are in, into the layers of the earth below you, and on down to the center of the planet, however that looks to you.

Are you still inside your head, or did you go swooping down to the center of the planet? You don't need to follow your cord around. Stay in the room in your head and direct your grounding cord from there. Your cord will obey you.

When your cord reaches the center of the planet, anchor it there so it is firmly attached. You can envision your cord as a long chain with an actual anchor, as a tree with roots that wrap around the center of the planet, or as a waterfall that has a constant, unwavering downward flow. You can also make up your own personalized anchoring system.

Feel the strong connection between the center of your gravity (your pelvis) and the center of the planet's gravity, and imagine solid attachments at either end. Call your full birth name down your cord three times, or see your name written all over the energy that swirls through it. This is your first grounding cord!

When you feel comfortable with being in your head and being grounded, *destroy your cord*. Drop it out, throw it away, burn it, make it vanish, or whatever. Just get rid of it. Let it go completely. You made it and you can make it go away. Let it go. Do it now.

Why? Because the world of spiritual information and communication has been either deified or devalued for too long, and when people first start to work with energy, they tend to become unbalanced. Many believe that dead relatives will appear or God will punish them or they'll see Elvis, but hey! This is just us working with our own energy in our own bodies. That's all. Again, I remind you that we have no language and no context in this culture to explore the spirit (I mean, *chakra* is an East Indian word; we don't even have the concept in English). When anyone starts to explore the spirit, a whole Pandora's box of hooey and fear tends to emerge.

We need to separate ourselves from all that reactive, uneducated fear of the spirit and remind ourselves that we are in charge of our own energy and our energy creations. Our energy tools belong to us, and if they aren't perfect the first time, or the right color, or the right size, we can destroy them and start over. We are in charge of the work we are learning here, and we can destroy anything we create and start all over again.

Now, ground yourself again in any way you like. If you can ground standing up, and don't need to place your hands on either side of your first *chakra*, good! Choose a bright color for your cord (it doesn't have to be red, even though its energy comes from the red first *chakra*), let it have movement and liveliness, and let it know you're in charge. Call your name down your new grounding cord.

There are only a few rules about your grounding cord: it should be securely anchored at both ends; there should be a constant downward flow so it can be used as a cleansing tool; and the outside edges of the cord should be rounded, without any holes, tears, or breaks to leak energy or trip it up. Beyond that, its size, color, and anchoring systems are up to you.

Get up with your grounding cord and move around. Jump. Run. Lie down. Does your cord come with you and move easily? If not, drop it out of your body. I like to snip a not-quite-right cord off just below my first *chakra* with imaginary scissors; I let it fall down to the center of the planet. Create a new cord with a better flow, or attach wheels to the one you have if you like it. Remember to call your name down each new cord you create.

If you are having trouble grounding, don't worry. It can be difficult if you've been out of body for a long time. At this moment, all you need to do is keep reading, and allow your mind to create a picture of grounding. The mind is wonderful at maintaining a conceptual reality until the body can catch up and create physical reality. Relax and read. You will be able to ground soon enough.

It took me months to get grounded, but I was very stubborn, and no one knew how to stop me from dissociating. You're luckier than I was, because this book has all sorts of grounding help for you, in each chapter, and in the Troubleshooting Guide. Stay in your head and keep working.

GROUNDING OUT ATTITUDES

When you're ready, sit down again and try this first grounding exercise: get in your head and establish your grounding cord. Relax yourself, stay grounded, and bring forward some small recent event that annoyed you. Think about the event until you get a vivid picture of the way you felt when that annoying thing happened. See if you can really work yourself into that feeling of annoyance again.

Now, speed up the downward flow in your grounding cord. Take your whole experience of annoyance (which, remember, you just called into your body out of nothingness!), wrap it into a ball, and drop it down the center of your grounding cord. Your grounding cord will speed this energy down and away, like a drain or a pneumatic tube would.

Stay in the room in your head and let your grounding cord vacuum the annoyance out of your body. Feel the tenseness leaving your stomach, feel the chatter leaving your head, and feel the annoyance leaving your body. Feel the cleansing whoosh as this attitude drains away from you, and you are left in the middle of your head with a million choices about how to feel right now.

As the energy of your annoyance travels downward to the center of the planet, notice that it loses its annoying identity and becomes simple, clean energy again. Notice that annoyance is something *you* attached to this energy. You could have used the same energy to be amused, to cry, to act, or to sleep, but you chose annoyance this time.

Watch your annoyance fall away. Watch it until you can see it as neutral, all-purpose energy again. When the energy reaches the bottom of your cord and the center of the planet, allow it to exit your grounding cord all shiny and clean, and let it go back to wherever it belongs. Notice how big this ball of energy is--in other words, check out how much energy and attention you converted into annoyance.

Consider, as you let this one simple situation go, that you have choices about what you do with your energy. Feel the difference inside you now that you are free of just one episode of annoyance. Perhaps you feel lighter and freer, perhaps not. That depends on how much you like to use annoyance in your life. If you miss your annoyance and you're not done with it yet, know that the energy will come back to you cleansed and ready to help you create a whole new level of supersonic mega-annoyance! Like I said before, you are in charge. You are in charge of how you use your energy.

You may notice, as you sit in your head and watch this cleansed energy leave your grounding cord, that the energy flies away from you completely and disappears. Congratulations! You have just grounded out *someone else's energy.*

What does that mean, *someone else's energy?* Well, all of us routinely pick up and nurture messages, attitudes, and ideologies that do not belong to us and are not growth-enhancing. The ideas can be as trivial as "Don't talk with your mouth full," or as deep as "People won't love you until you're perfect." These ideas and messages can be ones we learned in our families (getting sad or angry in certain triggering situations), something we learned in our gender identification (Nice girls don't..., Real men never...), or something we picked up from our peers (including our best friend, the media).

Part of the process of grounding and cleaning out our energy is finding where the stances and attitudes we take in life are authentic, and where they are artificial. Whatever the idea, if it is not comfortable or healing to us in our present-day life, it needs to be grounded out and examined from a more neutral, objective viewpoint. If the message or attitude or idea is ours, its energy will return once we've grounded and cleaned it out. If the message belongs to someone else, it will return to that person cleansed of our involvement.

When we ground ourselves, we remove our attachments from our own behaviors and free up clean energy for new attitudes (if we so desire). We also perform a service for others by cleansing out the messages and stances we borrowed from them. Before we give back another person's energy, we take responsibility for our agreement with their viewpoints.

In every moment of every day, we need fresh, present-time, examined responses to the world around us. With our grounding cords on and running, our bodies and our emotions will have a way to cleanse themselves in every moment. Our ability to Be Here Now will increase a thousandfold if we just keep grounding. We can begin to see ourselves as unlimited beings, unhampered by past behaviors, past actions, or old messages that trap us like flies in amber. When we are grounded, the silent strength and power we feel will remind us that we are the cause, and not the effect, of our busy lives.

By now, students of the martial arts have recognized the grounding cord as a form of *Chi*, or life energy. In most martial arts, students are first taught to stand correctly and balance themselves before they are ever allowed to jump and kick. In order to balance, students are taught to run the *Chi* inside their pelvic girdle downward, and to center themselves in their bodies and on their center of gravity.

Running the *Chi* creates the warrior stance, where the legs are firmly planted, the body is relaxed, and the awareness is finely tuned. The warrior stance in most martial arts is not aggressive and defiant, but watchful and aware of strengths and weaknesses. The martial arts' warrior stands firm, with all weapons sheathed, ready for anything that might come along, even though she is not particularly asking for a fight.

Grounding creates this same sort of preparedness in everyday work-force warriors like us. Our grounding helps us to stand firm within our own lives and psyches by keeping us centered and connected to the earth and to the present. If painful memories or repetitive behaviors make us want to withdraw from the present and leave our bodies, we can now stand firm. We can use our grounding cords to steadily remove the thoughts and attitudes that de-center and distract us.

GROUNDING OUT MESSAGES

Get in your head and check on your grounding. If there is any flimsiness to your cord, get rid of it and make yourself a new one in a day-glo color. Call your name down your cord again, and let's try another grounding exercise, but this time, let's get rid of something bigger than an annoyance reaction. Let's send a whole message down the cord and away from us. Choose an easy message at first, like a stereotypical parental rule, or a television idea about how your gender should behave.

This message can be in words or feelings, sensations or pictures. However you experience this message, get a complete sense of it before you let it go. As you let your grounding cord have this message, check and see if you feel like calling it back as you watch it slide down and away from you. If you feel a sense of loss, you may not be through with this message yet. Let it go anyway.

When the message has been cleansed and finally flies out of the bottom of your grounding cord, try to see where it's headed.

If you can't "see" any of this, don't worry. I'm not a visual psychic either. I just postulate and know that energy work is occurring by being aware of how my body feels. When I let energy go, my ears will pop, or my breathing will deepen and my body will relax. You can use your imagination and your body senses to guide you. Your body doesn't lie.

Watch or sense where the energy of your released message is headed. If the message shoots off easily, you're done with it. If it comes right back to you, it's a message you still need or believe. Study it. Now that you've grounded out its other-people, other-time identity, you can take a look at this message from the present, on your own terms. Perhaps the message makes sense to you on some level. If so, feel free to re-integrate this message, now that it's clean, into your present-day life.

If, in the next moments or days, the message doesn't feel quite right, go ahead and ground it out again. This time, remind yourself that if you picked up this message somewhere in your travels, you have every right and all the power to drop it back off again. You are in charge. When messages touch a cord in you (no pun intended), feel free to retrieve them, but ground out their past-time, other-people's energy before you do.

Here's an example: say your mother likes a clean house. I mean a really clean house. So do you, but it's hard for you to go through the actual cleaning of your house without thinking of her. You remember her cleanliness and pickiness, how all her books are in alphabetical order, how there's never any dust, how her lamp shades are perfectly straight.... All of a sudden you're out of time and your house is still a mess, and you get to hate yourself for being a slob *and* a procrastinator!

If you get into the room in your head and ground out your mother's picture of cleanliness, you'll see that you don't need to exist in her reality of home perfection, and that you don't need to be like her to love her. You can keep the nice aspects of her neatness, like knowing where everything is and making things beautiful and inviting, but you can send your mom a nice clean ball of her own intense, anal-retentive energy.

You can learn to own the spirit of cleanliness without needing to live your mother's life. Or, you can continue to be a slob in resistance to her. It's up to you.

Know that messages are just noise and ideas we've attached to energy. They're not laws handed down from God. Only our focused attention can give a message life in our hearts and minds, and only our conscious release can turn a message back into the nothingness it is.

Use your grounding abilities to look at the messages you live with every day. If the messages are hogwash, let them go. Remember--you have the right to individuate and to choose your own personal way to respond to the world, no matter what anyone else says or does.

Individuation is a life-long process of finding the meaning of our existence irrespective of others' needs, wants and demands. The early focus of individuation is not in finding "who I am," but in learning "who I am not."

Removing foreign messages and attitudes is a primary step in creating a quiet space where our authentic selves can come alive. By freeing us of thoughts, feelings, and behaviors that cause discomfort, grounding can make our present life more palatable, and our individuation more possible. With the knowledge that we can and do control our response to the inner and outer world, we will fit much more easily into the world as it truly is. We will not need to expend energy controlling the world around us, because our energy will be focused on being clear and authentic in each moment.

If we can go back to the Garden analogy for a moment, we can see grounding as a constant process of weeding, pruning, and re-examining the growth of our inner selves. If you've ever gardened, you know that new plants that should have been hardy sometimes need tremendous attention and care in relation to established plants. Some plants require constant pruning, some attract insects, some have to be moved into better light, and some can't handle your soil mix. If you are unaware of your garden, you will waste a lot of time, energy, and money on plants that just won't make it. You must be present with growing things, especially when they are being introduced into an already established system, and you must observe the entire system as it readjusts to the new life within it.

The same holds true for the gardening we are doing now, especially when we introduce our little rescued one into our lives. The messages and ideas we accepted unthinkingly when we were dissociated will now have to be examined if we are going to provide a whole, nurturing life for ourselves.

When we live inside our bodies with our little ones nestled inside our rooms, grounding is vital. We simply must be aware of all the messages our little ones send, and we must be aware of how our established lives respond to those messages. Grounding connects us to the earth and gives us a constant support system, and a constant chance to move out old messages, old ideas, and old ways of living.

Grounding makes the work of individuation easier because it throws the focus inside, on us and us alone, right here and right now. Grounding helps our spirits rest in our bodies safely and easily. When that happens, we will always Be Here Now.

GROUNDING OUT PAIN

Grounding, you will soon find, works for all kinds of things, including physical discomfort. Try this exercise the next time you have an ache or a pain: get in your head and check that your regular grounding cord is in place. When you are comfortable with your main grounding cord, create a second grounding cord directly in the center of your discomfort. Allow this second cord to grow from within the energy of your pain, then let the cord travel downward to the center of the earth.

Instead of anchoring this second grounding cord inside your body, let it drain the painful energy away from you, like a rope unwinding off the edge of a table and finally falling off altogether. Notice how attached you are to this pain as it leaves your body, how much energy you gave over to it, and how you feel about living without it.

Remember that pain, physical or emotional, is only a signal. It is not an entity that needs to be feared and fled from, or drugged into submission. Pain is a signal that something is wrong. If we had no pain, we wouldn't be aware of danger in our environment or illness in our body, and we would traipse blindly into things that could cause us real damage. Pain alerts us to danger and illness when we are not being totally aware, and it alerts us quite suddenly, with no subtlety or subterfuge. Pain doesn't play games, and neither should we.

We're not supposed to pretend to adore pain, bargain with it, or imagine that it feels wonderful so it will magically disappear. That's not the shift required. We are simply supposed to quiet down and listen respectfully to our bodies. The best response is to remove our dramatic attachments to the idea of suffering, and to focus our healing energy and attention (or the attention of our doctor/healer) on the painful area.

Grounding is an excellent way to address pain, because it focuses healing energy and lets the body know: you're home and aware, you're listening, and you're acting on its messages. As you continue with your energy work, you'll be surprised to see how many aches and pains your body manifests just to get your attention back inside you and centered on the present. You can identify this kind of pain very easily—it goes away when you ground it--as if by magic!

Keep your main grounding cord attached and running at all times. In the beginning, it's good to get in your head and check your cord at least twice each day. You don't have to find a quiet room—just sit or stand still for a moment, get into the room in your head, and ground yourself. It should only take you a few seconds. If your grounding cord is flimsy or unreal, let it go and make a new one. Change your cord every day if you like—it doesn't cost anything, and it can be fun to coordinate your cord with your attitude or your outfit.

Stay grounded as you drive, eat, sleep, and exercise. Check into your grounding when you're at work, at a movie, or in the middle of a fight. Work on your grounding when you're sick, when you're balancing your checkbook, when you're cooking, when you're dancing—and especially when you make love.

Because your cord is inside your pelvis, it can help you to clear out some of the energy you get from your lover during sex. If you're thinking ahead at this time, you're on the right track; grounding from this *chakra* can also help you release the energy and messages you got during sex with your molester. More on that later; we need to be comfortable with our basic skills first.

If it's very hard for you to get and stay grounded, don't worry. Because the grounding *chakra* is right in the center of the sexual assault "crime scene," as it were, some survivors just can't focus their attention there.

If you need some support, you can ground yourself in the shower by training the flow of water on your back or pelvis and following the downward movement in your mind. If this doesn't help and you still cannot ground at all, skip ahead to the chapter in Part III called *Advanced Imaging* and check into the special healing for your first-*chakra* area. This should make grounding much easier.

There are more grounding skills, rules, and ideas in the chapter in Part III called *Advanced Grounding*. Specifically, there is an auxiliary grounding technique that attaches your back and spine into the central grounding cord, which can make grounding much easier. If you are currently able to ground, but you feel unbalanced and need more grounding support right now, look up the Sciatic Grounding technique in *Advanced Grounding*. Women will also benefit from the Ovary Grounding technique in the same chapter.

Please feel free to skip forward, but beware of confusing yourself with too much input. It is perfectly normal, and even expected, to have difficulties with grounding at first.

Remember, if things get difficult, enter the room in your head and ground, first thing. The more you ground, the easier it gets, because your body becomes clearer and cleaner each time you ground. Soon your body will be clear enough to keep its grounding cord going without your constant help. Bodies like to be grounded, and the first *chakra* is an excellent little work horse that loves to have jobs to do. In a very short while, your body will stay grounded all by itself.

If you find yourself in a heavy effort mode, groaning and straining to ground and stay in your head, you're on the wrong track! Energy work takes application, not effort! Energy work is created out of gossamer and magic and willingness. It doesn't require blood and sweat. If you are exerting a lot of effort, stop. Relax. Tell yourself an awful joke and start over. Lighten up, read through the grounding exercise again, and have some fun with your own energy. The trauma is over; this is summer vacation. Relax.

BASIC GROUNDING RULES

A note before we go on: if grounding works wonders for you, that's great! I'm sure you think it would work wonders for other people in your life, and it would, if they grounded themselves. Nevertheless, grounding other people is not okay at all.

First off, it's the height of bad spiritual etiquette to heal anyone without asking--and grounding, don't forget, is a healing. Secondly, your personal grounding cord won't work for anyone else. You'd be putting the energy of your healing and your answers into their lives. Bad manners! No one but you needs to learn your lessons and experience your grounding!

If you know someone who is crying out for grounding, let them borrow your book for a few days. You can teach them what you know, but do not ground them! Do not become responsible for other people's spiritual growth. It won't work! Take care of yourself, please.

For further information on grounding rules, and on grounding in unusual situations, please see the chapter in Part III called *Advanced Grounding.*

BEGINNING MEDITATION & HEALING

DEFINING YOUR PERSONAL TERRITORY

With the rescue, the room in the head, and the grounding cord, we have been attempting to cleanse our internal world so that we can begin to live inside our lives once again. Once inside, though, we need to be sure that we have a clear sense of where our new-found world begins and ends. It is not enough to live within our own truth. We must also be sure that we are protected and defined so our lives and our truths do not spill out onto others, and the lives of others do not spill onto us. Realistic self-definition, or the definition of personal boundaries, is a vital step in individuation.

Survivors of sexual assault usually have difficulty with the concepts of self-definition and personal space. Many will play with their weight, either becoming very large and imposing, or very small and not really there. Some will expend inordinate amounts of time and energy on physical neatness and control, while others will live like slobs with their possessions strewn all about. Some get addicted to physical security and triple-lock their doors, or purchase intricate security systems to keep the dangers of the world at bay; others will invite undoubtedly dangerous people right into their lives.

More often than not, survivors of sexual assault exhibit their lack of personal boundaries by becoming co-dependently involved in relationships or situations in their lives. Because they do not know where they begin and end, these people will take personal responsibility for almost anything, from their friends' emotional states to the state of the environment. They find definition in how much they affect others, not in how effective their own lives are.

People without boundaries are often extremely active in and concerned about politics, religion, business, and finance. This is not a bad thing in and of itself, but in their relationship to these exterior activities, you will be able to identify boundary-free people. I call these hyper-active people without boundaries *runaway healers*.

Runaway healers differ from regular healers in a few very important ways. Runaway healers are often phenomenally good at what they do, but a close look at their inner lives reveals emptiness and chaos. All of their energy pours out of them and into the things and people they heal; they make no time for themselves.

A good test to use to identify runaway healers is to ask them what they do for themselves—how they rest and nurture themselves. Regular healers will rattle off a list after a small hesitation. Runaway healers will be rendered speechless, or will drone on about their *selfless mission*.

Selfless is exactly right. Runaway healers attempt to deal with their pain by de-selfing, by becoming unimportant footnotes in their own lives. By constantly healing others (or situations) and ignoring their own needs, these people try to remove themselves from their trauma, even if they become ill or die in the process.

In healing others or going up against impossible relationships or situations, such people are at least trying to keep their healing energy flowing, but because they don't have or understand boundaries (and are probably heading towards physical or mental illness themselves), their healing attention can be damaging to others.

Runaway healers cannot let other people sit with their own pain (if they could, they might have to sit with their own, God forbid). Runaway healers will often whisk away all blockages and difficulties before their heal-ees have learned the lessons tied into their personal discomfort. Runaway healers mean well, but they usually create unworkable dependencies because they *must* heal--they can't let others or the world simply be. They've always got to be finding new missions and new problems, usually by starting with *your* life and all its difficulties.

The basic force behind runaway healing would seem to exist to rid the world of suffering, but really, the force exists to rid the healer of the memory of his own pain. Because of this, runaway healing work tends to come from a very driven and stressful place, where the healer's very self-image is inextricably tied to his healing ability.

Runaway healers tend to end up in unworkable relationships, jobs and causes, and though they get a lot accomplished in these places, they seldom rest on their laurels. As soon as they fix one unfixable thing and lose another part of themselves, they're ready for more!

Forget their needs, their health, their homes, and their finances; they're on a mission! This mission is a sad thing. Because runaway healers always burn themselves out, mentally or physically, they have to stop healing, sooner or later. At that inevitable moment, runaway healers are disconsolate. Without their ability to heal, who are they? What do they have? What can they do? How will they survive?

If runaway healers can stop themselves *before* their breakdown and focus their incredible energies towards their own lives, they can turn their decay around quite swiftly. Getting in their own heads, grounding their own bodies, and defining their own personal territory is a great start.

When runaway healers discover their boundaries and begin to work with their own pain, they can generally accept the pain of others, and then stop interfering with—I mean *healing*--others. The first step is to stop them from healing others—completely—because they are almost certainly unable to say no, unable to rest, and unable to accept nurturing. Until they can learn to set strong boundaries, and respect their own bodies and lives, these people are more of a hazard than anything else. Only after reasonable self-care is undertaken and understood can a once-runaway healer begin to practice in a more respectful way.

A runaway healer's peace of mind will come not from a world filled with justice and devoid of pain, but from her own ability to deal with the inner issues that cause her to expend all her vital energy on anything but herself. Such a healer must be able to create inner justice and personal relief from pain before her help will be truly valuable. She must heal herself and have a real, everyday connection to her own balance and wellness before she can help manifest peace and justice in the outer world.

An individual with a strong sense of personal space does not look for his self-worth within his ability to heal others or to create external justice. He makes sure he is well enough to offer competent help first.

A person with boundaries does not heal others unasked. He is too busy living his own life to become co-dependently enmeshed in another's. He heals others naturally, by example. A person with boundaries is physically safe because he cares for himself, because he grounds out his own distress, and because he places himself in supportive environments.

A person who knows where he begins and ends does not use weight or lack of it for physical safety. His physical and emotional boundaries do not compromise his health. He is not compulsive or excessively careless about his personal belongings, and he does not believe that the world needs to be locked out or wired for intruders. A person with boundaries is not obsessive about possessions, because everything of real value resides within the room in his head. A person with boundaries has a comfortable, spacious, spiritually defensible place he calls home.

It may surprise you to learn that each of us has a God-given home boundary system already in place. It is the aura, and though it has had some unfortunately wacky metaphysical connotations attached to it, the aura is simply the outer boundary of your personal territory.

If you have ever felt but not seen someone looking at you, or coming up behind you, then you've had a physical experience of your aura's energy boundary. In its simplest form, your aura's energy "feelers" can alert you when people enter your physical area, whether you have visually detected them or not. With a little bit of practice and attention, your aura can help to make you aware of your emotional and spiritual territory as well.

Awareness of our aura and personal boundary system tends to grow with us as we move through childhood and adolescence, and away from the protection of our families. Further awareness usually comes when we have the experience of losing and then regaining our boundaries in relationships, jobs, higher schooling, and healthy sexual contact.

As we mature, we seem constantly to come up against new and novel experiences which prompt us to lower or even drop our boundaries. We get to gauge if this new person, idea, or experience is one for which we should change ourselves or our viewpoint. With a suitable support network, most people can come through these challenging and exhilarating moments with a stronger sense of who they are, and a stronger knowledge of where their newly examined and restored boundaries fit into the world at large.

Okay, that's how it works in the theoretical construct called a "normal life," but "normal" people didn't experience one of the most powerful boundary stealers of all: unhealthy sexual contact at a completely inappropriate age. All sexual contact involves the removal of physical and emotional (and sometimes spiritual) boundaries, but in the process of healthy sex, the boundaries get put back.

Healthy sex is a process of letting go and becoming one with our lover. When we enter into a loving, evolved, and safe sexual relationship, the simple act of letting down our boundaries has a profound effect: it makes us aware that we *have* boundaries. Emotionally safe and healing sex gives us a place where we can totally unwind and unmask. In this process, we and our lover can meld and cleanse our energy bodies, get grounded, and renew our connection to the sensual, earthy world.

It is very easy to live in the moment and in the body during healthy sex. I mean, who'd want to be anywhere else? After such joyful physical bonding, both lovers naturally disconnect, ground out most of each other's energy through sleep or eating, and re-form their boundaries with a fresh perspective. It's a fantastically healing thing, for their relationship as a growing entity unto itself, and for their individual lives.

Unhealthy sex (sex with strangers, sex that requires you to do things you don't enjoy, sex with someone you don't respect, and guilt-ridden "mercy" sex, to name a few examples) is another story altogether. Unhealthy sex connects us to people we might not like, know, or even trust. If we can't trust, we won't let down our boundaries (if we *have* boundaries), and we probably won't be grounded, so we won't be able to experience the healing release that healthy sex brings.

In unhealthy sex, our partner's energy comes into our auras and bodies, but it doesn't meld with our energy and cleanse us. It only clogs us up, because we haven't done the important, trust-based releasing and grounding work required of us--without that, sexual healing is unlikely.

We walk away from unhealthy sexual encounters feeling empty and dissatisfied, teary and remorseful, extremely wakeful, or dead tired. We may turn to drugs or food to numb the discomfort of unsafe and unfulfilling intimate contact.

These self-medicating distractions are symptoms of a body in distress, and an aura in tatters. We usually snap out of these symptoms in a few hours or days, but continuing in a relationship like this will eventually create a big jagged rip, inside and outside of us.

When sexual contact is trivialized, and boundaries are ignored and devalued, our inner Gardens are self-trashed. Spirit work and life work become much harder. Fortunately, most unhealthy sexual relationships can end without too much tragedy (Just say, "Go!"), and healing can be accomplished in a reasonable amount of time.

In totally damaging sex like rape, molestation, and assault (including that which occurs inside marriage), our boundaries are ripped away and we are simply invaded. After the invasion, we often can't find our boundaries--or our sense of safety and individuality--anywhere.

Our bodies are raw, our spirits are disconnected, our grounding is gone, and our foundations seem to disappear completely. Healing can occur, but not without an understanding of the energy body. It is especially difficult for children to recover from such trauma.

Adults, in most instances, can recover from assaultive or imprisoning trauma more effectively than children. Kids seem to do better than adults in their recoveries from illness, loss, and death, but I feel that's because they still have such a tentative idea of life here on earth. Most children are still connected to the angels and the fairies; they see pain, death, and loss in a more philosophical way than do most adults.

Children, however, do not seem to do so well with de-selfing events like torture or sexual assault, because their in-the-body selves aren't fully developed yet. Adults healing from adult-onset assault, torture, or imprisonment generally have a better recovery because they have a remembered life and self--a self that has been tested, revised, and amended through more usual boundary-impairing passages and challenges. Though it is by no means easy for an adult to recover from such an experience, it is possible.

Children do not generally have anything to fall back on when they experience boundary-destroying events. On a spiritual level, sexual assault does this: it removes the grounding cord and the aura in insidious, sneaky, and sometimes violent ways, and it disrupts the *chakra* system. Sexual assault can also install an unconscious life-program that invites more abuse and assault into the child's sphere.

Without their basic energy-body foundations, assaulted children essentially walk around without skin, without bones. Some split into a number of alternate selves or exist in a dream-state, some learn to use certain emotions to keep people away from them, and some try to control their home environment through taking on whatever role is missing in the family.

What these children almost never do is grow normally from the onset of the assault. How can they if their wonderfully, naturally incomplete core self is dangerously exposed, fragmented, and lost to them?

Therapy from a mental place can help these kids understand what happened to them in a somewhat detached way. Therapy from a physical place can release their bodies from remembered pain. Therapy from a socio-emotional place can help them amend their emotional postures into ones that work better, but healing three out of four aspects is not enough. The spirit, the soul, the energy body, or the Garden, whatever you want to call it, needs rebuilding as well. Without this fourth aspect, the healing of this essentially spiritual trauma is unlikely at best.

Damaging sexual encounters dramatically affect a growing spirit; the trauma generally lingers until a healing occurs and the boundaries the spirit had at birth are restored. Without known boundaries or a safe grounding system, it is very hard to live and grow in this world, and very hard to deal with or benefit from intimate, trust-based human relationships. The foundations just aren't in place, and as the child matures, he does so without real protections. The onset of adolescent or adult sexual relationships, which require a healthy and fluid boundary system, usually de-center him even further.

For childhood-assault survivors who have no connection to their auras and grounding abilities, sex can become another in a long series of intrusions on their bodies and in their lives. Even if their partners are gentle and respectful, many assault survivors can't get near enough to their bodies during sex to experience a healing.

Many assault survivors become excellent puppeteers when sex is "happening" to them; they pull the right strings and make the right noises, but they are not present at all. They are off in a dream world, or up on the ceiling. What they get from this sort of truncated sexual experience is a clogging of their partner's energy in their lower *chakras*. This clogging manifests as excess or insufficient weight, male or female reproductive illness, chronic back pain, or mental illness.

Other survivors develop sex addictions, and while we may joke about nymphomania, it is one of the most tragic life dramas imaginable. A sex addict's body is clogged like a puppeteer's, but because of the frequency of sex and the number of different partners, an addict's congestion is so severe that their body is simply not fit to live in.

When sex-addicted people feel pain, they look to sex for healing—they go back to the scene of the crime, to find the power they once lost. With each unhealing, distrustful, ungrounding sexual encounter, they get further and further away from ever being able to find that healing, or that power. As their pain escalates, they often turn to drugs and isolate themselves dreadfully.

Cheerful stuff. Nevertheless, there is a way out--we're on that path now. We keep working, we keep centering, and we become proficient at grounding and staying in our bodies. We clear a space for the room in our heads and the memory of our Gardens, and we get in touch with the healing boundary we've had since before we were born.

As we learn our basic skills and become familiar with them, much of our healing will begin on its own. In the second and third sections of this book, we'll use our tools to address all the wretched issues we've had to deal with in our lives. Right now, though, we have the time and the space to learn about our spirits and our energy bodies.

DEFINING YOUR AURA

Here's how to define and cleanse your aura: ground yourself and get into the room in your head. Stand up and envision a large oblong bubble completely surrounding you. Light the edges of the bubble with a very bright—even garish—neon color. See the bubble above your head, below your feet, behind you, in front of you, and on either side of you. The distance from your body to the lit-up edges of the bubble should be a constant twenty-four to thirty-six inches or so (arm's-length is best).

Now, stay in your head and envision your grounding cord. Notice it growing out of your first *chakra* and flowing steadily and calmly downward. With your aura lit up like this, you can now see how your grounding cord and your aura boundary interact: they intersect an arm's-length below your feet. Change the color of your grounding cord so that it matches your aura bubble, and be aware of the result.

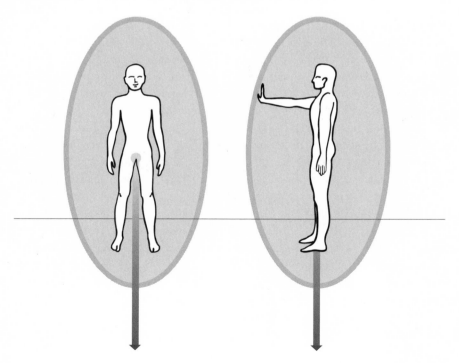

You may feel a shiver or a sense of release. This is a sign that your aura is using your grounding cord to release some of its unwanted energy. Great!

Stay in your head and study your aura. You just defined its area and gave it a bright color, but is it getting bulgy or changing color? Is it pulling itself closer to you or disappearing in spots, or do you see holes and tears in it? Are parts of your body feeling uncomfortable? If so, congratulate yourself. You are receiving communications from your aura! If you perceive no changes, congratulate yourself, too: your aura wants to be in the present moment with you right now. In either case, don't worry about what you see. We'll study the aura in more detail in a moment; right now, we're ready to do some aura cleansing work.

CLEANSING YOUR AURA

Here's how to cleanse your aura: sit in a straight-backed chair with your feet flat on the floor, your arms uncrossed, and your hands upturned comfortably on your knees. Get grounded and in your head, and light up your aura bubble. Match the color of your grounding cord and your aura.

Now, create another grounding cord, a very large pipe this time, with its opening on the floor around your aura bubble, and make its edges the same color and circumference as your aura. See the edges of your aura touching this aura grounding cord as you attach it at floor-level.

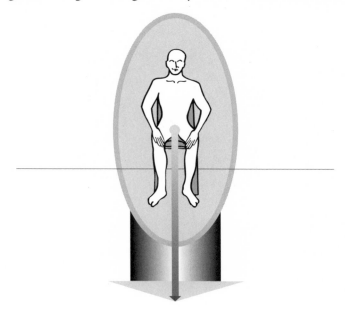

Stay in your head and be aware of your regular first-*chakra* grounding cord. Know that this main cord will stay right where it belongs, no matter how many other grounding cords you make.

Envision your floor-level aura grounding pipe, and allow the energy stuck in your aura to flow down and out of it, just as the energy stuck in your body flows down and out of your first-*chakra* cord. Let the clogged energy fall down and away from you. You may feel globs of stress coming away from your head, shoulders or stomach; your ears may pop or ring; you may get the shivers or feel hot and cold areas inside and outside of your body, or you may actually see people and events leaving your aura. Whatever happens, stay in your head and keep both cords grounding.

Read through this next step before you go on. It's not complicated, but it is a bit tricky to explain, which is why I've included illustrations.

Slowly bring the edges of your aura in towards your body, and as you do, notice all the old energy inside it being squeezed out and down your grounding pipe.

As you bring your aura in towards you, see the circumference of your aura grounding pipe shrinking along with your aura boundary until they are both drawn in towards you. The end result should give you a feeling of being closely enveloped in your own brightly colored auric field.

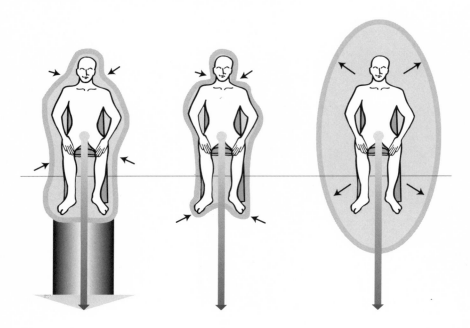

When your aura has been drawn in towards you, I want you to imagine the feeling of it all over your skin. Feel your aura above your head, behind your back, under your feet, along your chest and abdomen, around your arms, behind your knees, and so on. Stay in the room in your head and get a sense of this bright color touching and enveloping your body.

Know that there is no space or opening for old energy or information, because you've grounded everything out. Take a moment to become acquainted with your shiny clean aura.

When you have been able to feel your aura on your skin for about thirty seconds, thank your aura grounding pipe and drop it down and away from you. Stay in your head and keep your first-*chakra* cord attached.

Is your body grounding cord still the same color as your aura bubble? If not, change it back so that they match one another. Your first-*chakra* cord may have changed color to do something else while you grounded your aura with that larger pipe. This is great, but now we need your body's grounding cord to pay attention to our directions for a few minutes.

Notice once again how your aura boundary and your regular grounding cord intersect. Right now, with your aura drawn up to your skin, it and your grounding cord will intersect right below your first *chakra*, instead of at the normal arm's-length below your feet (see illustration).

When you've gotten a sense of being completely enveloped in your aura, plump your aura back out to its normal dimensions. You can pop it out, blow it up like a balloon, manually move it away from you, or just imagine it at its normal size. As you plump your aura back out, fill it with a pastel wash of the color you chose for its boundary.

For example: if you chose a neon yellow for your aura's boundary, you will create a pale wash of that yellow all throughout your aura. The pale yellow will touch your skin and radiate above you, below you, behind you, in front of you, and on either side of you.

Though your normal, cleaned, and re-sized aura boundary will not touch your skin, this light residue of its energy will keep you and your body connected to its protective and sensing abilities. This connection will make it easier for you to be aware of the many ways your aura protects and envelops you.

Connecting to your aura's boundary in this simple way will help you to be able to feel it and notice its functions, reactions, and fluctuations. This color-shading technique is an excellent way to make yourself conscious of the exact dimensions of your personal territory.

When your aura is cleaned-out and back to its correct size, get up and move around. Your aura should move easily with you, and maintain itself whether you stand, bend, sit, or jump. If your aura bubble doesn't come with you or move easily, sit down, ground yourself, and get into your head again. Change or intensify the color of your aura bubble and see if that makes it any more mobile. If not, cleanse your aura again, and it should become more fluid and flexible.

Take a moment to move around with your lit-up aura, to sit inside it, and to get a sense of it completely surrounding and protecting you. Become acquainted with your aura. If you can't get any feel for it yet, don't worry. For help, skip ahead to the chapter called *The Gold Sun Healing*.

Cleansing the aura and maintaining a conscious, present-time connection with it is as important as cleansing the body through grounding. The energy we store inside our bodies has to do with our feelings about ourselves; being able to ground, examine, and renew our internal energy helps us redefine our self-view. With grounding, we can actually move old attitudes and belief systems away from our inner lives so they can't haunt our present-day behavior.

The energy we store inside our aura, on the other hand, has to do with our feelings about our place in the exterior world, and about how others see us. If we connect with our aura, we can begin to identify exterior messages, and we can see how we have learned to act and react in the world around us.

Both our inner and outer energy bodies benefit tremendously from these simple acts of conscious energy-cleansing. When our bodies and our auras can rid themselves of messages, attitudes, ideas, and memories that do not serve them, both will begin to heal and live in the present moment.

If you are not comfortable within your newly cleansed and defined aura, let it go and create a better one. When you have created an aura you like, sit inside it and say your full birth-name out loud, or see your name in writing all throughout your aura.

Check in with your aura periodically throughout the day. Your aura should be bright and evenly oblong with no bulges, holes, or tears, and its edges should stay about an arm's-length away from your body at all points. With the help of this information from you, your aura can take good care of itself.

If you are receiving communications from your aura at this time (meaning that it shows you different colors, shapes, or distances than the ones you created for it), you may want to skip ahead to the chapter in Part III called *Advanced Aura Reading and Definition*. At this moment, we are not reading our auras, but giving them a healing.

In essence, we are at this point *telling* our auras how they should look, not asking how they feel. If you communicate this to your aura, it will most likely calm down and let you be in charge. If it continues to bombard you with images even after you make it clear that you are currently a beginning aura reader, then feel free to skip ahead.

Working with the energy of the aura is not quite like creating a grounding cord or a room in the head from scratch. Our auras have always been present, even if they have been totally ignored. What we are doing here is re-acquainting ourselves with our auras; we're reminding our auras, and ourselves, how auras should look and feel and behave.

If you begin to maintain and heal your aura, it will become more real and therefore more knowable. When you know your aura, you can begin to read it.

If your aura gets very big, it can mean you are trying too hard, taking on too many outer projects or too much responsibility, or not maintaining your distance from others. If your aura tucks itself closely around you, it may mean that you feel threatened, or out of place. If your aura has holes or missing pieces, it can mean that you are losing your boundaries, or unknowingly handing them over to others.

If you notice your aura changing, you can simply light it up and see it as whole, vital, and boundary-enforcing. This quick aura-brightening (it takes less than a second) will often nudge and awaken a temporarily unconscious aura, which usually fixes itself right away.

When you are in contact with your aura, you may notice how much time you spend out of your body and ungrounded. This is okay. Congratulate yourself for noticing your split, and keep doing your cleansing work. You've most likely been out of your body and away from your life for an awfully long time, because they've been unsafe, unsavory places for you. This split is to be expected; it's normal, common, and even proper for a survivor of deep trauma to be dissociated.

With the help of your energy-cleansing tools, you are becoming clearer and more powerful with each passing moment, even if it doesn't feel like it right now. You will soon have a body safe enough for your spirit to live in. You will soon be able to keep all of yourself in one place. Be easy with yourself, keep laughing, and keep working.

Each of these energy tools supports the others. For example, it is easier to ground if you're in the room in your head, easier to get into your head if your aura is defined, easier to define your aura if you're grounded, and so on. One or more of these energy tools may be impossible for you right now, but keep working with ease, relaxation, and humor.

Don't throw pointless visions of perfection at yourself. Perfection is for joyless drones who don't have any imagination, but this work is all about the imagination. Imagination makes growth and change possible. Growth and change don't look perfect. Sometimes this work is going to look and feel just terrible, and at other times you'll be the most competent and graceful being on the planet. Keep breathing and laughing and grounding, and it will all come together.

An aside about the aura: if you've read anything about the aura, you may be waiting for me to go into lengthy descriptions of all the colors and layers of the aura. Sorry, but I've never seen the point. Auras are living things that are in a constant state of change and flux and re-definition, not only in color, but in shape, size, completeness, and vibrancy. I've had about a hundred psychic aura readings, all completely different, and none very helpful.

I have learned to trust and read my own aura, and as its loving owner, I clean it, re-define its shape, and heal it when it's hurt. I don't obsess on its thousand fluctuations and peer and poke at all its layers. I believe in it and trust it to work.

My treatment of my aura is similar to my treatment of my body: I feed it and exercise it and heal it and give it sleep, but I don't take blood tests or MRIs every day. By taking constant, regular care of my body, I know that it is well enough and supported enough to tell me when it needs more attention.

Now, after saying all that, I'll back off a bit. If you ignore your body and all its little signals, it will eventually give you a nice big illness to deal with. At that point, you'll need to understand more about it, and taking blood tests and MRIs may be called for. The same is true for the aura. An abandoned aura needs more work at first, but ignored energy tools don't need the same sort of time-consuming healing rituals ignored bodies tend to require.

Clearly, I do include a chapter on reading the aura (*Advanced Aura Reading and Definition*, in Part III), but it's much simpler than most aura-work tomes I've read. I've found that the simple act of listening to what the aura tells me can be the best reading/healing of all, no matter what all its layers and colors are doing at that moment in time. Okay?

Your meditation at this point should go like this: you sit, ground yourself and call your full name down your cord, get into your head, and make sure your room is still there.

If you can't locate your room, re-create a new one in any style you like, but make sure to provide space for your little one each time. Better yet, let them help you create the room of your dreams.

Once you have your room established, give your younger self some favorite activity to occupy them while you learn the rest of your beginning healing skills. We'll begin to work with your little one later, so keep them happy and safe for now. They need the rest.

When you're grounded and in the room in your head, light up your aura in a bright color and see your grounding cord intersecting with it. At this point, you can envision your aura boundary and your grounding cord in different colors.

If your aura feels indistinct or wavery, though, give it a much brighter color and match your grounding cord to that color. When you do this, your grounding cord will naturally help your aura center itself and dump off its excess energy.

Don't worry about taxing your grounding cord with too much work. The first *chakra* energy is so boundless that it could do a hundred things at once and still make a flawless gourmet meal for twenty. Your grounding *chakra* can do anything you ask it to.

Once you've gotten your skills down, your daily healing check-in can take less than thirty seconds. Basically, it goes: sit, ground, get into the room in your head, light up your aura, and attend to any difficulties or incompleteness if necessary. That's it!

So far, you've learned to ground, you've created a meditation sanctuary inside your body, you've rescued a lost part of yourself and are protecting it from harm, and you're casually redefining your aura! Not bad for being halfway through a beginning class.

We'll be introducing a few more basic techniques before we move on to the more involved meditations and healings in Part II, but if you need to, stop here and catch up with yourself. If any of the skills tripped you up, go back and try them one more time.

Have fun and draw a picture of the room in your head and put it on your refrigerator door. Take your younger self to a movie or a circus. Change your grounding cord, or light up your aura with rainbow swirls. Play for a while if you need to, or better yet, let your younger self help you create and polish up your energy tools. Kids are much better than adults at this kind of thing.

If you're ready, then by all means, read on.

PART I

BEGINNING HEALING & MEDITATION

GIFTS FROM YOUR GARDEN

If you have done any metaphysical work before, you may have learned about the psychic protection systems called The Wall, The Mirror, or The White Light. These are barrier tools that some people use to protect themselves from others, or from any "evil" spirit energy that might come their way.

I have found that these barriers tend to create more problems than they solve. They often backfire on their users and foster a sense of isolation or spiritual victimhood. The isolation comes about when the barrier works too well and keeps *all* energy out, instead of just the so-named evil energy. The victimhood appears when these fear-based barrier users meet up with bored beings who like to hammer away at their boundaries for fun.

The Wall is an energy barrier that actually looks and feels like a wall of bricks. People who use The Wall are often rigid and inflexible in their dealings with the world. The Wall is erected as an impenetrable defense; however, many beings love a challenge and are drawn towards Wall people like moths to a flame. Though they truly want to be left alone, Wall people usually find themselves surrounded by off-center and manipulative people. Wall users do not realize that their defense system is riveting and/or insulting to others, who will try to break through just to prove they can.

Wall people rarely achieve the isolation they crave and are often heard to say, "How do these crazy people/jobs/relationships find me? Do I have a sign on my forehead or something?" Actually, since everyone is intuitive and completely able to perceive things like energy barriers, The Wall *can* be like a sign on the forehead that says, "Please bother me!"

The Mirror looks like its name and is a slightly less insulting barrier erected to send back whatever energy or attention comes towards its user. It is a way of saying, "Whatever you send to me belongs to you, so I won't become involved in your communications at all."

The Mirror is only partially effective, because while most people tire of having their communications come right back to them unchanged, others like to hang around and do their spiritual hair, as it were. Living behind a Mirror can be lonely, because very little gets through; it can also be annoying if the Mirror attracts spiritual narcissists who like to hang around the Mirror-user and look at themselves.

Like The Wall, The Mirror is dead and brittle. Neither one has any flow, and it's hard to get them into present time or invest them with any buoyancy or laughter. Because of their rigidity, both interfere with the health and fluidity of the aura.

The White Light is another story altogether. Essentially, The White Light is a brilliant white aura bubble erected around its user as an all-purpose protection system. The idea came from the world of spirit guides and guardian angels, whose energy usually appears as white or silver in an aura or a *chakra*.

Though these kind beings are fascinating enough to warrant a whole book of their own, we will only touch on them briefly because of the enormity of the subject (which requires an understanding of the afterlife, reincarnation, the superconscious, soul mates, karma, the *Akashic* records, and other things that will take us away from our chosen topic).

Essentially, guides and angels are beings who agree to watch over us in our lives here on earth. They often act as mediators between us and the information we desire, between us and God, and between our spirit and our immediate trauma.

In times of transition or shock, spirit guides will often provide us with a protective screen of white or silver energy. This spiritual security blanket is wonderfully healing, but it soon wears off so that our own natural colors and energies can re-assert themselves.

When people set up an all-purpose White Light barrier on their own (thinking that if some white light is good, too much is better), a type of auric rigor mortis sets in. The aura becomes rigid and unhealthy from the strain of maintaining one color at all times.

Soon enough, White Light people find themselves stuck—isolated from earthly energy, from their own energy, and from other people as well. Their spirit guides may even have a hard time contacting them, because the White Light's job is to keep everything out. Because the spirit guides can't get through, growth generally stops.

The White Light is very important, don't misunderstand me; it's great for emergencies or illnesses, but it was never meant as an all-purpose tool. In my own meditations, I never use White Light anymore, but leave its application to the discretion of my spirit guides.

When people come to me for classes or healings with these types of boundaries, I focus immediately on the underlying fear they imply. Generally, people with a need for these boundaries believe strongly in evil and spiritual danger, and have probably experienced a great deal of both. I know I did, that is until I began grounding and defining my aura. With the work we're learning now, I was able to get in touch with the projections I cherished: projections that helped me to live in a spirit world filled with evil and danger.

Here's my story: I was molested for two years or so by a neighborhood father, starting around the age of two or three. This dad also molested my younger sister, a number of other neighborhood girls, and most likely some of his own five children as well. When the molest was finally stopped (my older sister found out and told my parents, who took my younger sister and me to the police), I was around four-and-a-half years old. Going to the police station was a scary prospect, but the officer was so nice that I was able to tell him everything. My parents hired a lawyer, but none of the other neighborhood parents would bring charges, and the case was dropped.

So, the police did nothing, the courts did nothing, and my parents could do nothing. We continued to live across the street from my molester's jeering, angry family for another seven years, and everyone in the neighborhood knew what had happened. Many of the neighbor kids and some of their parents were ashamed of my sister (who was about three years old then) and me. Some even called us sluts.

My sexual assault and its devastating, empty aftermath did not fit into my idea of God and love. There was nothing I could do to reconcile the image of a loving God with the reality of my molestation. None of it made sense. God and child molesters could not co-exist, that much was clear, so that left me with one logical conclusion: if people could be allowed to molest children unharmed, evil had to be real.

I grew up being very interested in horror and evil, and when I got involved with spirituality at the age of ten, I saw myself encountering evil on many levels, which was exciting to me. Though my spiritual teachers all belonged to the White Brotherhood, I felt there must therefore be a Dark Brotherhood against which I would always battle in a grand apocalyptic struggle.

In my inner travels, I used all the aforementioned protection systems and anything else I could find to keep all the "bad guys" away. Sometimes the magic worked, but most times it didn't, and I got myself into a lot of psychic emergencies. Thankfully, one of those emergencies landed me on the doorstep of that psychic study center. There, I finally saw that my belief in evil had very much more to do with my beliefs about my molestation than they had to do with reality.

What I began to see was that because I didn't believe God could protect anyone, I lived in a world filled with unrelieved danger. Travelling alone without knowledge or connections, and armed with fear-based boundaries, I knocked around in the inner (and outer) world like an accident waiting to happen.

I lived in constant, unconscious fear, and drew fearful experiences to me like a magnet. I couldn't even recognize the positive, safe, and life-giving people and messages I encountered every day. I had no time for such lightheartedness--I was too busy ferreting out and destroying evil! I was going to heal the planet even if I lost my mind or died in the attempt. I was on a selfless mission!

Luckily, my mission was cut short by the skills I began to learn at the psychic study center (and by the chance to see the many tortured and unworkable missions in the psychics around me). As I learned to ground and define and cleanse myself and my energy, my defensive postures began to slip away. Nasty people and experiences stopped slamming into me with such frequency. I think that because I was no longer involved in the old fevered drama, it was less fun to bother me.

At first, I felt lost without all of the excitement and terror of seeing nasty spirits and being in constant danger. I was even bored! It actually took me a few years to really let go of my evil-fighting mission, which made it hard for other budding psychics at the center to be around me. I tended to trail crazy stuff behind me, and it was hard for anyone to stay centered or grounded when I came into a room.

I persevered, though, because it seemed that the skills I was learning put me in a different spiritual category than before, one that gave me more room to breathe. From within my head and behind my aura, I could now watch chaos without being compelled at all times to become *one* with it.

I soon became very proficient at healing, um, crazy people. It was very simple for me, comfortable even, to get into the mind-set of schizophrenia and visions and voices and paranoia. As a trained healer, however, I could use my new protection skills to get myself and my heal-ees safely back out of the craziness and onto solid ground.

As I worked on myself and healed others of their terrors, I learned a very important lesson: I began to see that the beings I once called fearful, crazy, and evil were more pitiful than anything else. Just like me, they stored a deep well of sadness and an unimaginable sense of loss just under the surface of their fearfulness. I stopped reacting to the ways they tried to frighten and control me (creating fearsome apparitions, repeating words over and over, and threatening me), and found we had a great deal in common. I was able to see scary beings as lost, frightened children who needed to go home and feel safe, and I addressed them from a similar place in myself. "Evil" became a quaint and simplistic concept when I began to understand the individuals trapped within its confines.

For a time, I did exorcisms and healed schizophrenics and so forth. With each tortured spirit I helped release, I was able to release more of my fear of the spirit world. Today I don't have much interest in that carnival type of psychic healing, but it certainly helped me then. These days, I spend all my intense healing and releasing energy in helping myself and others to learn to communicate with themselves.

As for the concept of God, that's been simplified as well. I began to see that God wasn't a human personality who did or did not love and protect me. Instead, I learned to see God as the overseeing energy behind all creations and all beings, including the "evil" ones (Lucifer started out as one of His favorite angels, after all). It became clear to me that each of us has to choose good or evil, and that it was up to me to learn to identify the dark beings and to stay out of their way, if possible.

I learned that if I paid attention to myself and my healing, I naturally got closer to God, and further from beings who were stuck in horror. Actually, when I began to tend to my inner Garden, I found that God and safety had been waiting in there for me the whole time.

The protection systems I now use do not stem from a fear of people or spirits, but from an understanding of their needs. When I need distance from others, I do not imagine that they are out to get me. I see them as having lost their way, or their God. If I erect huge, complicated, and fascinating boundaries, I won't really be protecting either of us. I'll just interrupt both of our journeys and draw our attention toward my boundaries, and away from our healing. I've learned instead to distance from people by living in my own body and behind my own aura.

When I sense an intrusion (which my healthy, present-time aura alerts me to by changing shape or color suddenly), or people and situations begin to get to me, I don't get frightened or enraged as often as I once did. I use a protection symbol and mini-healing that moves people away from me in a powerful way, without fear or insult on either side. I send living, loving presents. I send flowers.

The gift of flowers and plants has long been symbolic of love, respect, welcome, and recognition. Though other gifts have their intrinsic meanings, none conveys concern and attention more universally than living, growing, healthy flowers and plants.

Plants and flowers can be used to welcome a birth or mourn a death; to congratulate or console; to signal affection, ardor, or friendship; they can even signal the end of a relationship. Because of the universal symbolism of flowers and greenery, they are a perfect symbol to use in our self-protection and communications with others.

In the everyday world, such living gifts are generally accepted as a symbol of giving, concern, and devotion. The same is true in the energetic, or spiritual world. Because plants and flowers are non-obtrusive and non-threatening, their use does not require us to be in a fearful frame of mind; therefore, they will not draw fearful experiences to us. On the contrary, protection with flowers and plant life requires an entirely different attitude. This kind of protection system removes our reactive fears of others and the spirit realm by replacing knee-jerk reactions with compassionate separation tools.

The protection systems we can create with lively, colorful plants are very, very simple—so simple that it's hard to trust that they could actually work. At first, I had a heck of a time replacing my formidable Walls and Mirrors and White Lights with wimpy little flowers, ferns, and trees. In a very short time, though, I preferred my simple, effective Garden-y tools by far to the old clunky boundaries I once schlepped around. My living, growing protection symbols were the key to moving away from terror.

The first living protection symbol you will create is called the Sentry. Its purpose is to stand in front of you, greet everyone you meet, and ground out energy that comes at you. It will stay with you at all times, guarding the outer edge of your aura. First off, though, we'll get a little intuitive practice and do a mini-reading with our first creation, which is going to be an imaginary rose.

YOUR FIRST READING ROSE

Here's how to create your first rose: sit down and ground yourself, and get into the room in your head. Check on your little one and bring them up on your chair if they'd like to be there. If not, give them something nice to eat or to play with.

Light up your aura and make sure it's a smooth, oblong shape. If it's not, ground it and perform an aura healing before you go on. Be aware of the connection between the edges of your aura boundary and your regular, first-*chakra* grounding cord. Should they be the same color today, or can they clash? You decide.

Now, from behind your eyes and within your grounded body, look out at your aura boundary. It should be about an arm's length away from your face. See the edge clearly in your mind, and envision a large, long-stemmed rose just outside of the edge of your aura. See this imaginary rose's petals, leaves and thorns, note the color and the openness of its bud, and note which way the heart of the flower is facing. What you have just created is a graphic depiction of yourself as a spirit at this exact moment in time.

Let's study this rose before we go on. Because we will be using a rose like this one as a protection symbol, we will need to re-create it with a number of specific, protective attributes. Right now, though, it's helpful to know what each part of this particular rose means, and what this rose says about us right now. Here are a few generalities about reading roses:

SIZE & LENGTH: I asked you to create a large, long-stemmed rose, but I didn't give you any dimensions or illustrations, because I didn't want to taint this portion of the reading. I wanted you to go with the first rose that came to mind, because this first rose is an excellent indicator of where you are right now as a spirit.

The total size of your rose correlates to the space you are willing to take up in the world. If your rose is the size of a real-world rose, and could fit comfortably between your nose and your navel, you have a normal, well-adjusted fit in the world you inhabit. If your rose is much larger, you may need to look at the ways your energy and personality dominate the situations around you. A very large rose may mean it's time to move upward in your milieu so that your talents and abilities do not stagnate in an unchallenging environment.

If your rose is much smaller than average, you are very likely in a world that inhibits your growth as a spirit. Your task is exactly the same as the task of a large-rosed person. It's time to evolve up and outward to find people and interests that speak to your heart and create safety in your life. Your surroundings are thwarting you.

THE SIZE AND OPENNESS OF YOUR ROSEBUD signify your ability or willingness to listen to your own spiritual information at this moment. The size of your bud relates to your spiritual capacity right now, and the openness relates to your use of your own information.

You can have a huge bud which is tightly closed, signifying tremendous spiritual capacity, but a present-time unwillingness to open up. Or, you can have a tiny bud that is fully open, meaning your life hasn't given you the spiritual support you need, but that you are remaining as connected to your own information as you possibly can be.

If you're just a bud, you're beginning again, and probably clearing out a lot of garbage in your life before you open back up. If you're wide open, you're relying on your spiritual information, perhaps to the exclusion of the information in your physical life. Why? If your physical life is providing you with so little support, it may be time for changes, in diet or exercise, in career or relationships, or in the places you live and work.

THE LENGTH OF YOUR STEM has to do with your connection to the earth and your physical life. It also relates to your grounding abilities at this moment. A very long stem means you are very grounded, but a very long stem attached to a tiny or tightly shut rosebud can mean that your spirit-to-body connection is skewed very heavily towards the body. This can imply a distrust or fear of spirituality, or a lack of belief in God.

A very short stem points to an unwillingness to be grounded or in your body right now. It can also signify a lack of physical exercise or proper nutrition and health care (healthy, fit bodies tend to ground naturally).

As an inverse to the previous stem-flower connection, a very shortened stem attached to a large or very open rosebud can mean that the spirit-body connection is skewed very heavily towards the spirit at this moment. This often indicates a very unrewarding, chaotic, or even dangerous physical existence in the present moment, one in which you don't want to have much part. If your rose looks like this, get grounded! You can't help your body if you aren't in it, and you can't make the changes you need to make if you don't live in your life! Get grounded and get moving!

COLOR: I have included a brief overview of the possible meanings of color in the Troubleshooting Guide, but I have done so rather grudgingly. The experience of color is so tremendously subjective that I think it's just absurd to say, "Red is anger." Red means so much to so many different people; depending on the culture, red can signify almost anything.

Here's one small example: in our culture, black or dark colors are used for mourning; in other cultures, white and vibrant colors are—in those cultures, our tasteful black funeral suit would be absolutely insulting! It's just not possible in one small book to elucidate all the possible meanings of color. I won't even try.

Shade and intensity of color, however, are entirely different matters. Shade can indicate a level of emotional intensity or participation in life. If your rose is very light or pastel, that can signify a newness, a kind of soft uncertainty in your spirit right now. Deeper colors can point to a vibrant certainty, and very dark colors can signify a level of stubbornness that goes past certainty into a harsh law-making attitude.

Swirls of colors denote lots of action and information from many levels. Sparkling colors can signify a great deal of spiritual information coming through (or moving away, if your information is being re-assessed and renewed right now).

Beyond that, the significance of your rose's color is up to you. If you must peek, you can read about colors in the Troubleshooting Guide at the very end of this book.

DIRECTION & AGE: Which way do your petals face? If they are facing away from you, this may mean that you are looking for your answers in someone else's life. Right now, you're reading a book on spiritual growth, so your rose may be turned towards the book, or it may be facing upwards, seeking information from your spirit. Your rose may be looking down at its stem if you need more grounding, or it may face you directly, seeking your instructions.

How old is your rose? If it's brand new, much of your spirit has been through change and growth recently. If your rose is old and wilting, it can mean that you have outgrown your old ways of living, but you can't quite let go, even though the old ways don't work any more. You can easily replace your old rose with a fresh new one, but wait until we're through studying it. This rose is showing you where you are as a spirit right now.

LEAVES & THORNS: Leaves and thorns signify your capacity for growth and your willingness to protect yourself in healthy ways, respectively. Don't be surprised if your stem is absolutely bare right now; the capacity for growth and spiritual protection are aspects very few people are willing to acknowledge. Take a deep breath and ground yourself, and ask the stem of your rose to show you its leaves and thorns. It will.

Lots of leaves can denote a great capacity for growth, and also, a great need for it. Many leaves can mean that you are in or are ready to start a period of major growth and change. Having very few leaves doesn't mean you aren't growing or can't change, they can just mean that you are already doing so much for yourself that you've used up the leaves that were once there. Complete leaflessness means you don't believe in your capacity to grow, not that you haven't *got* the capacity.

Usually, a leafless stem is attached to a very light and unsure, or very dark and stubborn-colored rose. With light-colored roses, the lack of leaves is a lack of confidence in the self. In very dark-colored roses, the lack is a stuck, "can't teach an old dog new tricks" sort of belief. The belief systems that create this lack of leaves can very easily be grounded out.

THE PRESENCE OF THORNS signifies your ability to protect yourself. Roses themselves have evolved thorns as a very effective way of keeping people and animals from stripping each bush bare, but when horticulturists breed domestic roses, they generally breed the thorns out. If you've seen wild roses, you'll know that most are so covered with thorns that you have to handle them with gloves. Are you a wild rose, or have you been domesticated?

Lots of thorns of different sizes mean you have a nicely varied series of protection responses. Lots of thorns in only one size mean you've got one basic defense, but a lot of energy behind it. Very few thorns means your protective energies are at an ebb, and no thorns means you are at a loss right now as to how to protect yourself.

If you've got a very small number of very big thorns, it can mean that you are running out of energy to protect yourself, and may have started to yell or lash out at people or situations that just won't go away. If you've got thorns that are hazy, or appear and disappear, your main protection is probably dissociation right now. Don't be alarmed if your self-protection systems don't look so great right now. We'll fix them.

Thank your rose for showing you how things are right now, then make sure you're grounded, inside your head, and behind your healthy aura.

Now that you have looked at the rose that symbolizes where you are right now, I'd like you to thank it and let it go. This can be done by having it vanish, by draining it away, by burning it, or by the quickest method, blowing it up. Know that you can always put up such a reading rose for yourself or anyone you know, to get a quick look at your or their present-time condition. Just make sure your reading roses stay outside your aura, that you do not ground them, and that you make them disappear completely after you have read them.

Each time you create a reading rose for yourself, use the guidelines above to start off your reading, but follow your own intuition, please. My guidelines are very general. You will soon have much to add to them.

After you've dematerialized your first reading rose, you'll create a rose that will not be used as a reading tool, but as a protection tool. For this new rose, which I call the Sentry, you will now create the healthiest, liveliest rose you can. As you create this new rose, consciously invest it with the qualities your reading rose lacked; this is a mini-healing.

CREATING YOUR SENTRY

Here's how to make your first Sentry: make sure you're still in the room in your head and grounded, and that your aura is still lit up.

From within your room in your grounded body (you may sit or stand, whichever you prefer), create a large, healthy, long-stemmed rose in a warm, vibrant color. Place this rose just outside the front of your aura.

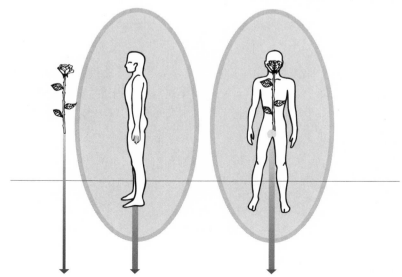

The rosebud should be fairly open and facing towards you at this moment. The flower should be directly in front of your face, and the stem should bear many healthy leaves and thorns and reach all the way to your first *chakra*. Envision the flower part as very large (as big as your face, if you can), so you can get a sense of hiding behind it to some extent.

Greet your Sentry rose, and attach a grounding cord to the very center of it (the ovary, or the rosehip). See this grounding cord moving down your rose's stem, reaching the floor, and travelling down to the center of the planet. Stay in your head.

See both ends of your Sentry's grounding cord as stable and anchored, and call your name down your rose's grounding cord three times. Now, turn the face of this rose away from you, so it faces the front like a good sentry. Stand up and walk with your rose in place; get a sense of it preceding you wherever you go. It will act as your energy bodyguard.

Your Sentry will stay at the front edge of your aura at all times and act as a primary protection symbol for you. This rose is meant to replace the Wall and so on; its function is to be an intermediary between you and the people you encounter.

Though you may find more suitable plant life for your Sentry in your own meditations, I chose the rose because it has something few other plants possess: a self-protection system. The thorns of the rose will, I hope, help to remind you that your sentry symbol exists to protect you and your aura.

Other plants and flowers may be more decorative or personally pleasing to you (and you can use them in the exercises in the very next chapter), but the thorny rose Sentry will help you to maintain a better separation for now.

Your Sentry works in many ways and on many levels. In its simplest form, this rose is a symbol of your beauty and love; it will transmit a peaceful, non-threatening greeting to everyone you encounter. Additionally, because it is grounded, your Sentry also has more complex functions and abilities. This symbolic rose can stand guard outside your aura and intercept other people much like a hostess (or a bouncer), by accepting and grounding out the energy sent your way.

Your Sentry can help you maintain a sense of peace and privacy, because its very presence tends to make people feel they have been communicated with and even validated on some level. Being met and greeted by a Sentry tends to calm most people down. Their own auric system notices the kindness and respect your rose symbolizes--often, that small greeting is enough to feed their soul. More often than not, people attempt communication simply to be noticed, and that's all.

Even very aggressive, bothersome people usually want only a simple, heartfelt "hello in there," which of course they won't get if they throw aggression around. Your symbolic rose communicates that greeting very effectively, and often, people will be able to interact with your rose, and not need to disturb you!

Though you set up your Sentry for protection, the message this living, loving symbol gives out is one of love and acceptance, which tends to make protection unnecessary.

At first, I didn't believe in Sentry roses at all. I preferred my Wall/Mirror/Light/Psychic Chameleon routine, even though it often left me exhausted. When I first started studying the Sentry, I lived and worked in downtown San Francisco and had to walk through the very rough Tenderloin section on my way to my bus home (at midnight, no less).

My usual survival technique was thus: I'd run a lot of adrenaline and intuitively read everything and everyone around me. Some eyes I wouldn't meet, some I'd have to; some men would become less interested if I acted young and soft, and with others, I'd need to act tough and "no nonsense." Sometimes I needed to act crazy and talk or sing to myself to fit in, and sometimes I just needed to hide in a doorway until the bus arrived. I always made it through unscathed, but what a performance I had to give!

One night, as a very drunk man stumbled towards me to ask for money, I readied my thousand defenses, but suddenly remembered my Sentry rose. I knew I could run away from this teetery guy if the rose didn't work, so I thought he would make an excellent first test case.

I quickly grounded and lit up my aura and put up my Sentry. The drunk man kept coming, but I stayed where I was, fighting not to put up my Wall, etc. Within seconds, the man staggered into my rose, turned on his heel, and without one word, walked away and left me completely alone. I was absolutely stunned. I forgot to ground my rose, so he took it with him. No big deal—I quickly made another. Not a bad trade--peace, privacy, and fresh air in exchange for one little energetic rose!

I used my Sentry rose exclusively from that night forward. Sometimes, I would send ungrounded flowers as gifts to particularly unbalanced people before I met up with them (sending free flowers or plants can help to calm disturbed people), but usually, the Sentry was all I needed.

An aside: other people shouldn't be allowed to take your Sentry if it's grounded, but you can always give out free flowers or plants to anyone, especially people who have a hard time leaving you alone. Make sure that your free "hello" gifts have no grounding cords attached to them.

If your free gifts are grounded, your recipient will get the message that grounding, safety, and psychic abilities reside in you and your symbols, and not in their own lives. This will undermine their abilities and turn them into ever more energetic, badgering pests, which will erase all the benefits of giving them a present in the first place. Your gifts should be just that, with no calling card or ulterior motive attached.

Remember, you can ground yourself, your aura, and anything you create for your own use, but you should never ground the symbols you send to others. People need to have the option not to accept the symbols you send, and not to heed the communication you give (though most people will accept your presents gratefully).

If your symbols are grounded, they are less ephemeral and harder to throw away. They also come at your recipient with a gift card, as it were, and the recipient now has the uncomfortable choice of accepting something unwanted or insulting *you*. Bleah. That's not responsible psychic communication; that's garbage.

This work isn't about controlling or intimidating others and forcing them to behave in ways that make you feel more comfortable. It's about getting in control of your own life and learning to create safety for yourself. You aren't in control of your life if you require other people to do your bidding, and other people can't move onward if they get the psychic message that beauty and peace reside in and come from you! Enough said!

Don't be discouraged if your Sentry experiences aren't quite as dramatic as my first try. In my case, I encountered a person in a severe state of altered consciousness. From that out-of-body state, energy tools usually seem more real than anything in regular daily life. Drunks and users see lots of things that no one else can see.

However, the less dramatic examples generally follow the same pattern: people think they want to talk to you for a specific reason, but all they really need is some love and communication. When they come in contact with the love and beauty of your Sentry rose, and it accepts and grounds their communication feelers, that is very often all the communication they need.

Keep your Sentry out in front of you and check it and its grounding cord periodically. If it's wilted or worn out, thank it for a job well done. If it changes or deteriorates, it has been intercepting the energy and communication of others. It's been a good Sentry, but it can be let go.

Create a new, beefier rose with a brightly colored grounding cord; make sure your new Sentry isn't too delicate for the job. If you like tiny pastel baby roses, put them all over your room and all throughout your aura, but use a meaty, thorny, deeply colorful rose for your Sentry.

Clearly, the symbol you choose for your Sentry needs to have a bit of an attitude! I envision mine as a broad-shouldered, nimble, highly aware, and energetic being with a goofy sense of humor. Nothing really fazes it, so I'm not constantly replacing or repairing it.

During your daily meditation check, feel free to re-create your Sentry at will. You can use other types of flowers or plants, and mix and match their colors to blend or clash with your aura boundary, your grounding cord, the walls of the room in your head, or your shoes.

Take the time during the day to check your Sentry's grounding, and to peek at it after you encounter people you love, and people you'd like to pinch. Note its appearance after each of your encounters in the days ahead, and make a note of the people who tend to damage it. They probably need a dozen free hello gifts from you in order to make their separation from you easier.

Know that you are safe behind your Sentry, even when energy-damaging people stomp into your life. Whenever your Sentry gets worn out, thank it, let it go, and create a new, industrial-strength Sentry with a new grounding cord. Know that, yes, people *can* affect your energy, but know as well that you can re-direct your energy and fix what's in disarray.

A note about destructive people: there are people who have received so much bad attention in their lives that all they can manage is behavior that draws more bad attention. You are free to be furious with people like this, but it will usually make you their new best enemy. Your negativity will attract them because they are used to negativity. You will feel like home to them.

Using Sentry roses with people like this can be frustrating, because they tend to destroy beautiful things, and it's very hard not to take the destruction of your rose personally. Don't. If these people can wilt or melt or destroy your Sentry, *they are doing you a favor!* They are showing you which energies your current Sentry can't handle.

Your job is to make a fresh, vibrant, beefy Sentry that loves a challenge. See your Sentry accepting destructive energy with relish, and growing stronger as it eats and then grounds out that person's energy. Remember, it's only energy.

Real plants and flowers grow more beautiful with fertilizer. Consider a destructive person's shitty energy as fertilizer for your Sentry. Know that anything thrown at you is just energy. You can work with energy. Your Sentry was created to work with energy, and intense energy doesn't need to scare it off or damage it. Use the challenge of energy-damaging people to create a lean, mean, Sentry machine.

I want to clarify something I suggested, which was to give free flowers and plants to destructive people. I know this sounds counter-intuitive. If someone is treating you badly, why should you do anything nice for them? Why not ignore them, or give them dirty looks? Why give them something beautiful?

Mostly, because it will surprise them. If someone comes at me with volatile energy, and they damage my Sentry, I immediately send them a dozen ungrounded gift flowers, *not* to reward them, but to avert their attention for a minute. I need that minute to re-create and re-vitalize my Sentry, and I need the destructive person neutralized for a moment while I do.

Then, when I am ready with a new, stronger Sentry, I see what the space-invader is up to. She may have destroyed all the gifts I sent and gotten her destructive energy out, or she may be in a state of shock that anyone would send her anything nice. She is almost never in the same place she started, and I am now ready to get out of her way, or to start again. The next round is usually much less intense, and may even evolve startlingly to a place of reasonable human contact.

Remember, everyone is intuitive, and everyone longs for spiritual communication, but our culture denies that. Any spiritual communication from you will be a breath of fresh air, even for crotchety, unloving souls.

Your responsible spiritual communication techniques will create a safer, more loving atmosphere around you, and people will begin to respond positively to you, regardless of whether they're unpleasant and unaccommodating to everyone else. For more help on dealing with unsettling, unsafe people, the next chapter, *Destroying Images* will be very useful.

Your daily meditation at this point should be to get grounded and call your name down your grounding cord three times; to get into the room in your head and check in with your little one; to light up your aura and heal it if necessary; and to create your Sentry.

Check in with your Sentry every morning. If it's healthy, just call your name down its grounding cord and change the color if you like—it's strong and doing fine as is. If your Sentry has taken a beating, thank it and let it go, and create a stronger, scrappier Sentry. Remember to ground your Sentry, and to call your name down its grounding cord each morning, and each time you create a new Sentry. You're done!

With only two more beginning skills to master, you're almost done with the basics of Meditation & Healing. If you are feeling overwhelmed, or confused about any technique, I remind you: skip forward to the Troubleshooting Guide. It will give you alternative techniques for creating your tools if you can't manage these more elementary ones.

Don't consider yourself a failure if you cannot master these techniques at once. I couldn't. I had to keep working at them because I had a serious spirit/body split throughout most of my life. Now, I'm back together, but it took work. It's good work if you can get it.

DESTROYING IMAGES

As you proceed with this work, you may notice that people are contacting you more frequently. Your parents and family members may call to check in, old relationships may pop up, and old animosities may flare up. People may intrude on your daily meditations by calling or coming over when you sit and ground, or by constantly appearing in your thoughts. One of these people may be your molester. This is all quite normal.

As I said before, spiritual communication and growth are generally invalidated in our culture; as such, any hint of them creates excitement, fascination, fear, and confusion. When you take on a journey of spiritual growth, you send ripples out in the psychic fabric of your life. Many people are intuitive enough to know where the ripples have originated, even if that knowledge is completely subconscious. They may not know why they're calling you or what they want to say, but they need to check in. They need to find out what's happening. They need to maintain the status quo and their sense of stasis.

If your molester senses that you are ridding yourself of his or her presence, he or she will most likely try to check in, either in your life or in your consciousness. Your work will threaten your molester if they have done no healing of their own, because suddenly, they will receive their own unwanted energy as you separate your energy from theirs.

Instead of being able to stay in comfortable denial, cherishing her insane rationalizations as to why she needed to molest you, your molester will be bombarded with the reality of what she did. If she thought she was teaching you about a healthy, lusty sexual life, she will now receive from you her actual lesson plan of gender hatred, dreary perversions, and a terror of adult sexuality.

If he thought he was controlling you and feeling his own power, your molester will now see you rising up and showing more true power than he ever could have dreamed of in his dreadful, truncated life. Whatever he thought he was doing when he hurt you, whatever story he told himself so that he could molest you without falling into uncontrollable remorse, whatever lies he cherished—all will come back at him with full force.

We know from our own experience that the return and destruction of our own lies was and is a painful but unparalleled opportunity for growth. When we had to stop pretending that we were okay inside, when that lie became excruciatingly unlivable, we could finally do the work that would make us truly healthy.

There isn't any shortcut out of lies. They're going to hurt until we look ourselves straight in the eye and say, "I lied. This thing (molest memories, damaging sex, controlling relationships, lack of security, disease, loneliness, etc.) has always hurt me. Not only am I not strong enough to deal with it, I don't even want to be. It hurts, I'm afraid of it, and I lied when I pretended I could deal with it." At that point, our own healing information will suddenly become available to us.

Before, when we were lying and couldn't receive true information, we couldn't move forward, and we couldn't heal. We weren't available to hear our own information because we were too busy covering up pain—pretending to be something we weren't, pretending not to feel. We weren't available for ourselves, because we were too busy lying.

Though it's not the most festive party gift, the return of a lie is one of the most wonderful things that can ever happen to anyone. Yes, it scorches us to confront the falseness each of us has dumped into our own hearts, but when we learn to honor our own true boundaries and our own true gifts, we experience a powerful, life-affirming healing.

If anyone, your molester included, shows up in person or in spirit at this time, they are probably asking you to stop rippling the psychic fabric, to stop stirring the fire and throwing off lies. If you are currently in an abusive relationship, the abuses may escalate or become more frequent as attempts are made to pull you back to a manageable, knowable place. Your healing ripples are probably beginning to affect the people who need to hold you back, especially when their own lies about you start to unravel. They are afraid, and think that if they hinder your growth, they can hold on to their comfortable and known agony. Sorry.

Even if people do get you to stop your work, the process of change and growth is already in motion, for you and for them. It will continue, whether they like it or not. My advice is to release them (with this chapter's energy tool) into the care of their own information, and continue on your path. Their fear, fury, and need for control belongs to them, not you.

Some people who show up will just want to say hello and study what you're doing (these are the people who will soon help you maintain your new-found skills, in all probability), but my suggestion is that for now, you keep your spiritual work to yourself. Nothing will gum up the works of an inner growth process better than having to get permission from others: permission to move on in life; permission to use spiritual healing techniques; permission to bring up your assault issues; permission to grow beyond the current level of your social milieu; and so on.

If people around you have noticed that the status quo is changing, and that you are moving beyond their established comfort-levels, you'll need a responsible, loving, and confident way to diffuse their stasis-seeking attentions. You'll need to be able to remove them, their needs, their hopes, and their wishes from your psyche. Once again, your symbolic gifts will come to the rescue.

We've worked already with hello gifts, which we give to people who like to be destructive. Our next type of separation and healing is called *destroying images*, and its work is more specific than the act of offering a free gift of a loving symbol. Destroying images actually allows us to move people out of our auras, and though it may seem startling at first read, it often has wonderful results.

DESTROYING IMAGES

Here's how to destroy an image: once again, get grounded and into the room in your head, inside a clean and colorful aura, and behind a strong and vibrant Sentry. Check your room and your little one, and if you want, ground your little one; they might like it. Get yourself into a comfortable, seated position, because you'll be here for a few minutes.

I'd like you to think of someone in your family—whoever comes up—and imagine an ungrounded gift plant or flower in their favorite color. Place this symbolic gift inside your aura, on your left or right side, whichever feels best.

Now, quickly place your image of this family member into the gift you made for them (I superimpose their image onto the plant or flower), move the gift outside of your aura and away from you, and destroy it as swiftly as you can. I explode my gift images with dynamite, but you may burn yours, vanish them with a POP, or see them disintegrating into a million tiny bits of nothing.

Check in with your meditative state: are you still grounded and in your head? How are your aura and Sentry doing? Could you maintain your energy tools and abilities around your awareness of this person, or during the act of destroying his or her image?

If you notice any disturbances in your energy tools, take a moment to fix them. These changes may be the normal effect this person has on your life (for instance, if you just lost your grounding, your aura definition, or your Sentry, you would probably do that in a face-to-face meeting with this person as well). The changes may also be the self-punishments you impose when you try to move on to new levels of awareness and break your ties with old relationships and modes of behavior.

If you experienced any weakening of your energy or tools, please re-ground and re-define yourself with stronger, more vibrant tools. Check in with your little one, and thank your energy tools for showing you, in this safe place, some of the ways this one relationship helps to keep you from moving forward.

If you noticed positive changes, such as a brightening of the colors in your aura or grounding cord, a reduction of mental chatter, or a clear communication from your little one, you have experienced the healing effect of removing people from your personal territory. It usually feels quite wonderful, and it brings us to a very important point in our healing path: the point where we begin to realize that other people and their needs for us should have no place inside our auras or our individual lives.

We're going back to individuation here, back to finding our authentic selves regardless of the controlling messages of the people around us. Grounding out and re-examining messages was our first step in making room for ourselves inside our own lives. Defining our aura and the room in our head gave us a finite area to care for and inhabit. Our Sentry delineated the edge of our owned area. Now, we have a way to remove other people's images from our well-delineated inner lives.

Inside our aura, there should be only one person: us! Our aura should not be a family reunion area filled with chatter, expectations, admonishments, and societal rules. Our aura will be at its healthy best when we live inside it, and it can talk to us without having to look over the heads of our parents or abusers, or around the shoulders of our siblings and friends.

No matter how much people love us, their energy does not belong in our aura or in our minds. Their energy belongs in their own aura. The act of destroying images makes that startlingly clear.

If you had a hard time destroying your gift image, don't feel alone. The idea of using violent separation techniques went against every idea of spirituality I ever encountered, but follow me here: when I create a gift in the favorite color of my intended person, I am offering them a symbol of love, acceptance, and beauty. When I place their image inside their gift, I am enveloping them in that beauty. I am surrounding them with love.

When I move someone swiftly out of my personal area and destroy their image, I am making a certain, clean, and lightning-quick break with them. Then, it's over. I'm through with the old image I had of them, and I didn't have to call them, plead with them, bargain with them, or make them feel bad. I simply let go, with absolute clarity. I let go from my side of the relationship, which is the only place I can ever effect any change. I set them free in a split second, and nobody got hurt. Now, our relationship has new footing, just like that.

How does it feel to have my own image destroyed like this? Actually, it feels wonderful, especially if I am in conflict with the person who is placing dynamite under my image. After their release, I can feel free to get back in touch, and to relate differently. I can do it right this time, because I feel released from my old attitudes, and from my image-destroyer's pictures of me. This is one of the most beautiful things about destroying images. It moves relationships forward.

An example: my best friend and I generally have a good relationship, but it has lately become one-sided. She has unconsciously taken on the role of protector, and I have become the person-in-need. When we talk, it's all about my difficulties and my struggle, and she spends most of her time advising me. I love her and value her insights, but I am starting to feel like a pest and a helpless little sister. She is uncomfortable too, because she has pain in her life that she would like to share, but she doesn't want to intrude on my long-winded, pitiful soliloquies. We are stuck.

One morning, she decides to put her image of me inside a bouquet of my favorite flowers and blow it up. She creates a number of freesias in my favorite color, and puts in a picture of how she sees me at the moment (helpless, clueless, time-consuming). My friend uses extra dynamite on my image, because she is frustrated with our relationship.

Suddenly, on my side of the relationship, I feel free, because that weak, snivelling picture I knew she carried of me is gone. I don't know that she has blown me up, and I don't feel sharp bits of flower shrapnel hitting me. I just feel freed from the weakness in myself and in our relationship.

I call her that morning, and for the first time in weeks, ask her about her marriage and her family issues before barrelling into my troubles. We are once again back on more equal footing, because she was willing to release me. Now, we are both able to try something new.

Since all people are intuitive, all people use intuitive communication. Maybe we know who's on the phone, or where a parking place will show up. Maybe we can sense another person's hidden bad mood, or just *know* when people are trustworthy. We all use intuitive communication skills. The destroying of images takes advantage of this fact.

People know (sometimes consciously, sometimes not) how we feel about them. It's like we carry around a picture of them that they can almost see inside us. If our picture is flattering, we have a friend. If it is unflattering, we have either an enemy, or a pest who can't leave us alone until our picture matches what they would wish for us to see.

In either case, people do know—even if it's in a completely submerged area of their psyche—how we view them. Our relationships are controlled to a certain extent by that view. The act of destroying these past-time-centered images in loving symbols helps relationships evolve.

By clearing out our old, limiting images of others, we can be in the moment, not only in our grounding and so forth, but in our responses to the people in our lives. The conscious destruction of images makes our relationship to the outer world as clean and present-centered as our relationship to the inner world.

Destroying images clears you out, certainly, but it also helps the evolution of the people around you, because it sets them free. Whenever you destroy your image of another person and release them, they get a healing of inestimable value. They get to move forward in consciousness because you were willing to release your old, past-time views of them. They get to come into the present and make new decisions about how they want to behave in relationship to you.

Your willingness to heal and change your relationships with others will give them a safe practice arena for making the same changes in other areas of their personal lives. When you release people in this way, they will be more able to go forward with you if they so desire, or move on.

Of course, people can also be stubborn and try to maintain the old status quo and the old images, but you can just destroy their image again. It takes almost no energy for you to release your limiting expectations of others, but it takes a ton of energy for them to be in resistance to change. They'll tire out eons before you will--even if they don't, you'll have a sense of freedom in the relationship. You will have changed it from your side.

The destruction of old images is the best way to deal with people who sense your psychic ripples and check in on your spiritual growth. Destroying images is a loving, responsible, and easy way to show people what you're doing on a spiritual level, without having to stop and explain everything in a logical, verbal way.

When you destroy their images, the people in your life can get a small intuitive taste of what it feels like to clean out and move forward in consciousness. Plus, you can have the spiritual peace and privacy you need for your healing without having to halt your process. Destroying images will comfort the people in your life, clear out the noise in your mind, heart, and aura, and give you the chance to heal and give without giving yourself away.

Your symbolic gifts and flowers, all of them, come from your inexhaustible spirit; as such, their use will never effect your day-to-day energy levels. You can bring forward and destroy images all day long and never run out or need to rest, because your gifts come from the constantly replenished nursery of your inner Garden. No wonder they're so beautiful.

Try destroying a few more images, but this time, revel in their destruction if that was hard for you before. Remember that your resolve in getting rid of old, limiting images of others relates directly to the quality of healing they will receive, and of the separation you will achieve. If your gifts flutter away gently or make a dainty little popping sound, you won't really be allowing the people inside those images to get on with their lives.

When your destruction of your image-carrying gifts is not certain and swift, the people inside them will feel a small, somewhat confusing communication from you—one that won't give them much direction. They won't feel the release that the real, serious destruction of your images would give them, and they won't really be able to move on.

If you can become comfortable enough to blast all the energy away from your old pictures and really mean it, you'll be doing your partners and yourself an irreplaceable service. Let go and allow yourself the freedom to get rid of old images, relationships, and expectations. Create beautiful, loving gifts, nestle your images of other people inside them, and obliterate them!

Remember to superimpose your image of people onto your ungrounded gift symbols *inside* your aura, and then to move the gifts outside of your aura to destroy them. These are important steps, because they help to remind you that the pictures you have of people belong to you.

The images you have of people are ones you create out of your experiences with them, but they are only imperfect and incomplete images that come from your current level of understanding and compassion. These images do not tell you the whole story about this person's spirit. They're just a tiny portion of the story; they're just the parts you can understand right now.

For example, your dad's spirited attention may drop in during your meditations, but your reaction to his presence and the images you create inside your mind will belong to you. The images are *your* creations, which are made up of your responses to your father. Your father is as many things and has as many different facets as you do. He is not just those aspects you perceive. He is a million things, and he is a spirit unlike any other. Your pictures limit his spirit, and depending on how important your views are to him, they can limit his growth as well--when he tries to measure up to (or resist) your views of him.

When you create a gift for his image inside your aura, you are taking responsibility for your view of your father. In effect, you are owning up to how you see him by projecting him symbolically, and enveloping that projection in a symbol of your love and spirituality. When you move your father's image outside of your personal territory, you are bringing that image into the light, where it can be released back into the psychic fabric.

As you destroy your father's ungrounded gift and the image of him that it contains, you will be examining your response to your father, returning his energy to him, and setting both of you free. You can begin again in that moment, and choose to see your father in his completeness, instead of viewing him in relation to your needs, your reactions, and your past limitations. Creating his image inside your aura, and then moving it away and destroying it with resolve—not some pseudo-spiritual gentility—will help both of you move on in the real world.

You can destroy images at any time and in any place, which is what I do. If people get in my face during the day and hello gifts don't calm them down, I'll blow them up right then and there. It's fun to talk to someone and keep nodding and saying, "Yes, I see," while I watch my image of them turn into shrapnel! What's hysterical is when they lose their train of thought and begin to relate to me more peaceably, for no apparent reason. Try it and see.

IMPORTANT: destroy your image of your molester on a regular daily basis, every time he or she comes up in your consciousness. The area outside your aura may begin to sound like the *1812 Overture* for a while, but it will feel very, very good to release this person from your life.

This whole book has been preparing you to identify your own body and aura so that you can identify and remove foreign energy, and nothing is more foreign than your molester's residue. Your molester's energy attachments will teach you, better than anything else could, to destroy images with certainty and resolve.

If you need special permission to have and use the anger or rage that may come up for you in these separations, skip ahead to the chapters in Part II called *Anger and Forgiveness*, and *Channelling Your Emotions*.

For fun, let your little one be in control of destroying your molester's image if they want to. Yee-ha, it's a wonderful feeling for them to be in control of this person's presence in your life. Finally, you and your little one will have a place to channel all that socially unacceptable explosiveness within you—and nobody gets hurt!

With only one more skill to learn, you are almost done with the first section of *Rebuilding the Garden*. The next skill, the *Gold Sun healing*, will give you a way to retrieve and re-dedicate all the energy you've been grounding and vacuuming and releasing and destroying. BUT, if you want to stay with destroying images for a few days, do so!

We have very little permission in our culture to move on by saying no, no, NO!, but this is precisely what molest survivors need to do. Much of the experience of molest is about having no choices, no power, no way out, and no help. It's good to stop at this point in the class and blow our molester's image to smithereens over and over again while we say NOOOOOOOOOOOOOOOOO!!!!

We know that this energy work is helping us to heal ourselves, but more importantly, it is helping us say no! to the continuance of the molest experience in our present-day lives. When we rescued our little one, we stopped the molest in the past, but we almost certainly haven't stopped it in the present, or our lives wouldn't be unrewarding and uncomfortable.

Our molester's energy still lives in our conscious or unconscious mind, and is probably very invested in controlling our lives and our reaches toward healing. Destroying images brings our molester forward into consciousness and returns the control to us.

This forced diet of unexamined energy can be painful for your molester to digest, but that's not your problem or your issue. Your job is to persevere in creating and destroying images—to give back to this person all their energetic traces. You don't need her images anymore, and your molester can't evolve out of her desperation and stupidity if you hold on to so much of her energy.

Let your image of your molester go, for your health, for his evolution, and for the evolution of the spirit of molest itself. Destroy the images of your molester as often as you can with a loud, explosive, but spiritually responsible NO!!

We will be doing even deeper release work with our molesters in Part II of this book, but destroying images is a vital pre-step. The destruction of images will help you experience the sensations and results of releasing people from within your aura. Feel free to move on to the *Gold Sun healing* if you are ready, but make sure you've blown up more than a few images *really well* before you do. Make sure that the images of your molester and anyone else who has victimized you in this lifetime are at the very top of your explosive list.

Your daily meditation at this point should be: ground yourself and your little one if they like, get into the room in your head, light up your aura and clean it out if necessary, check in with your Sentry and its grounding, and create and destroy ungrounded gift symbols for anyone who shows up in your consciousness. You can blow people up one by one, or you can destroy them in pairs, trios, or groups of whatever number you like.

Have fun blowing the stuffing out of your images of people, even (or especially) if you love them, and let your little one in on the process in any way you can. Children are much more proficient at energy work than most adults, and you are lucky to have the support of the child inside you. Let your childishness out and blow those old, tired, entrapping images away! You'll be surprised at how much fun you'll have. My inner three-year old thought this was the best part of the whole class.

PART I

BEGINNING MEDITATION & HEALING

THE GOLD SUN HEALING

Our work up to this point has been to separate ourselves from trauma by clearing out our energy. Now, we need a way to help cement the changes we are making so that old expectations and behaviors don't throw us backward into old ways of relating.

Getting ourselves and our little ones into the room in our head and behind our protected auras has helped define our territory. Grounding and releasing images has helped us to individuate from the foreign messages and energy surrounding us. Our next step is to retrieve the grounded energy and exploded picture fragments that belong to us. Our next step is to call our energy back into our lives, on our own terms.

The Gold Sun healing is a way to feed ourselves with our own cleaned out, rededicated energy on a daily basis. This healing is a constant reminder that our energy just is; it's not good or bad, healing or damaging, right or wrong. Energy just *is*, and it's available as currency with which we can purchase anything—love, happiness, grief, hatred, worry, laughter, insanity—anything. Energy can be redirected, renewed, rededicated, and reused. Energy itself cannot be created or destroyed, but the attachments we have to energy can be.

We already know how to redirect and rededicate energy. We've collected energy and turned it into grounding cords, gift images, and rooms in our heads. We've altered the edge of our auras, we've released energy from our pictures of other people, and we've drained the energy of old messages out of our bodies. We already know how malleable energy is, and how much it loves to move, flow, and transform.

The fluid properties of energy have formed the basis of our work, and have made it possible for us to move on. If we remain connected to our own energy source, and its fluidity is available to us at all times, then all movement, all transformation, and all healing is possible. Nothing can hold us back in life or consciousness if we have access to our own constantly rededicated energy.

The Gold Sun symbol is used to represent our endless supply of energy, with which we can create any kind of life we desire. The reason our lives often *don't* flow is that family and society usually need our lives to be understandable and controllable. Most of us here on the planet get stuck in some kind of stereotypical, societally induced, energy-wasting pattern essentially at birth. If we're a certain gender, we've got these thirty billion responsibilities, if we're a certain race, we've got *these* thirty billion, and so on into infinity.

Usually, by the time we're two years old, we've got huge slices of our Gold Sun dedicated to fitting in, making other people happy, living up to stereotypes, and not being any trouble. Children who try to break free, whose minds haven't got the correct amount of "fitting-in" synapses are often labeled hyperactive and drugged into normalcy.

Oftentimes, especially bright and powerful children are singled out by molesters, which tends to turn their vibrancy down to a more societally approved dimness. The spirit of molest seems to serve such a function in our denial-happy, sexually confused, fearful, and control-obsessed society: to contain vibrant beings and stop them from stirring up the family, the neighborhood, and society in general.

The Gold Sun healing, and all of the work of this book, exists to heal that containment and trussing of spirit in each of us. The Gold Sun healing also works through each of us to heal our society. Whatever release work we do has repercussions in the energy fabric, not only of our inner world, but of the outer world as well; however, we'll focus on ourselves and our own psychic fabric for now.

Our own personal energy is limitless. The symbol of the Gold Sun reminds us that our energy is constantly alive, constantly renewing, and constantly available.

We can't ever run out of energy, no matter what we do. We can give too much energy away and forget to refill ourselves, and we can clog our lives with other people's energy, but the vast sum of our energy remains available to us at all times. The Gold Sun healing gives us a way to gather and consciously feed ourselves our own energy, which contains our own information, our own healing abilities, and our own answers.

ENVISIONING YOUR GOLD SUN

Here's how to prepare for a Gold Sun healing: sit comfortably and ground yourself and your little one if they agree. Get into the room in your head, behind your clean aura, and behind your Sentry. Destroy a few images if you need to.

Now, envision a large, golden sun right above your aura, directly over your head. Feel the warmth of your Gold Sun, which symbolizes the limitless amount of energy available to you in this lifetime. Your Gold Sun contains your highest information, your healing powers, and your humor. Your sun contains an endless supply of energy that you can use right now. Your Gold Sun is also known as your eighth *chakra*, and its function is to oversee the energies in your aura.

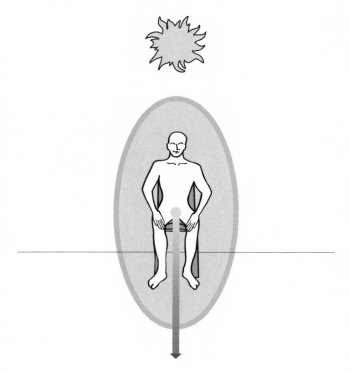

If my use of the word *energy* confuses you, replace it with the word *attention*. They mean the same thing. If your attention is on something, part of your energy will be there as well. Your attention requires a certain amount of mental and emotional energy, and the first part of the Gold Sun healing helps to remind you of that. When you are not paying complete attention to the present, your full energy won't be available, and you won't have the ability to function at top efficiency.

During this first part of this healing, your Gold Sun will act as a beacon for the energy you've lost or given away to relationships or situations in your life. When you ask it to, your Gold Sun will call back your energy and clean it out so you can re-use it. Ask your Sun to call back your energy, and stay inside your room as you watch it come back.

Don't be surprised if your attention is everywhere except inside your aura, and there is a virtual traffic jam of your lost energy in a holding pattern around your Gold Sun. Maintain your grounding and centering, and allow your energy to come careening back to you.

You might see the energy of disagreements or conflicts with other people, the energy of desperately wanting some material possession, or the energy of ignoring important tasks. You may also receive disjointed snippets of relationships, conversations, or emotional states. Stay centered and open, and just watch yourself.

As your energies come back, allow the attachments you created to burn up and fall off as the energies hit the edge of your Sun. Watch each bundle become clean energy again as it re-enters your Sun.

For instance: your energy may come back to you in the form of a remembered fight with a parent. You can either see or feel the quality of the conflict as the energy nears your Sun, but once the energy touches your Sun, the pictures burn up and fall away. The newly clean energy then becomes one with your Sun, and you now have that much more energy available to you. You can choose to revisit the old conflict with your parent in any way you like now that your energy has returned, or you can move on completely. It's up to you.

The purpose of the Gold Sun healing is to help you center on the present moment and call back all your energy and attention from wherever it was hiding. What you decide to do with your newly cleansed energy is your business.

If you can't see or feel anything coming back at this point, don't worry. Your Gold Sun will collect and cleanse your energy whether you can sense it or not. The Gold Sun is a powerful energy beacon, as is your grounded, centered state, your ability to release old images, and your ability to separate from others through the use of your aura boundary and your Sentry system.

Everything about you right now is already calling energy back. The Gold Sun is simply helping you to focus and get into conscious control of this process with the help of a visual and energy placeholder of sorts. Your energy and attention are coming back anyway. This Gold Sun healing is just a tool with which to collect, cleanse, and rededicate the energy that is already available and waiting to be acknowledged, accepted, healed, and re-used.

Each time you light up your Gold Sun, different energies and qualities of energy will return to you. You can observe the ways your attention is diverted from your present-time awareness, or you can trust your Sun *chakra* to do its collecting work, and relax into the healing.

When you really need to know why you're feeling antsy or scattered or deeply emotional, you can light up your Sun and closely monitor your incoming energy. This monitoring will be a simple process of watching your thoughts and emotions. Whatever comes up, that's where your energy and attention have been trapped. When you can see where your energy has been, you can ground out the attitudes that have kept you there, destroy images, or strengthen your Sentry so you can more easily keep your energy in one place. Or, you can let your Sun do its work on its own and know that your energy is now cleansed and available to you, no matter where it has been hiding.

THE GOLD SUN HEALING

Now for the second part of the Gold Sun healing: check in with your grounding and your general meditative state, and release a few images if your Sun work has brought other people into your consciousness.

If you need to, you can also dump attitudes down your grounding cord, change the color of your aura or your Sentry, or move your little one to a more comfortable place in your room. The changes you experience in the first part of this healing need to be addressed. Thank your Gold Sun for providing this self-healing practice arena.

If you experienced no changes in your meditative state, thank your Gold Sun as well. It is doing its work without needing to contact you or disturb you in any way.

When your meditative state is where you want it to be, make a small opening at the top of your aura, and let the energy of your sun shine in.

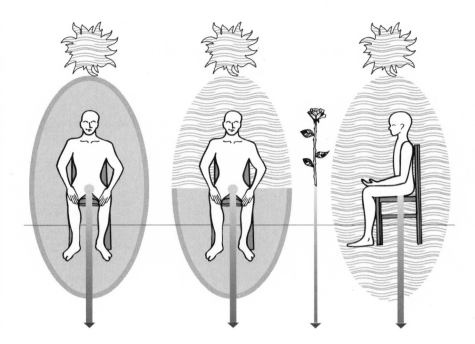

See or feel this warm, soothing, tingling energy filling your entire aura and covering your skin. Feel the warmth on your face, on your hands and feet, behind your back, under your legs and arms, and all the way out to the edge of your aura. Let your aura and its boundary become completely gold.

Breathe in the energy of your Sun, and feel the warmth as it enters your lungs. As you breathe, see and feel your Gold Sun energy travelling through your blood stream along with the oxygen you have just inhaled.

Feel your clean, present-time healing energy as it lights up your bloodstream, your muscles, your organs, and your bones. Feel your gold energy all throughout your abdomen, in your hips and legs, in your arms and hands, throughout the inner layers of your skin, and in your chest, neck, face and skull. Keep breathing.

Now, turn your grounding cord gold, and feel the energy inside your body flowing down your cord, cleansing the cord and your body, and re-dedicating your grounding cord with present-time healing energy. Stay in your head, and turn everything in your room gold—the walls, the furniture, the scene outside your window—everything. If your little one agrees, you can fill them with gold and invite them to move around and feel how wonderful present-time can be. Keep grounding and keep breathing.

Stay in the newly golden room in your head and shine your Gold Sun onto your Sentry symbol. Turn your Sentry gold, and change its grounding cord to match, and you'll give your Sentry a present-time healing as well.

Sit for a few minutes and experience your own energy. This warm, calming, tingly, wonderful energy is your own. It is constantly available at your discretion, absolutely free, and completely within your control. Feel it as it travels throughout your body, moving gently, lighting up each cell. Watch it as it moves through your aura and your energy tools, cleaning and rededicating your energy, and making each tool more real to you.

Watch your little one if they became gold, dancing around and feeling their own power and freedom. Get in touch with what it feels like to be authentic and safe in the present moment, surrounded by and filled with your own energy.

Now, check in with your grounding and make sure your cord is still gold. Running your Gold Sun energy through your body and out your grounding cord is a wonderful healing. As each portion of your body is lit up from within, old messages, pains, and stored emotions tend to dislodge and fall away. When you turn your grounding cord to gold, you'll be able to drain off a lot of old, clogged energy so your body can begin to flow into the present. Plus, healing your grounding cord with Gold Sun energy makes grounding much more effective.

When you are ready, close off the opening in the top of your aura, let your Sun disappear, and allow the golden energy to settle into your body and your aura. Keep grounding, bend over and touch the floor with your hands, and let your head hang downwards. Allow the golden energy inside your body to drain out of your hands and feet, or out the top of your head if that feels right to you. Stay in this position until you feel cleared out, then sit up again, slowly. Check your grounding, make sure you're in your head, check in with your little one, and you're done. Excellent work!

We always give our bodies a chance to drain out when we add energy to them. Bodies work very well on their own, thank you, and can be seriously disturbed when we traipse through them, adding light and colors and energy willy-nilly. Because they exist in the physical world, bodies are very different from our auras and grounding cords and images that live in the ethereal world.

Bodies have huge responsibilities, tremendous amounts of survival information, and much work to do on their own; our ethereal information may not jibe right away. In addition, bodies exist in real time, which means that their work proceeds at their pace, which is sometimes quite different from the pace our spirits can keep.

Though we nearly always mean well by it, adding healing energy to our bodies could be done in the wrong way at the wrong time, according to them. Our bodies need to have control over what they accept, and what they reject.

The Gold Sun energy shouldn't have any negative effects on our bodies at all, but we need to let our bodies decide how much of the golden, present-time energy they want to let go of, how much they want to keep, and where they want to store it. Bodies work with a different set of rules than spirits do, but they know exactly what they're doing and when it needs to be done. If our bodies need the spiritual energy we give them, they'll keep it. If not, we need to give them the chance to dump it off.

Don't throw energy work at your body. It may have been living without your attention for a very long time. If so, you can expect it to have its own way of doing things. Let it have the power to choose what it wants and needs. If you don't, your body may not trust what you're doing, and you could start up the old spirit/body split again.

Remember to bend over and give your body the choice of dumping out energy each time you meditate and use your Gold Sun. Your body may need to get rid of all your present-time energy while it works on an old illness, or it may keep every ounce of the golden energy you channel into it. Trust your body to make its own decisions. Work with it and not *at* it. Your body knows what it's doing.

Each time we call our attention back to ourselves and our Gold Sun, we are moving forward in consciousness. When we fill our auras and bodies with our clean Gold Sun energy, we are not only performing a healing, but alerting our body and our energy tools to the availability of new energy, new healing abilities, and a new level of consciousness.

After each Gold Sun healing is complete, our entire being knows where we are in evolution, because we've brought all of our tools into present-time awareness.

Now, our grounding cords and aura will know that we've called back our energy from this person or that situation, and they'll become stronger for it. Our Sentry knows where we are, and can transmit a clearer, more protective energy to people who want to check in with us. The room in our head has received a major spring cleaning, and our little one has received a healing. All of this helps to make the process of living easier, because each part of us is newly aware of and tuned into our current level of spiritual awareness.

The Gold Sun healing is a way to truly mend the spirit/body split we have lived with, because it connects our spiritual self to our body in a safe, warm, and real way. With this connection, we will suddenly have a number of safer and saner responses to the experiences around us, so we won't need to rely on runaway healing, emotional benders, fearful boundary-making, or dissociation. We will have not only the tools taught in this book, but the whole of our information as unlimited spirits, as long as we keep working.

Use your Gold Sun healing at the end of your regular check-in meditation, or any time you lose your boundaries. As with each of the other skills we've learned, this healing can take as little or as much time as you like.

In essence, as soon as you've got the gold flowing through you, this healing is done; however, you can choose to have your Gold Sun energy lighting and warming you for as long as you like, just as you can turn on your grounding vacuum, cleanse your aura, or destroy your images for an extended period. It's up to you.

A QUICK MINI-HEALING

If you feel a bit hazy during the day, you can put up a quick Gold Sun and fill your aura with gold energy, without going on to fill your body as well. This is a very swift way to redefine your aura, and it can be done at work, in the car, or anywhere else.

This simplified aura-fill is easy to do in the presence of others, because it's less involved than a complete Gold Sun healing. Since you don't bring the Gold Sun energy into your body during this mini-healing, you won't need to bend over and dump out, which can be hard to explain at a PTA meeting, or in the ticket line at the airport.

Actually, with a little discretion, you can do most of your meditation in public if you have to. None of these skills requires privacy, quiet, or even external peace, which makes them very useful for busy (and often harried) people like us.

You have now learned all the skills in *Beginning Meditation & Healing* and are ready to go on to the deeper work in Part II. Your daily meditation at this point should go like this: sit and ground yourself and your little one if they like, get into the room in your head, define your aura and cleanse it if necessary, check and renew your grounded Sentry if necessary, and release any number of relationship images. When you're done, light up your Gold Sun and feed yourself with your own energy. Finish up by bending over and letting your body dump energy out if it needs to—you're done!

Congratulate yourself for getting this far. You've learned a large number of skills, and you're ready to go on and do some serious separation work with your molest and your molester. Give yourself time to go back and revisit skills you didn't master, because the next section assumes that you can ground and work with your Gold Sun energy and so forth.

Don't undermine yourself if you haven't been able to work with some of these tools. Some skills will be as easy as anything while others could take a whole lot of practice, depending on where your energy is stuck. Skip ahead to the Troubleshooting Guide and look up your specific area of difficulty or your symptoms, and you should find the answers you need. If you are totally lost, you can contact me through my publisher, Laughing Tree Press, at the address on the back page. Otherwise, let's go forward.

Part II

Rebuilding the Garden

*Fitting in has often required
the agonizing, ham-handed excision
of functional portions of my personality.*

I realize now that the surgery was elective.

PART II

REBUILDING THE GARDEN

BURNING CONTRACTS

A quick review: we've rescued the assaulted person who has had to live through our trauma over and over again; learned to ground and center ourselves in a safe meditative sanctuary within our own bodies; and become proficient at cleansing and defining our auras. We've also learned to create and destroy images to release other people's messages from our inner lives; and created a Gold Sun healing to channel our own healing energy into our auras and bodies. With these foundations in place, we're ready to delve a bit deeper.

At this point, you already may have noticed a few relationships, attitudes, or ideas that you cannot ground out or destroy completely. In fact, some energies or relationships (especially those surrounding your molest experience) may show up in your meditations every day, regardless of how much releasing work you do with them. In these cases, it is very likely that you have entered into a psychic *contract* that needs to be examined, renegotiated, or destroyed.

When incompatible people relate with one another they often set up a series of expectations, behaviors, reaction patterns, and comfort zones in an attempt to create intimacy and connection. These postures and expectations often define the quality and scope of the relationship, and act as contractual maps or unifying placeholders for both participants. Through conscious and unconscious agreement, many relationships evolve (or decay) in precisely delineated, contractual patterns.

When people are truly compatible, and live in the present moment, their relationships do not require such contracts. Compatible relationships tend to grow, fluctuate, move, and change in response to the growth and awareness of each person.

If you have a friend to whom you can say absolutely anything, even if your paths diverge for months or years, you know the ease, freedom, and security such relationships provide. When people can communicate freely, contracts that specify rigid behaviors or expectations are unnecessary, and even damaging to the life of the relationship.

When people are not compatible, or not centered enough to live in the present moment, they often rely upon relationship contracts to create the illusion of closeness, or at least a reliable sense of continuity with others. In these instances, a relationship contract can remind people of how to behave when their own truths and needs are unimportant, or unwelcome, in a relationship. Work relationships or casual social acquaintanceships are perfect examples of instances where contracts can provide support when the true relationship does not. Relationship contracts are also helpful for people who would rather not be awake and aware in every moment.

Contracts can help to remind you to be serious with Mr. Baker, carefully emotive with David, funny but guarded with Jane, and so on. The problem comes when such contracts take over and force you to comply with their tenets, bylaws, and codicils. In these situations, authentic human communication and connection are swept aside—while the contracts grow larger and more rigid. In many relationships, people spend more time attending to their contractual obligations than they do in relating to their contract partner.

An example: we all know married couples who stay together for reasons we can't understand. Each person is miserable: they can't communicate, they are lonely and have affairs, or require tremendous support from their friends. But they don't split up and move on. Their relationship usually revolves around money, social obligations, or the kids, but their love for one another has no life or healing in it anymore.

What I see in this instance is two people bent under the weight of a gigantic, unyielding, 20-foot monster contract. Neither can reach (or even see) their partner through this behemoth called Their Relationship, nor are they capable of communicating around it. Still, both continue to feed and honor the contract, even though it creates despair. These two believe that it is honorable to obey contracts, and to live up to the expectations and demands of others, no matter what it does to them or their relationship.

Their unwieldy marriage contract is usually made up of societal and familial rules and regulations about how marriage should be. Often, both partners will unconsciously imitate their own parent's marriage contracts in a sad game of playing house. They will completely miss out on the excitement (and the work) of creating their own love and relating styles.

Such a contract will also be filled with trivial and often outdated information on each partner's likes, dislikes, and opinions—so much so that their conversations will center around reminders of how the other person is *supposed* to feel and behave ("You *hate* Mexican food... We agreed to have children *after* graduation... This never bothered you *before*...," etc.).

What these and all other relationship contracts do not contain is room for freshness, surprise, change, acceptance, or flow. Contractual relationships require conventional, reliable, and stereotypical responses. Relationship contracts exist to guarantee stasis.

Stasis is a natural and wonderful thing, just as change is a natural and wonderful thing; however, contracts do not leave room for the natural wonder of change. Contracts support only stasis; therefore, contracts are one-sided and unhealthy and should be avoided in an active, whole, and healing life.

Imagine how imbalanced and exhausted you would become if some agreement in your life required you to change constantly, no matter what. Your life would soon be unmanageable. The same unmanageability ensues when relationship contracts, which require a complete avoidance of change, are allowed to prevail over authentic human communication.

Contracts may seem to be workable support systems in the difficult realm of human relationships, but as with many systems that exist to make courage and honesty unnecessary, contracts soon become uncomfortable and incapacitating. Relationship contracts are often set up to make honesty in incompatible relationships nonessential, so that people who really don't belong together can manage their relationship on a superficial level. This may seem rational, and contract-building would be acceptable if human relationships were logical and rational, but because they're not, contracts in human relationships fail miserably.

When a contract is set up to help people avoid intimacy within a relationship, the people in it soon become *incapable* of intimacy or honesty. The rational contract becomes irrational in the real world as the people within it become trapped in webs of misunderstanding, frustration, and isolation. Release and freedom can only come when one partner is willing to take responsibility for their part in the agreements, and *burn the relationship contract.*

Let's use our unhappily married couple as guinea pigs: when the husband grounds himself and works through his meditation process, his wife may show up in his thoughts even after he has released her with a loving image. This will signal to him that he is holding onto more than just an old *image* of his wife; this will let him know he's got a *contract* with her as well.

From inside the room in his head, the husband will check his grounding, his aura, and his Sentry, and fix any problems he finds. Then, he will imagine a long piece of paper or parchment inside his aura, and place on it the qualities of his marriage contract. He may write his wife's name on the parchment, or a description of the emotional content of their marriage, or he may project a movie of their interactions onto the parchment. Whatever comes up for him in regard to his wife will be placed onto the paper, in plain view.

As he places his marriage agreements onto the parchment, the husband also places *his* stances, reactions, and requirements alongside those of his wife. As he does, his first parchment may soon become crammed with images and emotions. If this happens, he will move the first parchment aside a little, and create a second, clean parchment in order to continue with his releasing work.

When he feels a sense of peace and relaxation in his body, he will roll up his parchment or parchments so that the information on them is no longer visible. Then, he will imagine tying up each roll of paper with a healing golden cord or rope, and then moving the sealed parchments away from him. When the parchments are outside his aura boundary, he will set them on fire.

As he watches his relationship contracts transform into neutral, unreadable, unattached energy again, he will re-check his grounding and meditative state, and perform a Gold Sun healing to feed this newly available energy back into his life.

When he burns the contracts of his unworkable marriage, the husband will have examined, taken responsibility for, and released tremendous amounts of enmeshed, entangled energy. This step alone will help to heal his marriage, because it requires him to take responsibility for his part in the character and condition of the relationship. In addition, because his work involved a contractual agreement with his wife (which she agreed to on some level), his contract burning will help to release her as well.

If his wife is ready to move forward with him, this work will free both of them. She will no longer be ensnared by his stereotypical expectations and reactions; she may be able to respond authentically to him for the first time in years. If his wife is unwilling to move forward, and still wants to keep the old "You ruined my life!" pot brewing, his work will still have a freeing effect on both of them.

It does not matter if his wife refuses to burn her side of the contract. If the husband burns his portion, their contract will get smaller. It has to, and when it does, the wife's position will be less supportable, less charged, and less fun. It is not possible for his wife to maintain the old conflict with him if he won't fight, and it is not possible for them to have a damaging relationship contract if he won't sign it.

Regardless of the wife's wishes, the husband has moved forward. Because he is an individual, he has that right. The marriage contract they agreed to revoked his right to move forward, but he revoked the contract, and now he can make decisions based on his present-day needs, wishes, and realities.

The marriage may heal and renew itself, or it may end to allow both husband and wife to live again. The next steps, and the outcome, are as individual as they are. Burning their contract allows both of them to be individuals again, instead of slaves to a psychic document.

Contracts are everywhere. It is not unusual to have separate contracts for every person in your life, as well as contracts with emotional states like despair and fury. You can have contracts with gender identification and social standing, contracts with finances and security, and even contracts for how you live up to contracts! Assault survivors in particular tend to rely very heavily on contracts, because their general sense of dissociation leaves them feeling disconnected from the world around them. Sometimes, contracts are the only things that make a split person feel a part of the world.

Do not punish yourself for relying on contracts to pilot you through the tempests of human interaction. Contract-building is an important connection tool in instances where connections might not otherwise be possible.

We've already seen how casual relationship contracts can bring dissimilar people more comfortably into one another's spheres, but we have not yet looked at the support contract-building can offer to split and dissociated people. In many cases, contracts can be seen as lifelines that connect the turbulent, ungrounded spirits of trauma survivors to the earth and human reality. When I see numerous contracts in beginning

Garden students, I am actually more relieved than worried. Numerous contracts signal that connections to other humans and to in-body, human life are important; therefore, the work of grounding and connecting to the planet and other people in new and healthy ways will seem reasonable to them.

Though contracts are unhealthy in an aware and centered person, I much prefer to see a heavily contracted split person over a totally separate and isolated one. The isolated students usually have to fight at first to remain grounded and in their bodies, because they have no practice in reaching out and trying to connect to anyone or anything.

Once these isolated people get grounded and centered, they do all right, because they don't have a pile of unconscious contracts, or badly enmeshed relating habits to trip them up; however, they can remain aloof and separate for a number of years before they can truly trust in the healing aspects of human love and connection. Usually, their childhood experiences poisoned them in regard to love and connection, so they may need to spend a while burning contracts with their refusal to connect.

If most of your relationships require you to amend your personality, and your aura is littered with contracts, congratulate yourself for trying to connect before you despair over how much contract burning you will have to do. If you *never* amend your personality, and use very few contracts, congratulate yourself for refusing to connect in unhealthy ways before you despair over all the relational abilities you will have to cram into your being. In either case, it's time to get to work!

BURNING CONTRACTS

Here's how to burn a relationship contract: get into your grounded body and ground your little one if they so desire. Seat yourself in the room in your head, light up and cleanse your aura, and check in on your Sentry. Take a few moments to destroy the confining images you have of the people in your life, and be aware of which images come careening back into your consciousness. These are most likely your contract partners.

If you question the existence of a contract with anyone, create yet another gift in their favorite color, place them inside it, move their image outside of your aura, and release them again. If this person's image reappears after this second release, you've got yourself a contract.

Now, create a large piece of sturdy parchment paper in front of you and inside your aura. This parchment originates inside your aura to remind you that your views of people and your side of any contracts belong to you, not them.

Choose a warm and soothing color for this parchment paper. Bright or strong colors can be too reflective, and we want this paper to accept all our energy and projections without reflecting anything back onto us.

With the paper in front of you, allow yourself to think of your contract partner, and let your thoughts be transmitted to the paper. You can write your partner's name on the parchment, or you can write the name of the relationship (my wife, my father, my teacher, etc.). You can project your contract partner's image onto the paper, or transmit a video of their movements, actions, and behaviors.

If your first parchment becomes crowded with images, move it gently aside, and create a fresh page so you can continue to release the relationship. Some relationship contracts will require many parchment pages before you are through with them.

As you continue to work, your own image will begin to emerge alongside the image of your contract-partner. You will be able to see your conflicts, your body postures, your own attitudes, and your responses to your partner. Place those images and attitudes on the parchment as well. They signify your involvement in the contract, as well as your payoffs, and your reasons for agreeing to the contract in the first place.

Don't waste time abusing yourself if your reasons and justifications for agreeing with or reacting to the contract are less than wonderful. Stay in your head, observe yourself, and keep working.

Allow the energy of this relationship contract to flow out of you; use as many sheets of paper as you need. Your body and aura will signal the end of this session by making a shift of some kind. You may feel a sudden sense of relaxation, or the need to get up and move around. When you feel this shift, it's time to roll up each of your contracts so that all you can see are the blank, exterior portions of each parchment.

As you roll up each contract, tie it closed with a piece of golden rope. Binding your contracts with golden energy will remind the contract that you are now in present-time, where its rules and bylaws no longer apply.

When all your parchments are rolled and tied, move or toss them about three-to-five feet outside of your aura, gather or stack them together, and burn them up. Depending on your wishes at the moment, you may light one match under your contract or pile of contracts; you may set them ablaze with a flare or a stream of intense energy; or you may torch them with a militaristic flame-thrower.

When your contracts are blazing, stay in your head and watch their energy feed the fire as they lose their attachments and become neutral energy once again. As the once-important contracts turn to ash, know that they are no longer readable, viable, or legal.

Check in with your meditative state, and attend to any disruptions in any of your tools. When you are centered, perform a full Gold Sun healing. The burning of relationship contracts frees up and cleanses tremendous amounts of energy. Your Gold Sun will help you to gather, re-dedicate, and feed this energy back into your system.

When you have your energy back, you can use it to heal yourself, to forgive yourself, and to communicate authentically with your once-contractual partner. Remember to bend over and touch the floor at the end of your Gold Sun healing so your body can dump out any energy it doesn't want today. You're done!

Don't be surprised if your burnt-up relationship contracts attempt to re-animate themselves. Like any bad habit, contracts tend to hang around in the shadows of your being, waiting for the day when you become tired and unaware, and BANG, they're back.

If you can treat contracts like the untrained, immature animals they are, and gently but firmly remind them to "go on the paper (or parchment)," they will eventually get the message. If you give your contracts some respect as you create and release them, and realize what a valuable service they provided for you when you *wanted* to be unconscious, they will leave with more dignity and finality.

When you are less reliant on contracts, you will find that your relationships, even if they are purely social or work-related, will usually allow you the freedom to be yourself. Of course, this freedom in relationships comes only *after* you become centered and grounded enough to give yourself freedom in your own life, but the process of burning contracts supports the process of freeing yourself.

When you move away from contracts, relationship difficulties will become less prevalent. You will soon find it odd to be stuck and unable to relate, or in need of guidance and support in certain relationships. Difficulties with all humans will become a not-so-fondly-remembered thing of the past.

You won't need to identify yourself as unable to relate, and you won't need to use contracts to protect yourself from intimacy. You will begin to flow in and out of relationships that feed, instruct, or challenge you.

Your present-time energy will support you in saying what you feel, in asking for what you want, and in trusting the human experience.

Burning contracts won't suddenly turn the world into a safe or logical place. What it will do is free up your energy so that your inner world will become safe and logical for you. When this happens, your needs and requirements in relationships will change. You will release yourself from unworkably self-centered, "give me everything you have or I'll know you don't love me" expectations into a realistic, love-centered willingness to experience others. You'll be able to experience the fullness of another human without having to control, amend, objectify, or destroy them.

When you have the energy to meet your own needs, you won't require every relationship to be perfectly unwavering in its devotion to your specifications. When you burn your relationship contracts, you will free up the energy to meet your own needs. You will also free the people in your life so they can begin to meet their own needs, which will make them much less dependent on you, and much more able to relate authentically, *sans* contracts.

As you burn your contracts, take a few moments in each session to burn your contracts with the ideas, emotional states, identifications, and attitudes that hold you back.

For instance, you can create and burn the contract you have with your gender identification by placing all the pictures and ideas of how your gender should behave, dress, eat, parent, or make money onto a parchment. You can also burn your contract with depression by placing pictures of yourself in a depressed state, or by placing images of situations that depress you into a contract before you roll it and burn it up.

You can also burn contracts with your work ethic, your attitude about money, your fears of success or failure, or your reactions to certain religions, ideologies, or health regimes. You can free yourself from trapping, stereotypical relationships with anything or anyone.

We've already worked with grounding out some of the ideas and attitudes above, but it is very likely that some of the grounded items came careening back to us. We may have tried to ground and release gender issues or emotions and so forth, with very little lasting success. This lack of release signals a contractual relationship with the idea or attitude--a contract set up to keep you a controlled member of *the group*, whatever group that may be. Burn your membership card, please.

When we release our attachments and burn our contracts with ideas and attitudes, we certainly free ourselves, but we also begin to dismantle the ideas and attitudes in our culture as well. Any investigation of human history will show that many hallowed beliefs and practices simply disappeared when enough people examined and rejected them.

Some beliefs, like the flat-earth theory and the practice of medicinal blood-letting were rejected through scientific understanding, but some prevalent beliefs just lost their energy as people turned away from them. The wholesale beating of children in schools has never been proved or disproved as a disciplinary method, but it has disappeared to a great extent anyway, through the general disapprobation of society at large. Many ideas, inventions, and requirements that were concrete realities for our grandparents have no meaning to us today, because the energy and attention was pulled away from them. We can pull our attention and energy out of any of today's "concrete" realities, and live in our own reality.

Emotional states can also bind us contractually. We may become addicted to a certain emotion, and ignore the issues and emotions that caused the addiction in the first place. Rage, depression, and suicide are three favorite contractually addictive emotions that take up an enormous amount of energy which could be spent better elsewhere.

When we burn our contracts with recurring emotions, we free up our entire emotional body so that it can heal itself. When we burn our contracts with ideas and attitudes, we remove energy from them so that they do not have such a fiery presence in our awareness or our milieu. When we burn our contracts with gender, career, or financial identifications, we release energy from the fabric of those belief systems so that their intensity is lessened, and even less binding for others. When we release ourselves from contracts, we heal and release the people and energies around us.

When we burn our contracts, strangely enough, we actually become more connected to our world. We become more able to connect to the humans who share the world with us, because we move away from limiting rules and expectations, and into the flow of life.

I haven't said much about molesters yet, have I? Well, there's a reason for that. I'd like it very much if you would take a few days or sessions to become proficient at contract burning before we go on, because the release work we will do with our molest contracts can be rather intense.

If you are not yet proficient at contract burning, you may be overwhelmed by the release of the energy trapped in the contracts of your molest experience. You may freeze up in response to the energy, and you may forget your basic skills. If you are impatient like I am, and can't possibly wait to burn your molest contracts, will you at least commit to reading through the rest of this chapter before you attempt this next step? I'd appreciate it, and so will you.

LOOKING AT MOLEST CONTRACTS

Healing sex is a process wherein individuals exchange energy; they create life, bonding, and connection—in their bodies, in their emotional lives, and in their spiritual centers. Healthy sexuality allows the body and the spirit to meld as they create life, or add to the life of human relationships. Healthy sex heals by allowing lovers to connect and ground as they meld their energies inside one another's bodies.

Sexual assault, at the very opposite end of this spectrum, is a process wherein the creative, grounding, and bonding aspects of one individual are violated, sabotaged, and exploited by another.

Molesters require the same amount of physical bonding as anyone else, but at some point, their needs become twisted into diseased longings for inappropriate and unworkable sexual contact. Molesters prey on unprotected children because they cannot feed or manage their sexuality in healthy ways. Their sexuality becomes a lurid, power-wielding, secretive, and alienating action; each of their molesting contacts pulls them further and further from center.

At the outset of their careers, molesters can be seen as confused and tormented people. After repeated attacks, however, and after the repeated use of their bodies and their spiritual, sexual energies as weapons, they become quite insane.

Those of us who had the misfortune to be children in the sphere of a molester also have the misfortune of being energetically connected to them to this very day. Though their sexual acts were unbalanced, oppressive, and completely inappropriate, the fact remains that we were sexual partners with these people. Their energy entered our bodies and our spirits and melded itself with our energy. It is inside us right now.

Be aware of your reactions right now. *Stay in your head and keep yourself grounded.* Do not fly out of your body and dissociate. Keep breathing, pull your little one up onto your lap, and know that you are safe right now, no matter how much molest energy you have inside you. You made it through your molest, you have survived until now, and you can make it through to the end of this chapter. You *can* rid yourself of this energy residue. Keep reading.

When I first learned to burn contracts, I was not yet dealing with my molest in any real way. In my late teens, I went directly to intellectual release and forgiveness with my molester, because I could not and did not want to deal with my emotions. My favorite refrain was that I had understood the lesson within my molest experience, and could now go on to something else. Or so I thought.

When I finally examined the quality of my molest contracts in my twenties, I mean, really examined them, I was astonished by the power they still had. My forgiveness and intellectualizing had absolutely no effect on the psychic wounds I still carried. It was as if I had done no work at all. My molest contracts were as alive and active as ever, and I was living up to them in amazingly insidious ways.

Child molesters can most easily maintain their careers if they trick a child into thinking he is somehow seducing the molester, or controlling the molester's actions. If a molester can confuse a child into taking responsibility for the assault, they can avoid the horror a well-connected person would feel about coercing or forcing a child into having sex.

Many child molesters, who are often dreadfully overgrown children themselves, have the knack of knowing exactly what their victims are missing at home. A molester's offers of gifts, secrets, special privileges, and adult power lure children to them again and again.

My molester, a neighborhood father, kept me coming back by telling me lies about my importance to him. He created a tragic little sex-machine by meeting one of the serious needs I had as a member of a very large family: he told me that I mattered especially to him, and that he liked me better than anyone, including his own five children and his wife.

Our relationship was our special secret, and I as a three-year-old was even jealous of the other neighborhood girls he molested. His specially tailored message worked wonders for his peace of mind, because it kept me coming back while allowing him to place the responsibility for our sexual interactions onto me.

When I brought out our contracts more than two decades later, here's what they said: my molester was sad and sick and lonely, and no one loved or cared for him like I did. I got to heal him and be available while he taught me about sex.

He let me know he would not hurt me or get mad at me (even though he was very threatening to other people), because we had a special secret. I felt sick and scared and guilty when he did things to me, but he assured me that I was a grown-up, seductive, and exciting girl who gave him things he had never gotten before.

I know college-educated men and women who would fall—hook, line, and sinker—for that message. What chance did I as a toddler have of interpreting or refuting it? I wasn't just molested; I was carefully manipulated into believing that I had freely chosen to participate in this man's dreary perversions. I was lured and then entrapped into signing a contract.

When I, in my teens, forgave my molester because he was sad and misunderstood, and probably a molest-survivor himself, I was still living up to that contract! I was still invested in healing him by agreeing with his crazy message that he was sick, and that I or someone else was in charge of his decision to molest. I didn't get angry with him in my teens; I felt *sorry* for him! That would be funny if it wasn't so horrifying.

The contract my molester got me to agree to, and the things he taught me, stayed with me throughout my life. I learned that as a female, it was my job to be sexually suggestive, and to seek out unhealthy men and attempt to heal them with sex. I had a difficult time identifying with men unless they were sexual objects, and my attempts at friendships were shallow at best. If men weren't sick, or did not want me sexually, I had no time for them.

In my late twenties, after all that forgiveness schtick, I realized with a sick start that my molest contracts governed my entire life; my sexuality and relating skills were deeply twisted. Looking back from there, I knew: it was no wonder that I couldn't get to my emotions about my molestation in my late teens and early twenties. I could not separate from or feel anything about my molestation, because I had become a living, breathing testament to it. Through my continuing to offer sex to unhealthy men, through continuing to treat myself and men as objects, I had *become* my molester in my own body.

When I was able—through learning to ground and center myself—to examine my molest contracts, I became uncontrollably emotional. I would be sad and suicidal one day, furious the next, and empty after that. My molester's energy was everywhere, and I began to fear that I was going quite insane. I didn't know where I began or ended, and I wanted to kill him, or myself, or drive my car into a mountain. I couldn't stand the pain.

I knew enough to keep grounding, which calmed the tempest, and on that day I created the groundwork for the emotional channelling techniques that appear in the next chapters. As I burnt contracts and destroyed my molester's image (and grounded and grounded and grounded), I finally created some peace inside my body. Because I channelled my intense emotions into the releasing process, I was able to move decisively away from the molest contracts I could identify at that time. This gave me room to breathe.

Strangely, as the contracts disappeared, I experienced waves of sorrow and mourning. Even though my molest contracts were insanely destructive to me, I had integrated them so deeply that I felt almost un-anchored without them. I see now that my molest contracts, though revolting, formed the basis of my after-event, non-Garden life. My un-centered, dissociated adult personality was founded on the values and self-image I learned during the trauma of my assault. My molest contracts, to a great extent, formed my post-assault identity.

My work since that day has revolved around remaining centered in my life and aware of all my skills. My Gold Sun got a daily workout as I replaced my molester's energy with my own. I also concentrated deeply on releasing any subsequent relationship contracts that were based on my molest experiences.

It was hard not to be shamed by all of the casual sexual and social abuse I had invited into my adult life. It helped for me to remember that blaming myself for other people's bad behavior—and wondering why I didn't know better—was all a part of the contract that enabled my molester to keep hurting me.

When I was free of large chunks of my molest contract, I could finally see the molest for what it was. I know that I had no power there; I wasn't healing anyone. Now, I don't care if my molester was the saddest person on earth. Nothing gave him the right to use me.

I also see that my healing abilities did not fail my molester. He was far beyond help because he refused to take responsibility for his own illness. I know that there was nothing I or anyone else could have done for him, because his personal choices had driven him insane. I gave him back his craziness and ended our contract. I also burnt my contract with the idea that I somehow caused him to molest me.

If I could, I would have all sexual assault likened to shark attacks. Both offenses are startlingly, senselessly predatory acts, but somehow, shark attacks get better press.

Shark attack victims do not take the blame for the decisions of hungry sharks. No one suggests that they must have been behaving like lunch, or wearing a package of chum under their suits. Instead, these survivors are celebrated as veterans and martyrs of the gorgeous, uncontrollable sea. Shark-attack survivors often keep right on swimming or diving (because what could be left to fear?), even if they are missing major portions of their anatomy. They can even tell the story of their attack in public places without being shamed or studiously ignored by others.

In contrast, sexual assault survivors must deal not only with the horror of their assault, but with the emotional illiteracy of a sexually confused society. We have such an unreal relationship to our sexuality that we have a very hard time acknowledging the reality of sexual crime. Because of this, survivors of sexual assault are constantly beset with questions, spoken or not, about their own culpability in their assault.

It is a shame that assault survivors are invited to feel responsible for having been victimized, not just by their molester, but by society as well. In my case, one chowderhead figured out how I as a three-year-old could have been at fault in my molestation; it was my karma!

I actually believed it, too. Due to the way I usually felt about myself, it was easy to believe that I was some sort of monster who deserved to incarnate and be attacked almost immediately—as if my molester had no power to not molest me, because my karma overruled him!

My contracts helped me to feel responsible for the assault, not just in this world, but in the spirit world as well. My agreements with these molest contracts gave me near-total responsibility for the actions of my molester. My molester certainly appreciated my taking the blame; in many ways, I think society appreciated it too.

We know that molesters won't take responsibility for their actions. Unfortunately, our contracts require us to agree with our molester's irresponsible stance. We spend hours and years thinking, "If only I had been a quieter, nicer child... If only there weren't stresses... If only I could have helped my attacker...." Honestly, we spend our time and energy wondering which of our essential flaws *forced* someone to molest us!

We think we should have *known* better, or wonder what we as *children* could have done to stop the molest. These ideas seem so ridiculous when you reflect on them, but their function is not ridiculous at all.

Disconnected, un-centered people need to feel safe in the world, because they have no safe communication with their souls, nor a safe, personal experience of God. Often, un-centered people will grab for their idea of safety and security at the expense of everyone around them.

In our disconnected society, this desperate need for external safety, security, and rationality often fosters an unbelievably cruel attitude toward victims of crime, whose experience certifies that safety is often unavailable in the external world.

When we take, or are invited to take, responsibility for assaults upon us, we are providing security for the unwell aspects of our society and ourselves. We are agreeing with the idea that only the careless, stupid, impoverished, or improperly armed among us can ever be victims. We are adding energy to the idea that says there are real ways to keep the vagaries and traumas of life on Earth away from our doors.

When we sign our personal, "Yes, I *made* you assault me" contracts with our molesters, we also enter into a larger, class-action contract with all the frightened, small-minded, and callous souls on the planet. Our self-blaming helps them to maintain their assertions that they can keep themselves safe from external harm by being meaner, smarter, richer, or sneakier than the next guy. In order to maintain their life views, such people have to make people like us wrong, flawed, and imminently responsible for our sexual and psychic wounding.

It is very unusual for people to give responsibility for assaultive behavior to the assaulter! This is because people would really rather not face the fact that some people are completely uncontrollable. They hire more police and build bigger jails, but almost no one knows how to deal with the fact of human evil. It is much easier for them to pretend they have complete control over others, and that victimization only comes about when they are momentarily unaware or too lightly defended.

Though this is a widely accepted belief, it is not related to sanity. It is megalomania! We cannot control others. We cannot control others! We can't even heal others if they don't want to be well. We have no power over what other people choose to do. We control only ourselves.

Inside our auras, we are in charge of our internal issues, and of our relating skills and responsibilities. From inside the room in our head, we are in control of our reactions to anything that comes at us from the internal or external world. We are not in control of what comes at us. We are only in control of how we deal with what comes at us.

In our centered, adult lives, we can choose to leave or stay in abusive environments—in this way we control our reactions to what comes at us—but as children, we did not have that option. We were trapped and victimized because we were powerless; because someone took advantage of our position. There was no magic inside us that forced our attackers to break the laws of man and God and hurt us. Our molesters made the decision to molest us all by themselves.

It doesn't matter if children are seductive. Adults have a solemn, binding responsibility not to molest them.

It doesn't matter if you were naughty or noisy or stress-producing for your family members. Nothing in the world will ever excuse incest.

It doesn't matter what preceded the assault. The crime started *with the molester* at the very moment he or she began the attack.

It also doesn't matter if you went back for more, or "asked for it;" our molesters always had the power to refuse to molest us again. Nothing we did or could do made any difference. The assault happened because our molester decided to assault us.

In a nutshell, we experienced human evil, which is an inescapable facet of life here on Earth. We did not create the evil. We are not endowed with those powers. We were just caught swimming through our childhoods by a predatory, shark-like person. We survived the attack, and now, it's over.

You can swim once again in the waters of life, because, truly, the worst has already happened. There is nothing left to fear, unless you stay out of the water and out of your body forever, constantly reliving your attack.

In truth, you as an attack-survivor will now be a safer, smarter swimmer, because you will be able to sense and even smell shark-like people. Your little one holds that ability for you. He or she can spot unsafe people a mile away. All you have to do to avoid such people (to the extent you or anyone can) is to stay aware, centered, and in touch with your little one and your spiritual tools as you float through your life.

You now know what human evil looks like, and where sharks live. You can burn the contracts that draw you toward sharks, and learn to avoid the lagoons and waters where they congregate.

As you burn your contracts, you will also release the sharks that live inside you. You can release the molesting, abusive, and sanity-destroying residues of your assault contracts, and learn to channel your own God-given healing energy into your body and your life. You can swim in another direction—in any direction you like—as long as you maintain communication between your body, your spirit, your emotions, and your intellect.

Your spiritual healing work will not make everything in your external life magically smooth and wonderful, but when you have a clean, available, and lively inner life, your outer life will not have to be perfect.

Burning your relationship contracts releases others from the impossible task of providing for all of your needs. Tending to your Garden and burning your molest contracts will release the external world from the burden of having to be perfect before you will feel safe, comfortable, or happy. Burn your contracts and let them go--set your spirit free.

BURNING MOLEST CONTRACTS

Before you burn any molest contracts, make sure that your meditative state is whole and centered. Because these contracts are so foundational, the release of them can pull the rug right out from under you.

As you bring forward and burn your contracts, you may lose your grounding or your aura boundary, shoot out of the room in your head, misplace your Sentry, or forget about your Gold Sun healing. Please feel free to skip to the Troubleshooting Guide or the chapters on advanced healing techniques in Part III for help with any specific difficulties.

When you burn your molest contracts, you will also experience the release of a number of strong emotions or bodily sensations. Please skip ahead to the chapter called *Channelling Your Emotions* for support and guidance if your emotions become unmanageable.

The process of releasing your molest contracts can be a long one. Any contract with a sexual partner will be stronger and more complex than a casual relationship contract. In the case of a molest, the contract can be very entrenched, involved, and hidden in and around the body, and throughout the emotional landscape.

The size and complexity of molest contracts will vary from person to person. The quality of the contracts depends on your age at the time of the initial assault, the period over which any repeated assaults occurred, the connection your assaulter had to you or your family, and the emotional quality of the assault experience itself.

When a person is assaulted during childhood, his assault contracts will be tied into the learning and socialization processes of his particular age. If a child is assaulted in infancy or toddlerhood, his assault programming may be tied into his speaking and language skills, or to his sense of purpose as an individual. Later assaults may incorporate molest programming into gender and familial identity, peer socialization, body image and identity, or scholastic learning patterns.

In general, molest contracts are easier to identify and release if the initial assault occurred past the age of five or six. This is because the child often has competent language skills, and is more conscious of the adult world than a younger child is. Older children's molest memories will be more grounded and succinct, whereas toddler and infant memories may be hazy, incomplete, and stilted by their lack of language and discernment skills.

Usually, earlier molest contracts have deeper and more foundational roots than later ones, unless that later assault was continued for a period of years, or was a part of the family structure. Long-term molestations (or serial attacks by unrelated molesters), cross a number of developmental stages in a growing individual. As such, recurrent molest contracts have the same kind of depth and complexity one would see in the contracts of a survivor molested in infancy.

The contracts of a recurrently molested child, regardless of their age at the outset of the victimization, may involve destructive programming about life purpose, basic identity, personality traits, relational abilities, and even physical resistance to disease.

Assaults from within the family can go deeper still. Incest creates molest contracts that seem to attach themselves to the DNA of survivors. Incestuous relationships are far more insidious than non-family molestations, because the assaulter usually has ongoing, unlimited access to her victim. As such, this molest is not merely a horrifying event, but a regular, nearly dependable fact of family life and programming.

Incest survivors are often thwarted in their attempts to heal themselves because they still must deal or live with their molesters, who may also masquerade as parents, grandparents, aunts and uncles, or siblings. It can also be difficult for incest survivors to live in their bodies when they have inherited the eyes, the hands, the voice, or other physical attributes of their molester.

Another factor in the complexity of molest contracts is the emotional atmosphere of the assault itself. If the assault was sneaky, and deceitfully tied in with protestations of love and care, the survivor's relationship to love and care in adulthood will be very imbalanced. If the molester expressed or repressed strong emotions during the molest, the survivor's relationship to those emotions will be imbalanced as well.

These imbalances may take the form of complete aversion to the leading emotive quality of the assault, as the survivor tries to escape his memories. They can also take the form of a complete and addictive immersion in the leading emotion, if the survivor believes that his power resides in his molester or the molest experience.

If you are taking your molestation-intensity score right now, *stop*! It doesn't matter if you were molested by your father, starting in infancy, for a period of 7.2 years, with a leading emotion of rage; or if you were molested at the age of seven by a nice old woman, but never again. It is not good, or right, or healing to compare your experience of hell with the experiences of other people. It's all hell.

It is your own experience that you are attempting to heal now. Identifying yourself as a victim, and joining a group filled with similar victims is a very healing step, but it's only one step of many. If you spend too much time comparing your molest to the molest of another, you're off-track. Being off-track for a little while is a good vacation, but you've got to continue on your own path if you're going to heal your own pain.

It doesn't matter if someone else had a "harder" or "easier" molest experience than yours. However your sexual assault occurred, it was enough to throw you out of your body. For some of us, the break came through the emotional sphere, for others, through the physical sphere, and for others, only repeated molests could break their hold on life. We are all completely different, and our lessons, strengths, and weaknesses are completely individual; therefore, it doesn't matter how your molest-group-mates reacted. What matters is that you deal with your own experience, listen to your own child-self, burn your own molest contracts, and heal your own energy body.

Glorifying or minimizing your molest experience by comparing it to someone else's is a strange diversion. Do you seek further identification with your victimhood, or some sort of competitive molestation awards ceremony? Or do you seek your wellness? Wellness is a much nicer award.

As you work through your molest contracts, you may have to bring them out and destroy them once or twice a day for a period of weeks or months. They are that involved; however, they can and do move on if you will remain centered.

Each of the skills in Part I of this book will be called into action as you work, and you may be surprised to find your body and aura communicating with you in startling ways. Your head may ache when you are not in your room, or you may trip or become clumsy when you are ungrounded. Your aura may shake or quiver when you are not centered, or when your Sentry is breaking down. In addition, the relationships or experiences your psyche wants to release will step forward and boldly ask to be rescued, released, or grounded out. Your child-self may send you clear and even audible messages. Remain centered and available. Your healing abilities are awake, alive, and on task.

As you release your molest contracts, your body may bring illnesses, pains, and genital discomfort to your attention. At times, you may even be able to feel the molest as if it were happening to you in the moment. DO NOT LEAVE YOUR BODY. Stay in your head, draw your little one to you, ground the painful or affected area, and then protect and soothe the distressed area with your hands, and with dozens of strongly grounded Sentry images.

If pains, illnesses, or physical memories of touch come forward in your healing process, congratulate yourself and your body profusely. This physical release is an excellent sign that your body is coming into present time by moving trapped and damaging energy up and out of itself. Your body is placing itself in your competent hands, and asking for your help in releasing and understanding its stored and unhealed pain.

When this energetic shift occurs, it is a very good idea to find yourself an acupuncturist, homeopath, or ayurvedic practitioner to support this healing flow of energy through your body. It would also be beneficial to listen to the tapes called *Why People Don't Heal*, by Caroline Myss, wherein illnesses are connected to stuck, unhealed, contract-bound energy. You know how to release energy.

Though you may feel frightened, out of control, and scattered in response to the material coming forward, what you are experiencing is the healthy communication of your body and your awareness. As you move through your molest damage, this emotive and bodily communication will become clearer and more pleasant in nature. For right now, though, I would strongly advise you to support your body's willingness to heal with the expertise of an energy-centered physician. Such people can actually help to pull the molesting energy residue right out of your muscles, bones, organs, and cells.

As your assault contracts and their behavioral programming depart, you may feel strangely empty, confused, or un-tethered. You may not know how to behave without the support of all your contractual agreements, or how to live your life without their instructions. You may even miss them, or feel lonely and undefined when your victim consciousness begins to fade away.

These feelings are normal, healthy, correct, and expected. If you don't feel empty, you are not actually releasing the energy. The sense of emptiness is a sign that you are cleaning out and doing your work!

Molest contracts were entered into during a sexual relationship, which means that their rules and regulations came into, and then lived right inside, our bodies. If we grew up with them, they were also present for our growth and learning process, in our family relationships, and in our significant life passages. Our molest contracts most likely lived through our schooling and adolescence, through our college or career decisions, through our adult relationships, and even through our parenting of our own children. They were an integral part of our lives.

The loneliness, fear, and lack of direction you are experiencing now are just signs of the protective aspects of stasis within your own personality. The removal of these intrinsic and even innate contractual instructions is an extreme and profound change. Of course your body, your emotions, your intellect, and your spirit are going to react to that change. It would be bizarre for them not to react.

The way to support yourself in this releasing process is to ground, ground, ground, and ground. Grounding will keep you and your body in communication with one another, which will make the room in your head more comfortable. From inside your room, you can heal and redefine your aura, check on your Sentry, ground out pain and difficulty, destroy images, and burn your contracts. Grounding makes it all possible.

It is also vital to perform as many Gold Sun healings as you can during this time. Your Gold Sun energy contains specific, individual healing energy for you, as well as health information, behavioral guidelines, personal support, and information on your direction and your most healing spiritual path right now. As the old molest information and energy leaves you, make certain that you replace it with the cleaned out, healing, and supportive information and energy of your Gold Sun.

Remember, before you were molested, you were a complete, meaningful, magical spirit. You still are, under the soot and ashes. In a bizarre way, molest may give you a leg up in your adult life, because it allowed your spirit to split off and be hidden away until now.

Where other, non-molested people may have had the hope and determination they were born with eroded away in the course of a "normal" life, yours have been essentially untouched. If you can get rid of your old molest-centered contracts and shake off their dust, you will find an amazing treasure.

Along with your incredible, multi-faceted survival skills, you will now have access to the person you were before the trauma. This part of you didn't die; it hid in the shadows until it was safe to come out again. Now, if you want it, you will have the intuitive, silly, angry, loving, questing, snotty, powerful energy you had as a child. With it, you can accomplish anything.

When you add contract burning to your set of spiritual tools, you will become, for all intents and purposes, a miracle worker in your own life. When you can remove ideas, attitudes, expectations, once-cherished beliefs and other unwanted energies from your life, and then clean, retrieve, and repossess their neutral, healing energy, you will be a gifted psychic self-healer.

PART II

REBUILDING THE GARDEN

ANGER AND FORGIVENESS

As you burn your contracts, you may be inundated with strong emotions like terror and fury. All strong emotions are wonderfully energetic healing tools—and we will learn to use them in the very next chapter—but I'd like to take a special look at anger before we go on.

You may have heard that anger is a useless emotion; damaging, pointless, and immature. You may also have heard that forgiveness is a spiritually imperative act, without which no healing can occur. Well, you heard wrong.

I agree that unending anger is completely unhealthy, and that real, deep-level forgiveness is transforming, but anger and forgiveness do not stand magically outside the laws of positive and negative that govern all aspects of our universe.

We are all a blend of light and dark, of male and female, of love and hatred, of stupidity and brilliance. All aspects of our being share this blend, as do all of our emotions. Real sadness and real exhilaration can be exquisitely healing, just as unending sadness and unending exhilaration can throw us into imbalance. Both have their beauty and their shadow. Anger and forgiveness are the same. They have their healing purpose, and their destructive aspects too.

A beautiful and spiritual young woman came to my Garden class with no aura. Though her father had raped her for years, she had done vast amounts of work in forgiving and understanding him. Her only problem now was that her life had no joy or direction, and she could not see or feel her aura. She felt that she might be preparing to pass over to the spirit world, because she had little connection to her life, or to life on the planet.

I gave her a healing, and she was right. I couldn't find an edge or a color to her aura on any level. I marshalled some of the energy around her body into a small, makeshift aura, but after she left, I wondered what she could possibly learn from me. She seemed to have evolved past the need for boundaries; she seemed to be finished with her lessons, and ready to pass onward.

Two days later, she called me in a panic. She was enraged, shaking, and uncontrollably furious with everyone around her. She wanted to strangle her boss and stomp the high-heeled feet of the women in her office.

This formerly etheric angel of light was cutting off other drivers and swearing like a sailor. I immediately had her sit down and destroy images of both of her parents in the most violently explosive way she could. As she did, she calmed down, and was soon able to resume work.

In our healing session that night, I checked her aura again and found it strongly defined with a fiery red light. Her anger brought back her boundaries. Her anger *healed* her! Her forgiveness, no matter how well-meaning, was a disastrous lie for her at that point in her process. Forgiveness shot her out of her body and her life because it made her father's comfort—and a pseudo-spiritual concept of forgiveness—more important than her own reality.

Her subsequent use of anger, and the separation work it supported, restored not only her boundaries, but the wise voice of the little girl her father silenced when he maliciously initiated her into his illness. In a period of weeks, she was able not only to maintain her aura and grounding, but she was able to plan for a move and a complete change in career. Anger, that supposedly bad and immature emotion, healed her and set her free. It even may have saved her life.

Real anger and all real emotions have specific functions and specific healing properties. Real anger is momentary, boundary-enforcing, and non-directed. Real anger says, "This far and no further!" It does not attempt to hurt or degrade others; it only wants to protect *us*. Real anger creates a very clear delineation between our lives and beliefs, and the lives and beliefs of the people around us. Real anger offers us real separation, real healing, and true support.

Damaging, imbalanced, addictive, and destructive anger is another story; however, we all have such vast experiences with damaging anger, and so few examples of real, healing anger that the entire emotion has been categorized as negative. This is sad. It's like giving up on love because you could love the wrong person and get hurt. It's like giving up on grief because it might last longer than is comfortable.

The power of real anger is that it creates clear boundaries; the tragedy of misused anger is that it creates rigid divisions. The greatest tragedy of all is that our society invalidates all anger, which makes the work of legitimately angry people very difficult.

People who have lost their boundaries through assault, torture, or molestation need their anger so that they can re-create their boundaries and begin to heal. Survivors of trauma require their anger, but they are usually coddled or shamed out of it by well-meaning, but uninformed helpers. Such helpers place the concepts of forgiveness and acceptance above the true needs of the survivor; they throw anger out the window. Such helpers forget that there are real steps involved in real forgiveness.

My own case was not unusual; as I said, I went to forgiveness first. At the age of eighteen and nineteen, I studied child molesters and their psychopathology. I worked to understand their torment, and the flawed personality structures that led them to molest. I practiced saintly forgiveness and would have counseled anyone to do the same. Misery loves company.

We know that my early attempt at forgiving my molester was a part of my molest contract. I was still trying to heal him while I ignored the sick, dead feeling in my heart. Though my decision to forgive him sprang from within my unexamined molest contracts and illness, it made me appear very spiritual and advanced to casual observers.

Except, I was still suicidal, although my thoughts of suicide had evolved to include the possibility of karmic retribution for the act. My life was chaotic, my relationships were shallow, and I was soon to enter into an abusive and unworkable marriage. Forgiveness at that time did nothing good for me. Forgiveness helped me to stay very sick.

When I began to burn my contracts in my mid-to-late twenties, rage and fury came barrelling out of me to hurl forgiveness right out of my aura. At first, I was out of control. My anger was that of a three-year-old. I stomped and bullied and raged. It was not pretty, but it was real.

I learned to channel my anger and to use its intensity as a tool in my healing. I blew images away with violent glee, burnt my contracts on huge, thundering pyres, played loud music and danced until I was exhausted, and de-steamed in whatever way I could. I channelled my rages, and used their energy to free myself.

The emotional channelling we will learn in the next chapter is not like the emotional release work called for in some therapies. If I had counseled myself or anyone to go off and be angry, it wouldn't have done much good. Calling up anger or any other emotion is manipulative and counterfeit. It can also be damaging.

If you try to call forth or maintain a counterfeit and destructive anger, your body may fall into survival mechanisms that can be frightening. Please see the sections on *kundalini* energy in the Troubleshooting Guide if you have been manipulating your anger instead of honoring it.

When you are a competent emotional channeller, you will know that the time to channel is when your psyche brings an emotion into your awareness. Your emotions signal to you by pulling you into a mood or an intense emotional state. At that moment, your emotional channelling will offer you powerful healing information and opportunities. Until then, you need to leave your emotions alone.

Work with my real anger got me to acknowledge the loss of my boundaries, the fact of my victimization, and the ongoing difficulties I had to face because my molester chose to hurt and degrade me. When my anger showed me my real problem—that I was still boundary-injured and responding to insane contractual messages—I was able to fix it.

My too-early, unreal forgiveness sprang from a pretense that I never got hurt in the first place, and that there was nothing wrong in the present. I had nowhere to go from that forgiveness place, because it ignored the reality of my life. Forgiveness shot me even further from my body and made it impossible for me to move forward.

Very few people understand that anger signifies connection and importance. The existence of anger towards another is an honoring of their power in our lives. We do not get angry with people who mean nothing to us! Anger only comes forward in response to real, powerful boundary violations--violations created through the importance we give to our perpetrators. The stronger the anger, the deeper our connection to the boundary violator. The stronger the anger, the stronger our capacity to re-create our boundaries, burn our contracts, and move on.

With my real anger, I was able to see and destroy my molest contracts with certainty and resolve. I was also able to re-create a clear, healthy, anger-supported aura boundary between my life and the life of my molester. The "bad" emotion of anger made my spiritual journey easier.

Anger also revoked the permission I gave forgiveness to loom over me as it once did, nagging and poking at me. Forgiveness could no longer shame me into doing the "right" thing in order to look spiritual, instead of doing the real thing and dealing with my life as it actually was.

Even today, when my concept of forgiveness creates a rift inside me, I burn it up in a nice hot contract. I will forgive when I am through being angry about all of the travails I've had to endure. Until then, I'll be responsible for and responsive to my emotions by refusing to repress them (or expressing them all over the world outside me). Instead, I will listen to, honor, and channel my emotions throughout my inner self. I'll continue with the real process of forgiveness, and ignore the simplistic, prettified version so popular today.

Today, my real and healthy anger works for me in a number of ways. When people step over my boundaries, my anger reminds me to light up (or put up) my Sentry, right away. If the distressing or attacking person doesn't pay attention on an intuitive level, I speak out.

Often, my communication will be gentle, even funny, but when I set people straight on where I begin and end, it is always anger that supports my communication. Real and healing anger does not stomp and berate and escalate, it just says, "Hello. You are now entering protected space." Healing anger supports and enforces the boundary systems we set up in our meditations; it also lends certainty to our release and separation work. Healing anger is the warrior who stands vigilant, with her feet firmly planted, never needing to draw her sword.

And forgiveness? At some point, we will all arrive at a place of deep forgiveness of our molesters' actions, but it is a journey and a process with no shortcuts. We can't jump the line of emotions and rush to forgiveness. Emotions and bodily realities must be honored and accepted as real before they can be healed.

Forgiveness can only come at the end of a process of identifying, healing, and transforming the experience of victimhood. You can't go to forgiveness first! True forgiveness can only come after responsibility and blame are placed squarely on the shoulders of the perpetrator.

If you can't blame, you can't forgive, because there will be nothing *to* forgive. Anger and your authentic emotions will help you blame your molester. Your emotions will help you heal yourself and your behaviors. Then, when you're better, your emotional energy will help you release and forgive your molester and yourself.

We must move through the real steps of the forgiveness process, not just the saintly ones. We must reacquaint ourselves with our anger, or it will bring its exquisitely wrought sword down upon our heads in an attempt to be heard (see *Suicidal Urges* in the Troubleshooting Guide). Anger re-establishes the boundaries we need; without them, we won't be able to sit inside our lives, or become well enough to truly forgive anyone.

Use your anger to destroy some images of your assaulter or anyone else who won't let you experience the pain of your molest experience. Torch your contracts, and you'll know what it feels like to truly let go. True release has heat, and movement, and momentum. Saintly forgiveness is cold and lifeless--it doesn't move anything.

With the help of anger, the psychic message sent in your release work isn't, "Well, I guess I'd like to move on, if that's okay." When you channel your anger into releasing your images and contracts, the message is, "I am through with this pattern, I release all my energy from it, and I will never agree to be a part of it again!" Healthy anger helps us make clear, boundary-enforcing separations--without hurting anyone.

You have a right to be angry. And you have the responsibility not to hurt others. With emotional channelling, you can work with intense and socially unacceptable anger without hurting yourself or anyone else.

When you allow your anger to help you work through your real reactions to your assault, you can separate yourself from its energetic residue. When you have achieved some distance, you may then be able to see your molester as a small and tragic figure, instead of a looming, despised one.

At this point, forgiveness is good. When you can see your molester as a completely separate person who made a series of defective personal decisions in which you had no power, you are free.

In that quiet moment, when you have finally separated your energy from the energy of your first sexual partner, you may be able to see them as forgivable, and completely unconnected to your present life.

Which, by the way, they are.

I'll tell you a little secret: you've been forgiving people since the moment you learned to ground. Grounding, separating, releasing images, burning contracts, and taking back your energy; all are forms of forgiveness. Placing someone in a loving image and releasing them from your life is forgiveness! It's that simple.

Secret number two: each of your energy tools requires the use of healing anger as well as forgiveness. Healing anger creates your aura boundary and your Sentry rose, and the material in each of your released images and burnt parchments. Healing anger forms the protective boundary for your life. It also acts as the conveyor that takes unwanted energy out of your personal territory.

Each time you get into your body and take responsibility for your pain and reactions by releasing images or burning contracts, you forgive, and you release others from blame. You separate yourself from the trauma, which is the whole function of healthy anger--you become the warrior. You take the power over yourself back into yourself, separate from victim consciousness, and move towards real strength and spirituality. At this point, your anger is healthy, and forgiveness comes naturally.

Anger and forgiveness work together in the healthy, emotionally healed body. Anger and forgiveness, often thought to be fierce, completely oppositional enemies, evolve into intrinsically necessary, and completely supportive aspects of one process: the process of real, responsible, healing release. True anger and forgiveness support true evolution and healing.

When you have the real strength of living inside your body and your reality, no one can ever victimize or destroy you. If someone hurts you, it's real, but so is your ability to heal. If you sit and focus on your body and your injury, you will find relief.

You can rely on your emotions to help you separate from the assault or the assaulter. You can rely on your intellect to plot a way out of a life that invites abuse, and you can rely on your spirit to find your true lesson within the experience of your pain, or to show you the next step in your path to wellness. The only way another person or experience can cause you lasting pain is if you hold onto your suffering, and to your boundary-destroying victim identification.

As children, we had no choice about holding onto the suffering our sexual assaults caused. We were victimized by a predator because we did not have our skills yet. Now, we have the life skills we were missing, and we can move on.

We can release energies that haunt and torment us. We can examine and let go of cherished stupidities which assure us that life is terrifying and pointless. We can take charge of our own attitudes, emotions, healing abilities, and connections to spirit and God, and begin to live again. We can be angry and forgive at the same time.

PART II

REBUILDING THE GARDEN

CHANNELLING YOUR EMOTIONS

I don't know what has happened to emotions in this society. They are the least understood, most maligned, and most ridiculously over-analyzed aspects of human life. Emotions are categorized, celebrated, vilified, repressed, manipulated, humiliated, adored, and ignored. Rarely, if ever, are they *honored*.

Many psycho-rational therapies, religions, and New Age teachings split emotions into good and bad categories, and then spend extreme amounts of time and energy teaching their respective disciples to agree with them. In order to truly fit in, followers must court, seduce, and stay in the teaching's accepted emotions while they shame, ignore, pray away, and run from the forbidden ones.

The only problem is, the therapies and teachings can't seem to agree on which emotions are right, and which are wrong. Some religions and eastern teachings shun all emotions, while others shun only anger and fear. Most New Age teachings make do with one emotion (joy), and strive to remove, affirm away, or ignore the rest. As in any perfection-instead-of-wholeness regime, the damage caused by the denying of true human emotions creates truly inhuman problems.

Psychologist Alice Miller points out that in pre-Nazi Germany, the bad emotion was childhood exhilaration. After a lifetime of repression, these obediently unexhilarated children grew up to create the Third Reich. In our society, the bad emotion is grief, and after a few hundred years of repression, we are a cold-hearted people mesmerized by, but incapable of accepting, death.

Disallowed, repressed anger turns to inner rage, torment, and suicidal urges, while denied fear turns into panic attacks, spirit/body splits, and an underlying distrust of people and life in general. These are the rewards of repressing the emotions.

Expressing the emotions is better than repressing them, because doing so allows a flow of truthfulness in the body and spirit; however, if emotions are very strong, expressing them can create both exterior and interior turmoil. The exterior turmoil comes about when we pour our strong emotions all over some unfortunate soul, and try to make them responsible for our mood. The interior turmoil comes about when we realize we have startled or hurt someone with our outpouring, which makes us feel dismayed, and ashamed of ourselves.

Often, our strong emotions will have us lash out and blame others for our feelings. This blaming will trap us into believing that someone else is in control of our emotions: "You *made* me angry, you *made* me cry!" Expressing strong emotions can be damaging to our egos.

So, what's left? If we can't repress emotions without getting into trouble, and we can't express them either, what do we do, live in a cave?

Nope. We *channel* our emotions. By channelling, I do not mean to suggest the New Age idea of calling forth disembodied spirits. When I say channelling, I refer to the actual meaning of the word, which is to direct, apply, and channel an energy in a specific way.

When we express our emotions, we hand them over to the outside world, where we hope they will be noticed, honored, healed, and transformed into something bright and beautiful. Emotional expression relies on the exterior world and other people to decipher and transmute emotional messages into action.

When we repress our emotions, we hand them over to the interior world, most often our bodies, where we hope they will be taken care of, healed, and transformed into something more acceptable to us. Emotional repression relies on the unconscious, interior world to accept and *do something* with the emotion.

Neither hand-off works for very long. Emotional expression makes us unworkably dependent on therapists, books, friends, family members, clergy, and external action for emotional relief and release. Since all of these exterior people or supports can leave or be taken away, we emotional expressers can become stuck with a life full of feelings, but no emotional skills of our own, and nowhere to go with the feelings we have.

Emotional repression, on the other hand, makes us unworkably dependent on a body or unconscious that can only hold so much repressed material before it has to get rid of something. When you hand off your emotional responsibilities to your body, it will store them someplace where they'll eventually show up as pain or illness.

If you hand off to your unconscious and tell it, "No anger or grief, okay?" your unconscious will work very hard to obey you, but it will have to create something else with all your angry, grieving energy. Something like suicidal urges usually does the trick. Emotional repression may also help you to create an attention-getting addiction so you can pretend that your pain is coming from something besides your refusal to feel.

So, both the expression and repression of emotion have serious drawbacks. The hand-off never works; however, when you listen to, honor, and channel your emotions, you won't need to hand them off to anyone or anything.

Emotional channelling lets you handle your emotions yourself. When you are able to take care of your own emotions, they will take care of you in ways you may not be able to believe right now.

All emotions are messages from our unconscious aspects to our conscious ones. Emotions may spring from within the body, from our assaulted child, from our deep memories, or from unused and unnoticed aspects of our psyches. Emotions carry with them the absolute truth of the sending party or aspect.

Strong or uncontrollable emotions carry not just truth, but absolutely all the healing energy we need to deal with the imbalances that brought about the strong emotion in the first place. Strong emotions store, and then contribute the energy we need to heal ourselves and evolve.

Expressing and repressing emotions are subtle ways to leave your body and your experience, and to squander your energy. Though you may remain grounded and in the room in your head while you pour your emotions all over someone (or ignore an unacceptable feeling), expressing or repressing emotions are not centered or aware actions. You can get away with either or both for a while in a grounded and centered body, but eventually, your refusal to accept and honor your emotions will activate the old dissociation process again. To circumvent any further dissociation, let's learn to honor and channel our emotions.

There are two kinds of emotional channelling: one that can be used in any normal healing and meditation session, which channels fleeting emotions; and another that deals with very powerful or repeated emotional states and requires a special meditation of its own.

The simpler method of emotional channelling is actually a lot of fun. All we need is the willingness to be aware of and available to any emotions that come up during our regular healing and separation sessions.

CHANNELLING FLEETING OR IMMEDIATE EMOTIONS

As we release our images and burn our contracts, emotions often spring forward. If we have learned that emotions are bad and unspiritual, their presence may interrupt our process—and end our healing session—while we use up all our energy in reacting to or suppressing them. If we learn to see our emotions as good, healing, and integral to us, they will enrich and support our process. Our emotions will not be in the way of our spiritual process; they will show us the way.

Releasing and destroying images with emotional energy is a very simple process. As you create the images you will release, be aware of the emotions that come up in response to the people you imagine. As you move these people outside of your aura, simply use the energy of the emotions they bring forward to help you destroy their image.

For example: if someone's presence in my awareness brings up my anger, I will destroy their image with fiery red-orange, angry energy. If another person's presence causes a fearful reaction in me, I will release them with a spiky green, frightened energy. If someone else's presence fills me with grief and sadness, I will let them go more slowly, with a fluid, dark, and grieving energy.

When I release people with the emotion I have in reaction to their presence, I honor the fact that I *do* react. If I pretend that I feel powerful and complete at all times, and try to use my spiritual separation skills to tell myself lies about my power in the world, or my power over other people and the supposedly "lower" emotions, I'll soon have a whopping spirit/body split.

Emotions exist to help the body protect itself. They also serve as a connecting link between the reality-centered body and the light-and-energy-centered spirit. Emotions, if properly honored and channelled, create a flowing, healing, and communicative link between the needs of the body and the knowledge of the spirit. If we can listen to, validate, and use our emotions in our spiritual healing sessions, our body and our spirit will come into closer accord.

Spirits are powerful and fearless because they never die. Bodies, on the other hand, have to expend enormous amounts of energy ensuring their survival. Bodies die, and are injured, and are made ill every day. Bodies are not all-powerful. Bodies are also not fearless, or emotionless.

Though the body is not lower than, or inferior to the spirit, its grounding in real time, real food, real money, and real life can make communication with its other-worldly spirit confusing at best. Conversely, the spirit's timeless, formless, and limitless information can sound like gibberish to a body in immediate distress.

The intellect does its part to translate and direct information between body and spirit, but without the fluid medium of emotions to carry the information, very little real work is accomplished. When body and spirit are at odds, and emotions are ignored, the intellect will often go into high gear. Such a situation creates a person who thinks too much, often to the point of tormenting herself with all her misused and overburdened mental energy.

The intellect was never meant to do the work we moderns have forced upon it. Its translating and explanatory abilities are absolutely vital in a working quaternity of body, spirit, mind, and emotion, but the mind can't magically run the quaternity alone. Without the support of the fluid conveyance of the emotions, which carries the mind's translated information between spirit and body, the mind can only escalate its process. It can't transfer workable physical information to the spirit all by itself; nor can it help the body understand formless spiritual realities without an emotional assist.

What the mind can do all by itself is think, think, and think, create fantasies and battle plans, go over the same issue hundreds of times, and generally torment both body and spirit, not to mention itself.

However, when the emotions are utilized properly in the healthy quaternity—of body, mind, emotion and spirit—the body's mentally translated information reaches the soul in a spiritually tangible, "So *that's* how life feels!" form.

Conversely, when the emotions are allowed to transmit mentally translated spiritual information to the body, the information arrives in a physically understandable form. The body receiving this information can say, "Oh, so acceptance feels like *this*, anger has *this* energy, and my reactions mean *that*. I get it!"

When the emotions are honored and channelled, the intellect can take its rightful place as the overseer of the spirit/body translation process, instead of being expected to actually carry the information from body to spirit and back again. Because it is being asked to do what it was meant to do, the mind in this system does not torment itself. It can rest, lie back and concentrate on its studies, and let the emotions do the walking.

When you begin to include your emotions in your healing work, you will be able to almost fly through issues that once kept your mind, body, and spirit in turmoil. You will have reserves of energy available; energy you used to throw away when you handed off and dishonored your emotions.

The emotions are exquisitely useful, and wonderfully wise. They make the body more aware, the mind more able to process in calm and centered ways, and the spirit more grounded and understandable. Channelled emotions also make separations swift and sure.

As you release your images and move turmoil away from your center, let your emotions give you a hand. The forte of emotion is the transportation of energy from one place to another. The emotions can make your separation work easier if you let them usher and transport unwanted or confusing energy out of your life.

As you burn your contracts, remember to place all your emotional reactions onto the documents, and to burn them with the emotional energy they bring up for you. The emotions you feel in response to your contract partners are the specific emotions needed to transport information about the contract between your body, your mind, and your spirit. Your emotions also contain the specific amount of energy required to truly release yourself from your contracts.

Anger can help you burn contracts hot and bright. Fear and anxiety can help you incinerate them in a split-second flash, and sadness can help you create a funeral pyre so you can mourn your losses properly as your contracts are cremated.

Each of your emotions will help you to release yourself and the people in your life from limiting pictures, contracts, and expectations. Your honored and validated emotions will help you to flow more smoothly through your life. Use them.

CHANNELLING DEEPER MOODS AND EMOTIONS

Channelling deeper, more serial, or intense and unrelenting emotions is not difficult, but it is unusual. The process requires us to dedicate ourselves and our territory to the emotion at hand.

During a deep channelling session, we will choose a color, quality and movement for the energy of our emotional state, but instead of releasing images and contracts with the energy, we will channel it right into our body, our aura, our grounding cord, and all of our energy tools.

Emotional channelling is very like the channeling we have done with Gold Sun energy. The only difference is that our emotional energy is not neutral like Gold Sun energy; it has something very specific to say! If you'd like to hear the messages your emotions have for you, wait until they pull you into a deep mood, then use this process to listen and learn.

When a mood or an intense emotion comes up, your being is signalling the need for serious release work. As soon as you can, please sit and ground yourself. Get into the room in your head, ground your little one if they like. Define your aura, ground your aura with its own grounding tube, and check in with your Sentry. If you have to stop and fix any of your energy tools, go ahead. Your emotion will wait for you.

When you are centered, allow your mind and body to bring your emotion to its fullness. Let your body feel its intensity, and let your mind describe the emotion in words and images.

From within your head, choose a leading color and movement for the energy of your emotion. Your anger might be a hot, swiftly moving orange energy; fear may be an electrically charged green swirl; sadness may be a drippy blue energy; and grief may be a solid and unmoving brown cloud. Your mind and body will help you choose your own colors for your own emotions. If you have trouble visualizing colors, get a feel for the shape or movement pattern of the emotion, and use that energy instead.

When you have envisioned the energetic quality of your emotional state, allow it to fill your body completely, and then breathe it out into your aura. Fill your aura with this energy, and change its colored boundary into the color and quality of your emotion. From inside your head, watch and feel the movement of this emotion's energy inside your body and your aura. When your body and aura are full of the energy of your emotion, fill your Sentry until it too is made up of this energy.

Allow the emotion to come into the room in your head, and to fill the floors, walls, ceiling, furniture, and plants with its energy. If your little one wants you to, you can fill his or her body with this emotional energy as well. For a few moments, sit in your head and watch this energy. Ask it what it wants to tell you, and listen to its answers.

You may experience changes in temperature or energy flow in your body or your aura. This can happen when your emotion alerts you to problems in your physical or spiritual circumstance. Your emotion may require you to speak, yell, scream, cry, or move around the room. Do it. Be available and keep listening, and if the emotional energy tends to gather around one specific part of your aura or your body, ask it why.

If another emotion emerges from within the energy of your chosen one, choose a color or quality for the new emotion, and channel that emotion into your body and aura as well. If you have relied on repression in your life (and who hasn't?), your emotions may run in pairs or packs for support and protection against your treatment of them. Forgive yourself, welcome the new emotion, and keep channelling. It too will bring instructive and healing messages.

After a period of one to five minutes, or however long you like, turn your first-*chakra* grounding cord (and your little one's, if you have grounded them), into a vacuum. Create a large grounding tube for your aura, and turn it and your Sentry's grounding cord into vacuums. Use these vacuums to suck the energy of the emotion out of you.

Let the energy leave the room in your head and watch it as it leaves your body. Let the energy of the emotion move down and out of your aura, and let it flow out of your Sentry as you watch it from inside your room. As the emotion grounds out of you, remember that its attachments will dissipate. When it exits your grounding cord, it will be clean, neutral, reusable energy once again.

Right now, note any places in your body where the emotional energy is stuck and resists grounding, if there are any. Ask the energy why. Know that you can release and ground these areas separately in a moment, but take this moment to discover where your body holds this emotion. Ask it why, thank the emotion, and let it go. You may need to attach a special grounding cord to the resistant area. Do that now. When you are done, and the emotional energy is drained away, turn off the vacuums in all of your grounding cords. Relax for a moment. Breathe.

All that's left is a Gold Sun healing to fill you back up with clean and neutral energy; however: *before you put up your Gold Sun, please drop the grounding tube out of your aura.* You don't need this tube unless you are performing a special healing that pulls energy out of your aura. Your aura grounds itself very well by grabbing onto your body's grounding cord just below the floor; it usually doesn't need any more grounding than that.

When you put up your Gold Sun, it's going to be hit with a large amount of cleaned-up, ready-to-use emotional energy. Welcome it back and know, as you channel your clean energy through your body and your energy tools, that you can use this energy in any way you like right now.

Please bend over and touch the floor to let your body pour off any Gold Sun energy it can't use right now. Get up, and you're done!

All emotions are tools for us if we accept them, channel them responsibly, and take the time to listen to their healing messages. Not surprisingly, the "bad" emotions can bring us amazing insights because they carry so much energy with them.

Anger and fury can signal a lack of boundaries, and then contribute the energy to rebuild those boundaries. Sadness and despair can signal an arid harshness in the self or the environment, and then contribute the healing fluidity required. Anxiety, fear, and terror can signal the presence of dangerously wrong people, ideas, or situations, and then contribute protection, or the energy to move out of harm's way.

Grief signals loss, and then contributes the energy to cherish, honor, and release the lost entity. Suicidal urges demand liberty or death, and when channelled, contribute the energy to kill off unworkable aspects of life, and to liberate the spirit from unendurable pain.

Although it can seem as if emotional channelling lets moods take over our lives, nothing could be further from the truth. Inside our heads, we, the central being, decide on the colors and qualities of the emotion. We direct the emotion's flow, we ask it questions, and when we are done, we vacuum the emotion out of our body and our aura. While it is true that we give over our body and aura to the emotion, this is a completely different thing than being *taken over* by one.

People who dishonor, repress, or irresponsibly express their emotions are taken over by them. We emotional channellers instead take the emotions over, and use their energy in our healings. Emotional channelling reminds us that a healthy psyche is a complete one. Completeness includes light, dark, good, bad, love, hate, perfection, flaws, solemnity, silliness, wisdom, idiocy, and everything else.

If we attend only to the nice-nice parts of ourselves, we're dissociated, no matter how grounded we may appear. If we ignore our own emotion-filled shadow and try to hide it or throw it out with the trash, it may loom up and attack us with a sword created out of all our repressed energy. Ouch.

When we accept and channel our "bad" emotions, the sword transforms. It becomes a ceremonial dagger with which we may cut away the lies, contracts, attachments, and shackles in ourselves. When we honor the powerful wisdom of our shadow, we become multi-dimensional, whole human beings (for information on the shadow, please read through the chapter called *Advanced Aura Reading and Definition* in Part III).

We can still express our needs, feelings, and moods to the aware and supportive people in our lives, but emotional channelling offers a stronger, and more personally empowering support.

When we work with the energetic material of our own emotions, we no longer need to rely on others to help us deal with or validate our emotional states. Emotional channelling is like a session with an excellent therapist, or an intense and intimate friend.

If you have been to a competent therapist, you will recall that in the office, all emotions, reactions, dreams, and ideas were acceptable. When you channel your own emotions, you can create this exact atmosphere for yourself at any time.

In the safety of your own meditative sanctuary, you can bring your earth-wise body, your energy-and-information-filled emotions, your intellectual brilliance, and your spiritual awareness to bear on any difficulty, question, mood, or opportunity that arises—and save thousands of dollars in therapy fees.

When you can bring your emotions to bear on your life's issues, you will move through them with a fluid ease and grace. Your fluidity may require periodic yelling, crying, reacting, and stomping, but these momentary reactions won't bother you, because you will have matured enough to accept your emotions as they are. When you accept, honor, channel, and refuse to punish your emotions, all of your life will move and flow more easily.

In order to remain whole and alive from this moment forward, you'll need an environment which lets you cry when you're sad; shout and jump when you're exhilarated; move quickly when you're anxious; protect yourself when you're fearful; stomp and snap when you're angry; dance when you're happy; and grieve when you experience loss or death. Whole people accept and honor all human emotions. Whole lives require them.

Your life right now may be far from whole, but when you commit to channelling your emotions, you will head toward completeness. Your inner life, at least, will be the environment where you will be free to feel. Your inner life will be the place where you can work with your emotions.

The wisdom, energy, support, and strength of your own emotions will help your spirit to center itself in your body, your body to center itself on the planet, and your mind to free itself from feedback loops. Channelling your emotions will help to integrate your quaternity.

What are you waiting for? Go and destroy a few images and contracts with your emotional energy right now, or channel any mood that keeps you stuck. The rest of the book will wait. Your emotions have waited long enough.

You may notice that I haven't gone into detail about what your emotions may tell you. I feel very strongly that your emotions can do this for you far better than I can; however, the Troubleshooting Guide at the very end of this book contains definitions of more than a dozen different emotions. You can skim through them before you get started on your own emotions. You don't need to, but you can peek if you like.

As a support for your emotional body, I cannot recommend the Bach Flower Remedies highly enough. These English flower essences were created to bring emotional balance to the body and spirit, and their healing abilities are nothing short of remarkable. One of the best books on the subject is *Bach Flower Therapy*, by Mechthild Scheffer. Forget psychotropic drugs; these remedies actually work!

PART II

REBUILDING THE GARDEN

SEX IN PERSPECTIVE

There is a theory about sexual healing for assault survivors that sounds suspiciously like the homily about getting right back up on a horse after you fall off. Many well-meaning people think that healthy sexual encounters will cure assault survivors of their trauma, as if getting back into the sexual saddle again will create courage and healing all by itself.

While I agree that people should not let old wounds stop them from living in the present, I cannot liken the experience of sexual assault to that of simply falling off a horse. More realistically, it is like being thrown from a horse who then tramples you, breaks your ribs, sets your hair on fire, and then runs off with your clothes, your wallet, and your car keys. This horse is not one a sane person would care to ride again.

Sexual assault employs sex as a weapon. Because sexuality (their own and their molester's) has been used against them, assault survivors are often understandably gun-shy about it. Their physical reactions to sex or the thought of sex can be nearly identical to the reactions of a once-poisoned body.

The body's defenses in a poisoning episode are caught dangerously unaware, and are thrown into emetic, painful, protective reactions. The body will not make that same mistake twice, and anything related to the episode will become repulsive to the body. One food-poisoning episode with fish can turn a fish-lover into a complete fish-avoider for months or years. One poisoned sexual episode can turn a naturally sensual child into a repressed, asexual being for decades.

The asexual (or uncomfortably sexual) assault survivor needs to be able to avoid sex without guilt and recriminations, just as the poisoning survivor needs to be able to avoid fish.

No loving person would throw a shark attack victim back into the sea, and no lover should require their sexually assaulted partner to jump into sex if there is discomfort. If the relationship begins to revolve around demands for sexuality, it is no different than molest. The survivor must be allowed to say no to sex, just as a non-molested person can.

The problem is, without sex and the bonding it provides, the adult survivor may find it impossible to maintain love relationships. Their mates may feel not only powerless to help, but unattractive, unloved, and unwanted as well. These mates may even fall into the unworkable position of wondering what they can do, say, offer, or avoid in order to make the assault survivor wish to have sex again.

We as sexually confused survivors must be certain that we do not allow our mates to sign a contract that places the responsibility for our illness or our healing onto them. Though it might be nice to think our healing will come from some magical aspect in our mates, such thoughts place crushing burdens on people who just want to love us.

It's hard to live an adult life without sex. If you are currently asexual, you may think you are protecting yourself from the dangers of sexual energy. A small psychic look at the clogged energy in your pelvis, genitals, and grounding cord will prove otherwise.

As your lonely mate will tell you, adult humans are at their healthiest when their sexual energy flows. This flow, and your willing partner, can help you dislodge and examine your molest contracts.

The release of your contracts will free up your pelvic girdle, help you ground, center you in your body, and allow you to move safely into the adult world. However, to get to adult safety, you need to allow sensuality back into your life.

The body is an extremely tactile and sensuous entity. Bodies need to touch and be touched, or they will become ill. In our society, friendly social touching like hugging, hand-holding, and back-rubbing is not prevalent; if we go off sex and lose our only source of touch and bodily connection, our bodies can fall into ill health. They may put on a lot of weight to protect themselves, or drop weight as their energy depletes itself.

Our untouched bodies may become filled with pain and disease, and may become unable to communicate their needs. In response, our spirits may rely on dissociation to escape the pain of the untouched, non-sensual body. Touching must be restored, and if no safe touch exists in our lives, we must restore the touching ourselves.

How often do you touch and care for yourself? If you stub your toe, do you rub and kiss it as a loving parent might, or do you swear, kick the object that hurt you, and ignore your painful toe completely?

If your clothes are too tight, do you change them, or do you let your body spend an entire day in pain? When you sit on the toilet, do you leap out of your head, or can you remain present when your genitals are naked? Pay attention: take note of how much loving, concerned touch and innocent sensuality you allow in yourself.

Certainly, massage, facials, and other forms of body work can help your body to feel touchable and wanted, but if you don't even bother to provide the basic comfort of self-touch for your body, no amount of body work will heal you. You've got to make friends with your body again.

Pat your knee right now.

Did you pat your knee with loving energy, brush your hand across it because I told you to, or refuse to touch it because this is an embarrassing and idiotic exercise? How do you relate to your body?

Whatever your relationship was, it belongs to the past. We are now in an entirely different world than the world we inhabited one paragraph ago. We can pull out and burn a contract with our unwillingness to treat our bodies with love, and then channel our powerful, warming, love-filled Gold Sun energy into each and every one of our cells. We can change our attitude right now, and never go back to it. We can treat our bodies, right now, in the ways we long for other people to treat them.

We can become our own lovers, massage therapists, healers, and loving parents. We can make ourselves nourishing food right now, massage our own feet right now, rest when we're tired instead of pushing on right now, and surround ourselves with things that we love, right now.

We can pay serious attention to the sensual world of art, design, music, wood-or-metal-working, gourmet cooking, or sports and exercise, and in that way bring a sensual healing into our lives.

We can cut favorite pictures out of old calendars and magazines and tape them up on the wall if we love art, but have no money. We can read more books. We can listen to more music. We can design or build the things we need. We can do our sports or exercise.

We can change the way we eat the very next time we eat, and change our diets the very next time we go shopping. We can do our art, our craft, or our sport today, instead of waiting for schooling to make our expression acceptable to others. We can move onward this very second and head in another direction while we remain grounded, centered, and aware of our needs.

If you used to practice self-abuse regularly, you can practice self-support now. Both self-abusing and self-loving actions require underlying attitudes to give them the energy to survive. You can change your underlying attitudes and create a new self-treatment energy right now.

If you're not sure about your own self-abusing habits, write down ten traits of abusive people. See if any traits apply to your own treatment of yourself; if they do, burn your contracts, channel your emotions and your Gold Sun, and change the underlying energies that give those traits life.

Don't be surprised or dismayed if you discover you have abused yourself. Self-abuse and self-denial are national pastimes with deep roots in the pioneering, Calvinistic foundational energy of our society. Self abuse and self-denial are also foundational energies for molestation, but we can rely instead on the foundational energy of our own spirits, and move on from self-abuse to something more reasonable and worthwhile.

We can also move on in our relationships to sex, gender identity, and sexuality. We can bring out and burn contracts for any attitude we have about our sexual nature, and we can channel any emotions that come up for us. We can cleanse our sexuality of destructive, foreign contracts and messages, and repossess the creative power of our own sexual energy (for physical assistance, please see the sciatic and ovary grounding techniques in the chapter called *Advanced Grounding*).

Healing sexuality is beautiful, connecting, powerful, and good. Your body still knows this, even if its current, molest-centered programming says otherwise. Let's face it, your body's sensual and sexual information has hundreds of thousands of years of evolution behind it, while your molest programming has only the span of your post-trauma life. Which energy do you think would win in a fist-fight?

When you can clear yourself out and get back in touch with the true foundational energy of your body—which is naturally sensual, tactile, sexual, and pleasure-loving—your healing sexuality will once again become available to you.

It is vital, when your body feels queasy, frightened, and unsure about sexual contact, to immediately bring forward and destroy images of your molester or your assault experience, and to ground out your physical discomfort as you work. When the molest memories come forward, you must make a conscious connection between this genital pain and your molester, or this queasy stomach and your assault. In this way, you and your body will begin to equate bad sex and fear with your specific assault experience, and not to the experience of sex itself.

Through your conscious energy work, and your willingness to stay in your body, your body will begin to know that there is help and healing available. Your body will learn to rely on you, and it will begin to heal.

As you work through your assault residue, programming, and issues, your genitals and reproductive organs may release pains and memories at strange moments. No matter what you are doing or where you are, you can settle into the room in your head, check your aura boundary, ground yourself and your little one, and destroy unwanted images while you soothe your body. It is imperative that you do so.

Nothing is more healing and supportive than a body willing to release its pain. Staying in, cleansing, and supporting your body in these moments is vital. When the body, mind, spirit, and emotions work together, all healing is possible, and all knowledge is available.

When your body is grounded and aware, and able to release old attitudes, memories, energy, and programming, it will be able feed you information about relationships, work environments, health concerns, diet and health routines, and more. It will also let you know when, where, how, and with whom it wants to have sex. Honor it.

Honor, as well, the fact that you are hurt by unloving or abusive sexuality, whether that lack of love comes from within or without. You already know what exterior sexual abuse looks and feels like, but what about *interior* sexual abuse?

Sexual self-abuse appears in many forms. It can appear as asexuality, an addiction to sex or masturbation, a condition of obesity that de-sexualizes the body and obscures the genitals, or in conditions of de-sexualizing emaciation, where the body is too thin and frail to reproduce.

Sexual self-abuse also appears as an unwillingness to sensually care for the body. Such self-abusers push their bodies past pain and sanity, live uncomfortably in messes or hyper-clean, sterile environments, and either follow punishing health regimens, or no health regimen at all.

Sexual self-abuse and degradation are a normal, accepted part of everyday life. Consider, as you bathe or shower, that you have special cleansers for your face, hair, hands, nails, and feet, but none for your bottom or your genitals. There are creams, lotions, pomades, and salves for every part of the body, but none for the anus, the penis, or the labia.

All the genitals get is fungicides and hemorrhoid sprays, suppositories, purging douches, or synthetic deodorants—even though their skin is as sensitive and fragile as the lips and mouth, or the skin around the eyes. And none of us asks why. The abusive, repressed sexuality of Victorian society didn't die off after all, did it?

All abuses can end today. As you burn contracts with the energy of sexual self-abuse, remind yourself that your molest programming almost guaranteed your future as a self-abusive person. Your first sexual partner filled your body and spirit with abusive programming. You can change your programming--it's only energy. You know how to work with energy.

Make this moment a non-abusive moment. Make today a non-abusive day. Yesterday is over and gone. Tomorrow will come, no matter what. Today and this moment are all that matters right now. Listen to your body, clean out old energy, stay centered, bring your Gold Sun energy inside you to fill up any empty spots, and know: you are in charge of yourself and everything you do.

If you exercised too much this morning, you can rest and massage your sore muscles and joints right now. If you chose to ignore your messy house or office an hour ago, you can pay attention to it right now. If you ate or did something last night that does not agree with or heal you, you don't have to eat or do it again. If you had unloving sex, or masturbated too much this week, you can cover your genitals with your hands and apologize right now. This is the present. The rest of that stuff happened in the past. We aren't controlled by the past.

In the past, sexual issues were a problem for us, but this is the present. Here, we can honor our bodies and our sexuality by approaching sexual relationships with trust—with the willingness to learn, grow, and heal.

Right now, we can listen to our bodies, and choose partners who will honor us with love and gentle respect. If no such partners are available, we can learn to masturbate and stimulate our own sexuality with love, honor, and respect.

Sexuality has a lot of different uses for a lot of different people. Its power invites all sorts of attention, rules, abuses, fantasies, by-laws, emotions, difficulties, and insanities. Modern society says that sex is either naughty and fascinating, or disease-filled and deadly. Some religions say that sex is pro-creational only, or filled with sin, while other religions use sex or celibacy as tools to reach Nirvana.

It can be very hard to come to a personally fulfilling agreement with sexuality when so much harsh and conflicting sexual energy slams around in the psychic fabric. No matter how difficult it may be, it is both possible and necessary to create our own agreements with our own sexuality. This will occur naturally when we are safe inside our heads and behind our healthy, protected auras.

Your body knows what its personal sexuality requires; when you get into your body and clear it out, it will tell you all about it. Then, your body will support you in creating a sexual life that will heal it, your emotions, your intellect, and your spirit. Your sexuality will not fall into any proscribed social or religious category, but some teachings may help you move from an abusive sexuality to one closer to your healing reality.

When you are ready to enter the realm of healing sexuality, you may need to work alone, on your own sexual issues, for a period of time. Through the cleansing of your own sexual energy, you will soon be able to identify healthy sexuality, and healthy sexual partners.

Healthy bodies require aware, gentle, comfortable, trusting, and supportive partners. Such partners do not come along every day, but if you do your work, you will find them soon enough.

When a healing sexual relationship is a possibility for you, your new awareness will protect you. You will be protected from shooting out of your body during sex and becoming a puppeteer, or from falling into sexual addiction to prove that sex doesn't touch your soul.

Sex does touch your soul. It touches your heart, all your *chakras*, your aura, your grounding cord—everything. Sex invites your lover right into your energy field, into your body, and into your life. Your experience with the horrifying sex of your childhood has proven that fact beyond a shadow of a doubt. Today, you can honor the power of sex, and allow only honorable people, and honorable self-actions to touch your sexual life.

When you masturbate or make love today, you can be sure to ground yourself and stay in your body throughout the whole experience. You can even teach your partner to ground.

After your lovemaking, you and your partner can release each other in loving symbols and separate your energies until your next love-making session. You can remain spiritually centered and aware of your body, and add sexuality to your pantheon of healing tools, attitudes, and abilities. You can begin today. You can begin right now.

It may not seem fair that survivors of childhood sexual assault should have to do so much work to get well, and then have to be careful, awake, and aware about body-care and sexuality for the rest of their lives. I don't know.

I used to believe that every single thing about molestation was dreadful, destructive, meaningless, and wasteful. Now, after a lifetime of learning the hard way about what safe and healing body-care and sexuality is, I have found an irreplaceable treasure.

I have learned that I have a Garden at the very center of my being which can be accessed by others through love or during sex. I have seen in bloody technicolor what life is like if I do not care for or live in that Garden, and through rebuilding it, I have rebuilt a strong, centered, joyous, and meaningful life for myself.

My early need to rebuild my Garden and protect myself sprang from the need no longer to be sick and crazy. My present Garden tending springs from the knowledge that I have a lively and unrepeatable inner world that feeds me, my family, my loved ones, the planet, and God. Now I care for, live in, and protect my Garden simply because it is the center of my life.

I still think it's unfair that I had to learn about my Garden by losing it in such a horrifying way, but now that I have it back, I wonder: if I had my life to live over, would I choose to avoid my assault if it meant I would not discover my true power through the assault's specter of powerlessness?

Would I want to be a "normal" adult woman and let people casually trample through a Garden I never saw as special, as if it, and I, were unimportant? Or, if it was the only way I could learn to honor my spirituality this lifetime, would I choose to go through my molestation again in order to learn that I have a soul worth protecting, and a Garden worth tending?

Hmmm. The answer is pretty clear when I ask the question that way.

PART III

ADVANCED MEDITATION & HEALING

The glory is not in never falling,
but in rising every time you fall.

Chinese proverb

PART III

ADVANCED MEDITATION & HEALING

GOING ONWARD

I have no intention of dropping you off the end of this book without a number of safety nets. Though I tried to keep things fairly simple during the beginning stages of this book, real life is complex and confusing. We all need access to more advanced skills as we traipse through our time here on the planet.

In rebuilding our Gardens, we were able to dislodge our molester's energy from its place in our bodies, our auras, and our brain stems. That was actually the easy part. Moving ourselves away from a long-held belief in our victim status can be somewhat more laborious. Retraining ourselves to respect our own dreams and wishes in the present moment can be difficult, especially in a circle of family and friends who have probably come to rely on our being selfless and other-directed.

At this time, I suggest making your healing journey and intentions known to the people in your life. If people truly care for you, they'll let you grow, even if they don't quite know how. Let them screw up, and accept their apologies, but keep going. Don't let anyone's stasis-seeking stop you in your tracks.

Use your gift symbols and your contracts to get rid of old images of yourself and of the people in your life. Stay in your head and behind your strong aura, and check in with your little one if you become confused about where you need to go. Or, channel the energy of confusion, and let it help you destroy your images and contracts.

If you can channel your emotional reactions into the upheavals in your life, your path will have clearer meaning, and greater rewards. Consciousness is not a smooth journey--your emotions will help you to stay on track even when no track is in sight.

Moving on from the molest experience means moving beyond its grasp, both in the past and in the present. Your unexamined molest contracts kept you ungrounded, out of your body, and out of control for years; it's very easy to understand how your life kept attracting unsafe people, dismaying situations, and shocking events. No one was home to keep them out.

Now, you are home, and it's time to clean house. Unsafe people and experiences will still come knocking for awhile, but you don't have to invite them in. Every time you say no to uncomfortable, untruthful, and unhealing people and situations, you'll separate from those energies. You may become hypersensitive to abusive energy for a while as your healthy aura and *chakra* system become aware of your intention to heal, but soon, the energy of abuse will feel very foreign to you. When abuse surprises you and no longer feels normal or par for the course, you will be free of its shackles. You will have moved on.

The trick to moving on from this moment is to learn to be comfortable with comfort, to be happy about happiness, and to feel secure about security. Most molest survivors chase safe, positive experiences away with the ferocity of attack dogs, but we aren't most molest survivors any longer. We are ourselves.

We are now people who know how to protect our bodies, our energy, and our auras. We can work with our emotions. We can calm and center our intellect. We are no longer a pile of molested junk to be kicked around at will. We are worthy, connected, aware, loving, safe, and strong individuals who deserve truckloads of comfort, eons of happiness, and oodles of security. God knows we've gone without for long enough.

In this third section of the book, I want you to have a quick reference guide to flip through after you've completed your main Garden work. In reality, none of the exercises in this book were created specifically for assaultive trauma; they were all meant to be used regularly by anyone at anytime. So, once you're back into your body and your life, you'll still need to get grounded, maintain your aura, burn contracts... just like anyone who undertakes a conscious spiritual journey. Don't feel alone if you forget or ignore your skills. Often, beginning students point out that I am neither grounded nor in my head, to which I reply with a spiritually advanced, "Oh, shut up!"

If you're not lucky enough to have people reminding *you* to get grounded, you can put this book in a very visible place and flip through it whenever you drift out of your body. Or, you can leave it unopened on the coffee table, where it will glare at you when you're not grounded. You can then yell, "Oh, shut up!" at the book. What fun!

A special note: in the pages that follow, I will often refer to on-path and off-path behaviors. When I refer to path in a healthy and centered individual, I refer to the set of experiences, tragedies, and triumphs for which they prepared themselves before they incarnated. Path can be seen as the map your spirit gave you to navigate through the often rough and uncharted waters of life on this planet. Every path is completely distinct and separate, and based on the needs of each spirit.

When a child is molested, his path is often lost to him as his spirit and body spiral into survival-based dissociation. Though contact with a molester may have been an unavoidable part of his spirit's destiny, the experience of molestation often pulls away the foundation of his spiritual connection. This can obscure his map, and his path, from view.

Once the work of re-centering begins, path re-asserts itself in the life of the molest survivor. In the vast majority of cases, spirit path is significantly different from the current life. It is often so different that it appears to be ridiculously unattainable.

In these cases, all of the skills learned in Parts I and II of this book will need to be brought to bear in releasing the current milieu and stepping onto the true pathway. The skills in this third portion of the book will make walking the path for the remainder of your life much easier.

The journey from here to the center of true path can become a harsh journey if you desperately grab onto stasis and resist the changes that will bring you back to path; however, the harshness will pass if you will commit to staying centered and in the present moment. When you live in the moment and use your own skills, your return to path will be an adventure instead of an ordeal. Read on.

ADVANCED GROUNDING

When your body is grounded, it's easier to live there. Simple. The same is true for your home, your workspace, your car, the room in your head, your aura, or anyplace else you are. Grounding creates a connection between your spirit, the grounded object, and the center of the planet. Grounding also provides a spiritual dumping ground for energy, and a constant source of safety, renewal, and awareness. However, awareness requires responsibility. We must therefore learn the rules of grounding.

GROUNDING RULES

The grounding rules for areas, objects, machinery, and possessions are similar to the grounding rules for people. Just as it's not okay for you to ground someone else, it is also not okay for you to ground someone else's house, office, car, computer, or whatever. Things, buildings, machines, and possessions have their own energy, their own karma, and their own destinies with the people who own them. The energy of your grounding cord would interfere with those destinies.

If you ground other people's things, you will interfere in their life. This is a bad thing. Didn't we just go through this whole book to train ourselves to pay attention to our own energy--to stop trying to live other people's lives? Grounding machines and possessions transmits your attention, ownership, and responsibility to a grounded object. If you do own the thing, machine, place, or portion thereof, you have every right to ground it. Otherwise, leave it alone.

Before we learn how to ground places and objects we own, let me give you a few specific exceptions to these grounding rules.

Grounding your area: if you live in a room in someone else's house, or inhabit a space, cubicle, or office in someone else's work building, you have every right to ground your area. Your sleep and work areas should always be grounded, but don't worry about transitional places in someone else's area. For instance, you shouldn't ground the communal kitchen in a rooming house or office building, because it's not your private space. Your own personal grounding cord will be enough to keep you centered while you're making meals.

If you have no private area of your own in anyplace you live or work, take care. Keep yourself and your aura grounded so you will have some privacy and distancing available, and do what you can to find a situation that respects your separateness and humanity. Privacy is a necessity.

Grounding your responsibilities: when I borrow objects from people, use their car or their computer, or caretake their house, I become responsible for those things. I want my own energy in charge of what goes on during that time, so I ground those objects. I look at it this way: if anything happens to something in my care, I'm going to have to deal with it, financially or otherwise. I'd like the things that happen to have something to do with my energy, my path, my lessons, and my karma. I don't want to have to deal with another person's theft or damage fears when I have to rely on their possessions, so I ground the objects or machines I am responsible for as soon as I get them. I also renew my grounding each time I use the objects.

When I return the borrowed item, I remove my grounding cord (by dropping it out of the object). This is a vital step, because just as I shouldn't have to deal with another person's energy in any item or machine I use, other people shouldn't have to deal with my energy once their possession is returned to them.

As far as alerting people to my psychic safety techniques: I tell people about what I am doing with their borrowed item if they understand grounding, and I keep it to myself if they don't.

Grounding your tools: this is a combination of the first two exceptions. When you are working with tools, machinery, and other skill-requiring objects, you are expected to be responsible for them. Therefore, it is best to ground them even if you don't own them. The drill press or computer you use already has an energy connection with you, and that connection will be stronger, safer, and more real if you ground the tool during use. Grounding the tools of your home or workspace helps protect you from accidents, and them from breakdown, misplacement, and inadvertent borrowing.

Within the category of tools, I include any vehicle you use for work, including commuter planes, fleet cars, rental construction equipment, and even elevators if they make you queasy. Work machines and vehicles are in a hazy gray area of these grounding rules, because no one person really owns or relates to them individually; however, I think we aware users do these metallic beings a great service by grounding them and giving them our focused attention. We do ourselves a great service when we allow our centered awareness to connect and protect us in all the places we go.

Grounding your healing area: I always ground any place where my body is being worked on, including massage rooms, my acupuncturists's treatment room, operating rooms, and so on. I ground these places because when I pay for a professional healing service, I want real healing to occur, with no foreign energy getting in my way. I also want my body to feel completely safe so I can let go and receive the healing I asked for.

If you have a special place where you read this book and do your meditations, make sure it's grounded, and it will be easier to keep yourself centered. I always ground rooms where I give classes, because I have to be very open and receptive in those situations. Once again, I want to protect and center myself as much as I can when any healing work occurs.

Now that we have gone over the basics of grounding rules, let's look at some advanced grounding techniques:

HOW TO GROUND ROOMS OR AREAS

This skill is hard to explain, but not to master. Please see my illustrations.

The grounding cord you provide for an area will help to define its territory; therefore, it doesn't matter if the area is a room, a whole house, a partitioned cubicle, or an oblong lean-to. Your grounding will define it as a separate, protected area.

In grounding of rooms or areas, you will identify the psychic boundaries of the area you wish to ground, and attach energy cords to the uppermost and bottom-most corners of your chosen location.

Starting at the ceiling, visualize four cords of golden, present-time energy, and attach them to the uppermost corners of your room or area. When these cords are attached, allow them to reach down diagonally to meet one another at the very center of the room or area. This center should be at about eye-level.

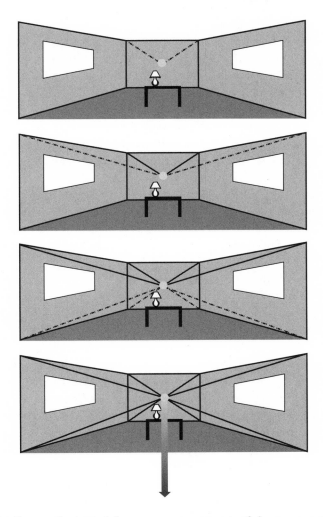

Attach similar cords to each bottom-most corner of the area, and visualize these cords travelling upwards to the center of the room, where they will meet and connect with the cords you brought down from the ceiling. These eight cords will reach their mutual apex at the very center of the area you wish to ground.

Now, attach a brightly colored grounding cord to this cord apex (pretend that this energetic apex is the first *chakra* of the room). Send this cord down to the center of the planet. Anchor this cord, and your area is now grounded.

You will need to check on your area grounding cord a few times to see that it stays put. If it disappears regularly, there may be an ungrounded person using the area and grabbing your cord unconsciously. It is a good idea to use gold cords if this occurs. Gold is a neutral, de-personalized healing energy. If someone inadvertently picks up your gold area-grounding cord, they won't become trapped in your energy. They'll get a nice healing, sure, but if you use gold grounding cords, they won't be able to identify you as the source of that healing unless they are very intuitive.

Remember, when grounding your portion of a public area, to surround your portion with a blanket of ungrounded gift images or roses. This symbolic blanket will help to define your area, and stop people from snatching your grounding cords and undoing your work. This blanket usually stops cord-snatchers, who will instead walk off with an armful of your free gifts or flowers. Since the gifts are there for the taking, your visitor has every right to them. Ungrounded gifts are easy to replenish.

I ground my healing area or office space each time I arrive, and I don't even check to see if my previous area grounding still exists. I want my portions of other people's space to be freshly grounded each time I use them. In my home, I check my grounding much less often.

I find that my customary body and aura grounding cords tend to freshen my home's grounding, and vice versa. Also, maintaining a grounded home, office, or area around me helps me to stay in the room in my head, to remember my Sentry, and so on. Once again, the use of each of these energy tools tends to support the health of the others.

In addition to surrounding your home, workspace, or general area with an aura of ungrounded roses, it is always a good idea to place a grounded Sentry symbol at the door or entryway to your grounded area. The act of grounding is very noticeable in your local psychic fabric, and people may be inexplicably drawn to you. Your free gift blanket will give these people the communication and healing they seek, and your grounded Sentry will help them to remember that you are a protected individual in a protected area.

Without the help of a gift blanket or Sentry, you may find that your grounded area is the new hang-out, and that you have to replace its grounding cord every few hours or so.

Once again, if you notice a few people who can't seem to stay away from your grounded area, and they really need a healing—don't stop your forward progress and slow down to heal them! Let them borrow this book, or draw them a picture of grounding, and continue with your own healing and separation skills, please.

HOW TO GROUND CARS AND OTHER MACHINES

Some people have an uncanny way with cars and machinery; machines don't break down on them. Though they're not usually mechanics *per se*, they always seem to be able to remedy mechanical problems. My father is like this. Very few of his machines and possessions break down, even if they logically should, given their age and condition. The reason for this is that Dad is a naturally grounded person; his grounding generally extends to anything he touches or uses. His grounding of machines works just like the grounding of energy in an electrical current; it tends to make machinery run more efficiently, and therefore more safely.

My mother, on the other hand, used to be somewhat ungrounded. If a machine was going to have a difficulty at some point in its life span, it would usually wait until my mom was in control. Her cars always did the goofiest things, but when she'd have my father look at them, there wouldn't be a hint of trouble. Today, I see that Mom's lack of grounding helped create mechanical and electrical difficulties in the machines around her, while Dad's strong grounding actually drained the quirks and difficulties right out of the machines. Mom knows how to ground now, and she is no longer a hazard to machines.

It is wonderful to learn to ground your machines, and to become a person who doesn't create chaos in the mechanical world around you.

Grounding machines and things is very like grounding areas. You will attach four cords to the upper corners, and four cords to the lower corners, of the machine or thing. Then, you'll bring all eight cords together in an apex at the center of your chosen item. Attach your main grounding cord to that central apex, and you're done!

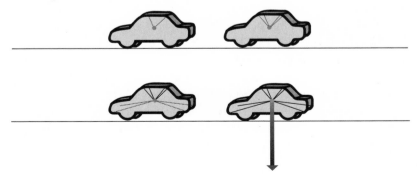

We can ground our cars, computers, tools, and appliances. By grounding, we not only create a safer arena for the electrical and mechanical beings in our lives, but we increase our present-time awareness as well. When we are able to ground and connect with all the mundane and useful items in our everyday lives, our meditation and healing will not have to stop when we're driving, working, cooking, or doing all those mundane, real world things. The real world will be a part of our spiritual world, and we will continue to ground, heal, grow, and process--no matter where we are or what we are doing.

Though these auxiliary grounding skills are very useful, grounding your own body is by far the most important skill taught in this book. If you forget everything else and simply ground from your first *chakra*, your life will travel along more smoothly. All the other skills have their importance, but the ability to ground is the centerpoint of everything we have done and will continue to do.

When you are grounded, you live in the present moment, and in your body. When you live in your body, you are aware of and available to your surroundings; therefore, you notice your needs, your thoughts, your reactions, and your emotions. You begin to care for yourself. When you care for yourself, you protect yourself and create separations, *et cetera*. It all starts with grounding, so feel free to go on an all-out grounding binge, especially when you get a little out of sorts. You can always get back to center when you ground yourself.

When you are centered, your ability to ground yourself (and all your stuff) will make staying present in your body and your life much easier. When your world and the stuff around you is cleansed of past-time, excess, or foreign energy and expectations, peaceful awareness will be far more available to you.

A little note about all of your rooms, areas, machines, possessions, and stuff: if your life is filled with stuff and possessions, the act of grounding all of them may help you to see them anew. In a more spiritually attuned life, you will begin to realize that you are responsible to and for each of the things you own. Whatever you keep becomes your responsibility, and a portion of your energy will be dedicated to that responsibility.

As you begin to ground your possessions, you may notice that you have too much stuff to keep track of. Good. Remind yourself, as you move things out, that you are clearing the way for peace, simplicity, beauty, and comfort. In this way, grounding will not only help you move old, unworkable energy out of your body and your aura, it will help you move the clutter out of your home and life.

If you hoard old energy, your mind and heart become cluttered; if you hoard old things, you not only get stuck in a cluttered life, but you keep your possessions from moving on to people who could use and honor them on a daily basis. Grounding your possessions will often wake you up and help you to honor yourself enough to release your clutter.

Grounding all of your possessions can also help you to step away from the fear of the loss of your personal belongings. Remember that true wealth, especially in a time as troubled and poverty-stricken as ours, is measured by the number of things you can let go of, leave alone, and do without.

Most people who are heavily security-and-money-conscious also fear the loss of self. They usually feel ripped-off emotionally, but can't get to that knowledge consciously, so they pour a bunch of energy into keeping all their material possessions safe from harm. The problem is, their "mine, mine, MINE!" energy attracts thieves like flies, which sends these fearful people into an ever more frenzied, endlessly vicious cycle of loss, fear, stinginess, over-protectiveness, and more loss.

Let's look at the energy of theft. People who steal have a number of difficulties, but lack of money is, surprisingly, not the major issue. Thievery is an interesting topic in and of itself, but the lowdown is that thieves are people who don't want anything that rightly belongs to them.

I have known a number of career thieves who, when a previously stolen item became too familiar, would fence it, unintentionally break it, or have it stolen from them. Thieves don't want and can't have anything that is theirs; no, they want something that clearly belongs to someone else. It's an important part of their process, and of the thieving sub-culture, to take things that are very important to and enmeshed with the energy of their owners. If your possessions throw off an intense energy that squeals, "Mine, mine, MINE!! Don't steal me!" a true thief will be drawn to them as a moth is drawn to flame.

When you ground your possessions, the energy drains right out of them, and they won't transmit crazy, possessive zeal. Thieves and vandals tend to pass by grounded objects as if they are not there. I have seen it time and time again. Grounding seems to create a non-possessive neutrality which is all but invisible to thieving or mischievous energy.

So, letting go of old unworkable mindsets and becoming responsible for the energy you transmit creates a safer, saner life. Go figure!

As you move through your day, feel free to ground as much or as little of your milieu as you see fit. If your body and aura grounding are strong, you may naturally and unconsciously transmit your grounding, like my father does, to everything you use. It's very comfortable to be on the planet when you get to that level of grounded-ness.

If your area or object grounding cords disappear, be aware that someone in your life needs grounding, and that your areas or objects are giving them that grounding. If you react emotively to the theft of your grounding cords, use your emotional energy to re-create the missing cords in more vibrant and energetic colors. Then, place an ungrounded gift blanket and a grounded Sentry just outside of your grounded area or possession. This should correct the problem.

It is okay for people to take your area or possession grounding cords a few times, but it is not at all good for them to make a habit of it. If you allow that, you will be teaching others that grounding resides in your life, and not in their own. You'll also be allowing them to perpetrate against you, which is a very irresponsible thing to do.

Please allow your natural emotional reactions to come up in these instances, but channel your emotions appropriately so they can lend their decisive energy to the re-creation of your external grounding tools.

Protect and honor your life by making it safe from unaware people. If you think it will help, you can talk to grounding-cord thieves about learning to ground for themselves. You could also place a copy of this book where they will be sure to see it. In any case, protect and separate yourself, and go on with your own healing.

As an advanced Gardener, your grounding abilities may change and evolve as you do. Fluctuations in your skills and abilities are normal and healthy; however, if your grounding does not feel real to you, even at this point in the game, I would suggest that you add the grounding supports below to your daily meditations.

SPECIAL TOPIC: SCIATIC AND OVARY GROUNDING

Your first-*chakra* grounding cord may not provide all the grounding support you need. In men, this is signalled by a forward-leaning body (often with a protruded belly), a lack of ease in the pelvic area, and difficulties with the bladder, the lower intestine, or the prostate. For women, more grounding is necessary when the pelvis is tight and inflexible as well, but also when the ovaries, uterus, and vagina are manifesting discomfort or disease.

Because the energy of male genitals is expressive and outward-directed, assault residue does not tend to hover around the penis or testicles. In men, the physical residue of molestation tends to scatter throughout the aura, around the buttocks, or up through the spine.

Grounding the sciatic area helps to drain energy off the back and out of the anus—while the first-*chakra* cord attends to and grounds out the energy stuck in the sexual glands and the center of the body. This extra grounding support often helps clear the aura of foreign energy.

Because women's genitals have a receptive and inward-directed energy, the residue of assault is often lodged inside their sexual organs. Females who were assaulted as children have a phenomenally high rate of reproductive diseases and cervical cancers which are not scientifically explainable in terms of recognizable risk factors. Such diseases are easily understood by psychics, though. When foreign energy is allowed to lodge itself in the body, diseases are far more likely.

Our first-*chakra* grounding cords are already draining the energy of our molest, but they may need more help. Please try these simple auxiliary grounding techniques for a few days. If you like them, add them to your regular meditations, and make them a permanent part of your grounding. For those of you who understand the *chakra* system, these new cords create an outlet for the stuck energy in the second *chakra* or the *hara*.

SCIATIC GROUNDING FOR MEN AND WOMEN

Please sit down and center yourself. Get grounded, and ground the room in your head with the room-grounding technique we just learned. Check in with your little one (ground them too, if they'd like that), light up and heal your aura if necessary, check on your Sentry, and destroy a few images.

At this point, this series of steps should take no more than a minute, but you can take your own time if you aren't in a hurry. This meditation was created to help busy people maintain their spiritual awareness in a minimal amount of time, but you can work through each step at a languid and unhurried pace if that suits you.

Seat yourself inside the room in your head, and make sure your first-*chakra* grounding cord is firmly attached inside your body, and firmly anchored to the center of the Earth. You may choose to ground your aura with its own grounding tube, but it is not vital to do so.

Now, place your hands behind you, right over the dimples above your buttocks. If you know anatomy, please place your hands over the sciatic nerves on either side of the upper sacrum. You should feel small depressions or dimples on either side of the bony plate of your sacrum. Attach a grounding cord to each depression, and direct both cords diagonally downwards toward your first *chakra*. Attach your sciatic grounding cords into your first-*chakra* grounding cord, and you're done.

As these cords do their work, you should feel energy draining off of your back and spine, as well as out of your buttocks and anus. Both men and women tend to carry a lot of psychic weight on their shoulders, back, and hips. Sciatic grounding allows this heavy and often stress-filled energy to flow down and out of the body. Molest survivors usually love sciatic grounding, because it helps to release trapped sexual energy from within their pelvis, rectum, anus, and spinal column.

I can almost always identify a molest survivor by the complete lack of pelvic sway in their walk. Theirs is not the tight-assed walk of most Americans, but an almost impossibly immobile form of conveyance. The hips may move slightly from left to right, but they almost never sway from front to back. This is not only an avoidance of sexualized movement within their pelvis, but also an unwillingness to stir up or release molest energy within their bodies.

First-*chakra* grounding clears out some of this stiffness. Sciatic grounding clears out more. The burning of molest contracts ensures that the molest energy will not settle back into the pelvis, and the channelling of emotions keeps the pelvic girdle flexible and protected. In many cases, the gait of grounded molest survivors will loosen and begin to flow in a matter of days or weeks.

OVARY GROUNDING FOR WOMEN

After you attach your sciatic grounding cords and get them working, please move your hands to the front of your body and place them over your ovaries. Your ovaries are on either side of your pelvis, approximately three inches below, and four inches to the left and right of your navel.

These positions will not differ if you are missing one or both of your ovaries. Your energy body still contains ovaries at the site of your missing ones. As such, grounding your energetic ovaries is still possible and advisable. Keep reading.

From within the room in your head, study the energy of your ovaries. What color are they? Often, because they trade ovulation duties every other month, one will be active and vibrant while the other is resting and dormant. If you have passed through menopause, though, both of your ovaries may have the same energy vibration.

Attach cords of colored energy to each of your ovaries. If your ovaries have differing energy patterns right now, they may require different colors. The active one may like a vibrant cord while the sleepy one might prefer a quieter shade. Ask each ovary what color cord it would like. Each one will send you feelings or pictures of its preference.

When cords are attached to each of your ovaries, channel the cords inward and down to your first-*chakra* grounding cord. Attach each ovary grounding cord directly to your first-*chakra* cord.

At this point, you will have two sciatic cords attaching to the rear of your first-*chakra* cord, and two ovary cords attached to the front. This may seem complicated. It's not. Once you get your entire pelvis grounded, you won't have any difficulty maintaining your auxiliary cords. They tend to maintain themselves.

Your ovaries are connected to your emotive, clairsentient, empathic second *chakra*, which is located between your navel and your pubic bone. Ovaries tend to sponge energy off of people and situations in an attempt to heal others, or to rid the environment of unsafe energy. As such, their need for the release of grounding is often very great.

As the ovaries release their runaway-healing, trapped sexual and creative energy, they free up the second *chakra* for present-time attention and duties. When the second *chakra* is cleared out and awake, the emotions become more accessible. As the emotions become knowable and available (and can be channelled), the work of separating from molest contracts and assault residue becomes much more possible and real.

When women can ground their sciatic area and their ovaries, a great deal of the molest contract residue will dislodge, ground out, and come into conscious awareness. The remedy for the dislodging caused by this new grounding is... you guessed it, more grounding.

If you still have difficulty grounding, or with your auxiliary grounding techniques, please refer to the special healing for the first *chakra* area in the chapter called *Advanced Imaging*.

ADVANCED AURA READING & DEFINITION

As I mentioned before, most of my education about (or experience with) aura readings has been confusing at best. I think I could easily take my aura to a dozen otherwise competent psychics in one day, and get a dozen or more conflicting diagnoses. The reason for this is that auras are very much alive and constantly changing, so it's really hard to nail down what each color, movement, nuance, or fluctuation means.

I believe that a competent study of the aura might require an exhaustive, encyclopedic series of books, because each aura contains a wealth of information. But, the study of the body also requires encyclopedic knowledge, and most of us get along quite well without having to be consciously aware of each of the untold thousands of functions therein.

When we live in and care for our bodies, they tend to require less external healing or expert advice. Health-building is easy when we listen and let our body tell us what food, exercise, environment, emotional state, or relationship it would prefer.

If we live in and listen to our aura, it will very clearly tell us what healing or attention it needs. We will become excellent aura readers, not by studying all auras at all times, but by being aware of the specific needs of our own energy boundary.

Auras, like bodies, are individuals. While there are auric similarities that can be relied upon, blanket statements like "Purple auras mean spiritual advancement" can send an aura reader down a very precarious path. Though I do include a list of the possible meanings of color in the aura, I don't want you to take them too seriously.

As I said before, color interpretations are (and should be) extremely subjective. If I tell you that green in the aura means change and evolution, but the green in your aura reminds you of frustration, then your green *is* frustration. It's *your* aura, which means it understands your inferences and experiences. The colors and images it shows you will have personal and specific meaning to you alone.

When I read or heal other people, I try to respect their privacy, so I don't usually their read aura colors. In a sense, I put on blinders. Instead of reading specific colors and trying to guess what they might mean to each person, I feel around (with my open hand *chakras*) and get a sense of where each aura is in relation to each body.

When I read auras, I check for hot or cold spots, holes, completeness, bulges, and so on, which I talk about as I work. Usually, the person's aura will begin to mend and reshape itself as I speak, but if not, I shape and fill it with the person's own energy. I trust that their aura will do the rest of its work once I've helped define the area it should inhabit.

Each aura I see is completely different, both from other auras, and from itself from reading to reading. Auras are, as I said, malleable, changeable, and completely individual.

Some auras are quiet and placid as I move them around, and some are so excited to be read that they start throwing funny pictures at me (I felt a rip in a woman's aura once, and her aura showed me a husband-shaped hole, just like in a cartoon). Some auras anticipate my next move, and complete their healing before I lift a finger, and some are stubborn as all get-out.

The only thing all auras have in common is that they always exist in some form or another. If they do not appear right away, the energy normally hovering around the body can be fashioned into an aura (through the lighted aura-bubble technique we learned in Part I).

This placeholding aura will provide protection until the real aura can right and re-form itself. I've seen some tremendously drug-and-psychosis-damaged auras, but they always hold on in some way, shape, or form, the little dears.

I have also seen energies or deviations in auras that had no meaning to me whatsoever. In those instances, I check in with my own aura, which sends me a feeling or a picture in *our* individual language to describe what that other aura is doing. This is an important point about the techniques used in reading for others. Psychics always read from their own understanding, even though they may get help from spirit guides and so forth.

The main trick to becoming a good psychic is to live fully and collect as many bits of knowledge and experience as possible. If you do, you (and your guides) will have a wide base of knowledge and experience to use in unusual reading or healing situations. Then, a good psychic simply trusts that the information being interpreted is correct. This is as true for self-readings as it is for the reading of others.

As we go through these aura-reading guidelines, I want you to feel free to replace any reading technique that doesn't work for you. I have very sensitive hands and do my readings through a form of empathic ability. You may have very sensitive eyes and be able to do your readings clairvoyantly.

If I ask you to feel the aura, and you can see or hear or sense it instead, use your own psychic abilities. Don't rely on my reading techniques if they don't work for you. Your intuitive abilities, like your aura, will differ from mine.

GENERAL AURA READING GUIDELINES

To read your aura, sit in your usual, grounded meditative state, cleanse your body and your aura of old energy by using your grounding vacuums, and light up and define the oblong boundary of your aura with golden light. Gold energy is present-time healing energy, which will be a signal to your aura that you want to see what it is doing at this very moment.

After you have established your correctly shaped, complete and golden aura boundary, stay inside your head and allow the gold energy to fade into whatever color your aura wants to show you. Be aware, too, of any shape changes, or other deviations that come about when the color changes.

If you can't see anything at this point, close your eyes and use your hands to feel the edge of your aura. Hand *chakras* can pick up color vibrations; don't worry that closing your eyes will give you a monochrome aura. Your brain can very easily receive and interpret color vibrations through your hands. It's the way a lot of psychics work.

Before you read through this color list, let me remind you once again that these ideas about the meanings of color are only general guidelines. Your own interpretations of the colors in your aura are far more important (and far more correct) than any list made up by a total stranger!

COLORS

PINK: Healing humor, protection from abuse, indecision.
RED: The physical body, power, anger, sexuality.
ORANGE: The emotions, the muscles, fury, sensuality, healing.
YELLOW: Intellect, immunity and protection, impatience, fear.
GREEN: Love, transformation, healing, frustration, loss.
BLUE: Communication, spiritual knowledge, mourning, separation.
INDIGO: Spiritual power, telepathy, victimization.
PURPLE/VIOLET: Spiritual certainty, release, religious confusion.
BROWN: Earth energy, grounding ability, past-time issues.
BLACK: Finality, death, rebirth, delay.
WHITE: Spirit guide presence, purity, shock, erasure.
SILVER: Spirit-world information, ungrounded-ness, uncertainty.
GOLD: Healing, neutrality, transformative illness.

As a rule, pastel colors carry a less intense message than their base colors, while darker colors carry a more intense message. Mixed colors carry a mixed message.

For example: a pale yellow in my aura could mean that I'm relying partially on my intellect, am slightly impatient, or am needing a light level of psychic protection in a somewhat unsafe environment. A very bright yellow would mean I'm thinking all the time, I'm very impatient, or I'm using a lot of protection energy because I'm in a terribly dangerous environment.

On the other hand, an orangy-yellow in my aura could mean that I'm trying to bring sensual realities into my thought process, that I'm trying to protect my sensuality, or that I'm impatient with my emotions. In your aura, an orangy-yellow may mean something entirely different. My suggestion is that you rely on the certainty you have when you channel your emotions, but reverse the process.

When you channel your emotions, you choose a color scheme and energy quality for the emotional state you want to heal, and then let that chosen color represent your emotional state as you work with your emotional energy. When you read your aura, you can reverse the process by allowing its colors or qualities to tell you what emotions or situations they represent for you.

To interpret the colors in your own aura, stay in your head and sense the color or quality of color surrounding you. Wait for your body to bring up an emotional state or memory in response to the color or energy in your aura. Your mind and body may help you interpret the energy of the color by bringing forward a series of images or explanations about the energy. Thank them, and move forward in your reading with the information they provide.

Don't get married to the colors you see in your aura right now, or judge yourself on their level of evolution up the vibrational scale. Your aura may be a scuzzy green and black right now, but it will be purple and gold later, and bright pink or electric blue in between. During this reading, your aura essentially freezes itself in place so you can see it. In normal situations, it moves and fluctuates so quickly that you'd never be able to keep up with it. The colors you see now are only momentarily valid.

What your aura is showing you right now are issues that require your immediate attention. Your grounding and centering *are* that attention, and the Gold Sun healing at the end of this aura reading will heal, cleanse, and process any issues your aura has right now.

Far more important than color, in my practical experience, is the shape and condition of the aura as a whole. Up to this point, we have redefined our aura into what I consider to be its ideal size and shape. The bright color we have chosen for our aura boundary is not a directive on color management. The color is a placeholder, for us and our auras, signifying where we would like them to be in relation to our bodies.

My bright magenta-bounded aura can be any color it likes inside the boundary, even if I create a pastel wash of that magenta inside my aura. My magenta energy does not force my aura to become magenta. My use of the magenta energy helps me to maintain a constant awareness of the completeness and integrity of my personal territory.

My magenta boundary lights up and defines the area I wish my aura to inhabit, which helps remind my aura of where it should be. The pastel wash of magenta is used to connect my bodily awareness with my auric awareness, not to replace my aura's natural colors with ones I might like better.

An aside: if you read about the hazards of using the White Light barrier, which *can* harm the aura, and are confused about what I just said, you're not alone! I always wondered why the White Light could disrupt an aura's natural color flow until I realized that the White Light is created from fear (often, repressed fear). If you've channelled your own fear, you'll know that its intensity is often overwhelming.

When fear is not honored, but instead formed into pseudo-spiritual energy barriers, its intensity can disrupt the balance of anything it touches. Our brightly-colored aura boundaries are not a part of any dishonored emotion; therefore, they don't disrupt our aura's natural functioning. That's the difference.

WARNING: The explanations and exercises which follow are included to give your aura a little help when it is out of sorts or stuck; however, if your aura is constantly whacked out and wavery, you may be experiencing the effects of drug use. This aura reading and the Gold Sun healing will help you, but not if you continue to abuse yourself.

If you are currently using drugs, including caffeine, tobacco, or alcohol, your energy will be quite chaotic, and this work will be very difficult. You most likely won't be able to maintain a healthy aura, a constant grounding cord, or a meditative sanctuary in your head. If you want to stop using, all of the tools in this book will make moving out of abuse easier, but the work we're doing (and in truth, any work) won't help if you're actively abusing your body and your energy with drugs.

When your aura shows you its color and energy patterns, it may also show you any deviations it has in its shape. These will be healed during the Gold Sun healing at the end of this reading, but first, let's take a look at what each shape deviation might indicate.

AURA SIZE

These size categories are in relation to the general twenty-four to thirty inches away from the body, oblong-shaped aura we've been defining all along.

TOO SMALL: A tiny overall aura boundary (anything less than sixteen inches from the body) indicates a reaction to a unsupportive, even life-threatening environment. If your invisible aura cannot take up its required room in your life or relationships, it's a certainty that you don't have the personal freedom you require for your highest growth and evolution.

Often, we will unconsciously choose engulfing environments, for two very ingenious reasons. First off, engulfing environments take away our ability to move forward, so we don't have to face the terrors of growth and change. Secondly, engulfing environments force our awareness into a smaller-than-normal area, which may keep us in or near our bodies most of the time. But, now that we know how to stay in our bodies, there isn't any need to squash or hinder our auras any more.

It makes no difference where you are in consciousness; your aura needs to be at its healthy size, and you need to be in an environment which allows your aura to take up its normal space. If your aura has been limited, attempting to plump it out already may have created difficulties for you in your presently engulfing environment.

Please, if you have a smaller-than-usual aura, care for yourself, burn your contracts regularly, and move on to a situation that allows you and your aura the space to live and breathe. I know it's not easy. It's just absolutely necessary.

TOO LARGE: A huge aura (anything larger than thirty-six inches from the body) denotes that a tremendous amount of your spiritual and physical energy is essentially being ignored. An aura boundary which is all over the room is the sign of a bored and under-utilized spirit, or a drug user (don't make me recite the drug speech again--just get your energy back together, okay?). A person with a huge aura is usually out of his body, mostly because his life has almost nothing to do with his true path as a questing, intelligent, immortal being.

Pulling this type of aura back in to the requisite area can be very uncomfortable if you want to continue to ignore your life path and fool around. You may suddenly feel terribly hemmed in and forced to make decisions that ask you to travel down a narrower path than you think you want right now. Those are fears talking. Choose a color for those fears and channel their emotional energy to learn what they have to teach you. Remember, the old cliche is true: what looks like death to the caterpillar is the beginning for the butterfly.

AURA SHAPE

Auras can deviate from the oblong in a number of ways, but before we look at specific deviations, I'd like to give you an overview of what each segment of the aura indicates.

THE FRONT: Any deviations in the front of the aura are related to the future and to the conscious mind. A person with a very large front section (and a small, close-to-the body back section, see illustration) is placing a lot of their energy into the future, in plans, schemes, or dreams.

This person is most likely out-of-body, ignoring the past and any unconscious messages, and living in a frenetic, jumping-out-of-the-skin state. Plumping out the back of their aura, and making room for the lessons and unfinished business of the past, may help to calm them down.

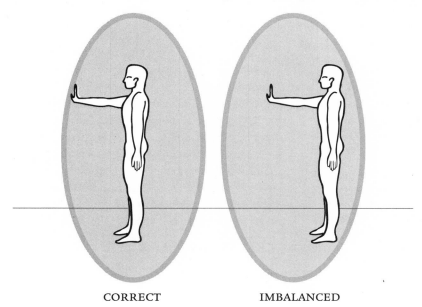

CORRECT   IMBALANCED

Injuries to the front of the aura may signify an upcoming trauma. Many of us have the ability to see clairvoyantly into the future to some extent. You can bring any foreseen situation into your conscious control by making and then burning your contract with it. The events of the future are always a probability, and if you want to, you can change the quality of the future by working, in your present-day life, on the issues you can foresee.

THE BACK: The back of your aura is the past, your unconscious, and the foundation upon which you base your current life view. A very skewed, too-much-back and not-enough-front aura signifies a person unable to move forward; they are focusing all their energy and attention on past issues. Because they do not have the support of the front, or forward-facing portion of their aura, they may not be able to bring these past issues into consciousness. The past may haunt them. Molest survivors generally have back and front skews of varying degrees. Bringing the molest contracts forward and running the emotions will remedy these skews.

Injuries and tears in the back of your aura signify past-time injuries that have not been addressed. Gold Sun healings and rescue scenarios will help to bring these injuries and issues into your awareness. You can then heal and confront these issues with your present-day abilities. Plumping out the front of your aura, which can make more room for you in the present and the future, will help as well.

THE LEFT SIDE: The left side of your aura signifies your feminine characteristics: your diffuse, intuitive, receptive nature. Feminine energy is equally present in men and women: there is no sexist monopoly on energy. When there are indentations or injuries on the left side of the aura, I look for a denial of the receptive feminine aspect of the self, or an interference caused by a person who runs a lot of feminine energy. The condition of your aura's left side denotes your ability to receive, from the spirit world of information and guidance, and the from the physical world of contact, support, and love. A huge left side to your aura infers a serious dependence on receptivity, while a squashed left side infers an unwillingness to listen, to remain still, or to receive.

THE RIGHT SIDE: The right side of the aura signifies your masculine characteristics: your focused, discerning, expressive nature. Masculine energy, too, is equally present in men and women. Injuries or deviations in this portion of your aura denote difficulty with masculine energy within you, difficulties with a person who runs a lot of masculine energy, or difficulties with your ability to give, to teach, to speak, and to express your inner self in the outer world. A huge right side to your aura infers a serious dependence on expression, while a cramped right side infers an unwillingness to act, to speak out, or to express yourself.

THE TOP (from chest-level to the upper edge of your aura): The top of your aura relates to your connection to your spirituality, and your comfort with the guidance or information you receive from spirit. Spirit can include God, your spirit guides and angels, or anyone you know who is not currently in a body. If the top of your aura is squashed flat around your head, it can mean that you don't believe in or trust spiritual information. On the other hand, a huge and elongated top portion of your aura can mean that you focus so much energy on the cosmic aspects of life that you ignore your body and your physical life.

Injuries and deviations in the top of your aura can signify a punishing religion, a rift in your belief system, or a separation from spirituality and the support it provides. Plumping out the upper portion of your aura can make spirituality more real and understandable to you.

THE CENTER (from your chest to your knees, all the way around your body): The condition of the center of your aura relates to your daily physical life. Deviations in this portion generally refer to physical problems and challenges that your aura is either alerting you to, or trying to heal on its own.

Sometimes, your aura will show you a blob of color or a pulse of energy right around a body part that has or is about to have difficulties. Channel your Gold Sun energy into that area of your aura and body, and go see your acupuncturist. Chinese medicine has worked with energy for over five thousand years, and it is invaluable in maintaining a clear, grounded, healthy spirit/body connection. Chinese medicines are also very energy-respectful--they won't throw you out of your body and create side-effects as western medicines usually do.

The center of your aura also points to the fit or communication level between you as a regular human and you as an immortal spirit. Central aura sections that are wobbly and indistinct usually denote a not-so-comfortable body/spirit relationship. Keep grounding. You'll get it.

THE BOTTOM (from the knees down): The bottom of your aura relates to your ability to ground. Incompleteness and deviations in the bottom portion of your aura point to an unwillingness to stay grounded, or an unawareness of grounding. Hazy lower auras can even denote a lack of exercise (which is naturally grounding), or poor care of the physical body.

Be aware of your top-to-bottom aura skew. Are you grounding very hard and pulling in the top of your aura so you don't have to listen to spirit, or are you pulling up your grounding so that the top of your aura can go flying off in search of magical answers?

A little tip: the magic is right here, and you'll find it faster if you're grounded, in your body, and connected to your spiritual information at the same time. It's fun to go off on a body-only, or a spirit-world-only afternoon every now and then, but being healed means being whole. We are all spirits *in* bodies, not just spirits, or just bodies. Being whole means working to keep all parts of ourselves in communication most of the time.

Any skews, tears, bulges, or insufficiencies in any part of your aura can be healed by re-forming your aura boundary with present-time gold healing energy, and then performing a full Gold Sun healing. As a matter of fact, you can consider any aura boundary definition and any Gold Sun healing as a quick reading and healing of your aura.

The more advanced reading techniques that follow are only called for when an aura deviation does not respond to simpler healings, and keeps showing up, unchanged, in your meditations. In that case, a full aura reading is called for.

DEVIATIONS IN THE AURA

Now that you have an idea of what each area of the aura depicts, let's look at what specific deviations and injuries can mean. Remember that in almost every case, healing of these injuries will be accomplished during the Gold Sun healing you have already mastered.

BLOBS: Defined blobs of color in an aura can signal trapped, unmoving energy, in the energy body or the physical body. See COLD SPOTS, HOT SPOTS, and PULSATIONS, below, if your blobs have specific attributes. If not, sit and ask the blobs why they are there. They will usually show you an unhealthy relationship or thought pattern, if they come from the emotional, intellectual, or spiritual bodies, and you can clear such blobs away by burning contracts or destroying images.

If the blobs are connected to your physical body, they will usually hover around an area where a disease or difficulty originates. Sometimes the blobs will show you a picture of a way that you hold your body, or a food that you eat which is causing difficulty. Pay attention to any blobs of trapped energy. For support, see your acupuncturist. Acupuncturists see the body as a system of energy meridians; they are usually able to find and release energy that is stuck and gumming up the works.

If your energy blobs show you pictures of other people, it usually means that you are in a contractual relationship which allows your contract partners direct access to your aura or your body. The blobs in these instances are actually bits of your contract partner's personal energy, which can't work in your aura.

Please burn your contracts and destroy your image of this person, and steer clear of him or her for a while until you've made a clear separation. Sometimes, it will take a few releasing sessions before you can truly break the connection and move on. As you work, remember to channel your golden healing energy into the area the blob once inhabited, and to cover your aura with a grounded Sentry blanket. These steps will make an unconscious contractual re-connection less likely.

BULGES: Bulging areas usually correspond to an aura skew, meaning that the opposite side or portion of your aura has an indentation which is either the reaction to--or the cause of--the bulge.

Bulges usually signify that a part of you is feeling trapped and indented by limitations (your own or society's). Your aura's opposite side will try to bulge out and take up more space in the world.

For instance: if you have an indentation in your right or male side of your aura, which means you don't have permission to express yourself or your masculinity, you may swing over and bulge out your receptive feminine energy in response. Such bulge-dent imbalances can be healed during the regular auric re-definition you learned in Part I, or in a Gold Sun healing. In either case, use your hands to pull in a bulge while you plump out its opposite indentation. Add lots of bright, healing energy to both sides of the imbalance.

BRIGHT SPOTS: Areas of bright light or color denote a portion of your being which is being examined, highlighted, and healed right now. The application of this light may have come from you directly, from your aura's own healing ability, or, if the bright spot is white or silver, from your spirit guides. I generally leave bright spots alone unless they are very hot (see HOT SPOTS, below). Hot spots signal awareness and healing, so I don't interfere with them.

COLD SPOTS: Auras should generally maintain an even temperature, but sometimes, brighter or cooler colors will change the temperature in their area. This small change is normal; however, if you feel a spot in your aura that is noticeably colder (by more than five or ten degrees), it may need attention.

Cold spots usually denote a part of you which has been allowed to die off through lack of use. A cold spot can also point to an area in your life where specific people can enter into your awareness and abuse you.

Please refer to the section on aura segments and their meanings, above, to get a handle on what this cold spot could signify for you. Cold spots need to be filled with a great deal of warm and healing golden energy, and surrounded with a grounded Sentry blanket.

Burn your old contracts with the cold, unused, and denied aspects of yourself (or with the people who have had permission to drain off your energy); incinerate them.

Keep an eye on this area through successive Gold Sun healings, and make sure to define your aura boundary with very warm and vibrant colors as you take this area back into your life and into your conscious awareness.

COLOR SPLOTCHES: Skittery and indistinct color splotches (as opposed to more distinct and slow-moving or motionless BLOBS, above) denote a great deal of activity in an aura, usually related to spiritual growth and transformation. Splotches are generally a transitory deviation, but if they show up more than once, or are all the same color, you may have energy damage related to drug or alcohol use.

Drugs and alcohol scatter physical energy, each in their own specific way, but they also do a lot of damage to the auric and *chakric* fields. If drugs are in your current or recent life, the work in this book will be very difficult, and splotches of color are probably about all your aura can manage right now.

Nurture your aura with lots of golden healing energy, and try to pull yourself together by cleaning drug energy out of your body and your life. See an acupuncturist, a nutritionist, and a rehab counselor for support.

DARK SPOTS: Dark spots in your aura signify areas of punishing, abusive harshness, from yourself or others. Entirely dark quadrants can signify a complete deadness in the darkened area, or an unwillingness to accept that aspect of your being (see the previous section on aura segments for an idea of what the deadened aspect might be).

I see dark energy as a place where the lights have been shut off, through punishment or fear. Channelling Gold Sun energy into darkened spots, and lighting up the aura boundary, can help make acceptance of the area or areas a much easier task. Remember: burn contracts with your old images of your darkened aspects, then light up and re-occupy the area as you create a grounded Sentry blanket for your entire aura.

DENSE ENERGY: Areas of dense energy, where you can actually feel edges or boundaries, often signify the presence of other people or beings in your personal territory. This presence is always contractually allowed, because no one can hang around in your aura without your permission.

Auras work best when their colors and energy patterns have fluidity, and freedom to pulsate, move, twist, and flow. Dense energy creates a blockage in the aura that has no flow--it's not conducive to healing.

Dense energy can feel hot, warm, or cold, depending on the level of intensity of the contract. Such contracts need to be brought out, examined, and completely burnt up. In addition to contract burning, these areas of denseness need to be grounded out and released.

To remove areas of dense energy, place a brightly colored grounding vacuum right in the middle of the denseness, and vacuum it out of your aura. As the denseness drains away, immediately fill your aura with Gold Sun energy, and see the golden energy pressing the denseness further down and out of your grounding vacuum. Use your hands to smooth your golden energy into the once-dense area, and surround the area with a blanket of grounded Sentries.

If you know who helped you create this denseness, burn your contracts with them again, after you have released the dense energy. If you can't identify your partner, place a picture of the size and quality of the dense area onto a contract, and burn your relationship with it. This will work just as well.

It's not always necessary to identify the contributors to your psychic distress. The only real necessity is to clear out old, unworkable patterns, and to replace them with better skills and a higher level of awareness. Blame is good to hold onto for a while, but taking decisive action to remove yourself from victimizing relationships is better in the long run.

DENTS: Dents indicate areas where you don't have the freedom you need to express yourself. Dents usually indicate that this lack of freedom originates in your environment, and not in yourself. Sometimes, though, dents are a part of an aura skew you have created through the belief that you can be one thing *or* the other, but never both.

I see a lot of people who dent off the grounded bottom portion of their auras so they can bulge out the portion at the top and become more spiritual (whatever that means). I remind them (and you) that we are striving to become whole, centered beings, not dissociated, one-sided reactions to our environment. Whole beings have earth and the cosmos, male and female, dark and light, peace and chaos, past and future, *ad infinitum*. Whole beings are one thing *and* the other.

Smooth out your dents and bulges by redefining your aura boundary as a solid, continuous, and well-balanced oval. Remind yourself that even if you are having issues with a certain portion of your being, your aura will be happier and more able to heal you if it has a healthy, workable, and wholly defined area in which to process your issues.

ELONGATIONS: Elongations (long tentacles or ropes of energy coming out of your aura) are areas where you are reaching out and trying to grasp onto a concept which you judge to be beyond your range of ability or understanding. This belief is a residue of your old out-of-body existence, where safety, peace, and information seemed to be anywhere but in your own life and experience.

Elongations need to be called back in to center as you remind yourself that all information, all healing, and all safety reside within you: in your grounded, protected body, and in the present moment. It is also helpful to manually smooth out the edge of your aura in the once-elongated area, and to attend to that portion of your aura in subsequent readings and healings over a period of two weeks or so.

Elongations can also be a sign of giving or losing your energy to some person or situation that has wounded you. As you pull your energy back, use your Gold Sun to clear and cleanse your energy while you burn your contracts with your wounds or your wounders. Remember that the only way someone or something can continue to abuse you is if you refuse to move on.

FLIMSY, WAVERY EDGES: Through your regular aura boundary definitions, your aura should be able to hold on to a fairly sturdy delineation between itself and the outside world. If instead you find a flimsy, indistinct edge, it can signal a lack of health, in your aura or your body.

Examine your sleep, diet, and exercise routines, but also check in with your interpersonal or work relationships. If your life is unsafe or unsupportive, your aura won't be as healthy as it could be. A beautiful aspect (or a scary one, depending on your point of view) of this inner work is that your suddenly healthy body, aura, and inner self won't put up with abusive energies anymore. You and they will begin to react strongly to abuse as you come out of basic survival and into a more conscious life.

Though you are truly becoming stronger and more alive, you may feel weaker and less free as your body says no to this lover and that food; as your little one says no to this job and that neighborhood; and as your aura says no to this relationship and that health regime..

When the edge of your aura is flimsy, it means that your health, both physical and spiritual, is at risk in your current milieu. You can certainly beef up your aura boundary and load on the grounded Sentry roses, but I'd also like you to realize that safety and support are available, right now.

You don't have to stay in a boundary- and health-compromising situation at this point in your life. Your molest is over and you can move on to other lessons. Or, you can stay where you are and discover all sorts of new energy tools for protecting yourself in unsafe environments. The choice is yours.

HAZY AREAS: Haziness in an aura signifies unexplored or confusing aspects of the self. The haziness may come from other people's refusal to let you explore the aspect, or from your own refusal to support yourself.

If you have no idea of how to express your feminine energy, and your aura's left side is hazy, or you just don't *get* spirituality and the top of your aura is wavery, a very healing process is this: put up your Gold Sun, and place in it a picture of yourself as a feminine person, a spiritual person, or a grounded, earthy person. Imagine an entire person made up of the aspect that is hazy for you right now.

See this person inside your Gold Sun, and as you bring the Gold Sun energy into your aura and your body, pull this whole self-created person into you. Let this person's legs fill your legs, let them sit into your pelvis, let their arms reach into yours, and let them look out from behind your eyes.

Allow this previously unrealized aspect of you to place gold energy in and around your aura, and give it a strong gold grounding cord so that it can stay with you. Sit and feel what it's like to be this feminine, or spiritual, or earthy person, and let yourself experience the wisdom and strength of this previously ignored or invalidated part of your whole self. Let this aspect of you speak and feel and live; let it share all the information, healing ideas, and life energy it has been forced to hide.

When you've gotten this lost part of yourself firmly installed in your body, let your Gold Sun vanish, and close off the opening in the top of your aura. Bend over and dump any excess energy out the top of your head. Be aware of how much of this aspect your body wants to keep. Don't be surprised if it wants all of it, and you feel completely comfortable right now. You've lived without this portion of yourself for long enough.

Let this aspect of you have its head for now, and try to listen to the stories, warnings, and feelings it has about your life. You may find its information to be counter to what you believe right now (or its area wouldn't have been hazy), but listen anyway.

Invite this aspect of you to help heal your aura during any subsequent reading and healing sessions. You may find your life and attitudes changing in surprising ways once you revitalize a hazy and unrealized portion of your being.

HOLES: Holes in the boundary of your aura are places where your energy can leak out, and other people's energy can sneak in. Holes can be a sign that your Sentry is not the right one for the situations you encounter, because the edge of your aura is becoming involved in the energy intrusions of others. A hole-filled aura needs a grounded Sentry rose blanket right now, and don't skimp on the thorns.

Holes also ask you to be more aware of the quality of interactions you have with the people or situations in your life. Step up your image-releasing and contract-burning until you can pinpoint any specific boundary-injuring people or events. If you ask them, the holes in your aura will often show you the shape of the person or situation that created them.

Once you identify the cause of such holes, you'll need to burn specific contracts, send dozens of hello gifts, and be aware and grounded when in contact with hole-making people or situations in your life. The advanced aura boundary definition called *Aura Stomp*, taught later in this chapter, will help.

Holes will also appear in your aura through your use of drugs, especially depressants, hallucinogens, and marijuana. All western drugs and mood-or-consciousness-alterers scatter energy. Sometimes that's called for in certain situations, but not nearly so often as we moderns tend to think.

If you use drugs, your aura will show it, and you will have a less evolved, less able, and less aware reaction to the many challenges of living in a body. You can choose to continue your drug use and fix your incomplete and unhealthy aura more often, or you can give your body a break and clean out!

HOT SPOTS: Areas with a rise in temperature of more than five or ten degrees denote intense concentrated energy, either from your conscious attention, from your aura's own healing ability, or from the attention of another person. Heat is usually a sign of intense healing energy, but its presence can disrupt the delicate balance in your aura and take healing energy away from other equally deserving areas.

A healthy aura needs healing energy available in all areas at all times. Hot spots denote a lack of clean, readily available, present-time healing energy. More frequent Gold Sun healings are called for in this instance, so that the aura can experience a constant flow of healing energy, instead of having to take energy from one area to heal another.

Ground out any hot spots to cool them before running your Gold Sun energy throughout your entire aura, and keep an eye on the area and on your body to see what is going on. A visit to your acupuncturist or other holistic practitioner would be wise as well. Remember not to compartmentalize yourself or your aura by obsessing on one spot or one aspect to the exclusion of all others. Keep your excellent healing energy flowing and available to all parts of you.

JAGGED EDGES: Jagged, spiky edges on aura boundaries (or in holes or tears), signal a serious need to pull in and redefine all boundaries. I usually see jagged spikes in the auras of what I would call "all-encompassing" people, or people who try to love, accept, and experience everything they encounter.

When you do not use your discernment to make separations between what does and doesn't work for you, your aura may have too much input to process. If you try to accept all beings, all external experiences, all contact, and all information without filters, you depersonalize yourself in the process. Though a sense of universal love and acceptance of all experience is considered paramount spiritual behavior, it can really get in the way of healthy individuation unless it is arrived at truthfully.

Real individuation requires real emotions like anger, jealousy, prejudice, fear, and exhilaration. Emotions and reactions help us to separate input into chaff and wheat, and that difficult and messy process helps us evolve. Opening up after reading a book on how to be evolved, or doing a weekend seminar on advanced *beingness* doesn't usually work well in the real world of specific life purpose, karmic patterns, and unsafe experiences. The process of opening up requires actual work, not just the denial of the supposedly unspiritual emotions or other boundary-enforcing aspects of your whole self.

Jagged edges in any part of your aura are a call for help. When your aura becomes spiky, it means that you are not giving it enough definition or conscious support. When an aura is undefined, it is unsafe, non-functioning, and endangered. Spikiness means the aura can't separate from the experiences and people around it. Without the support of your conscious discernment, your aura will create edges and points and straight lines to try to protect itself. Your aura will try to make up for the delineations you are not providing.

Don't get me wrong. I am not asking you to cut yourself off from humanity and hide behind your aura, but instead to engulf yourself in a protective blanket of your own individuality. Within your individuality lies your true path, your true healing, your own answers and karmic patterns, and your own ability to love and honor the world as it is.

It is much easier to love and accept people from within your healthy aura, because you can love as yourself, and draw your true friends to you. If you instead try to drop all your boundaries and your individual responses, and pretend to be some all-encompassing un-personality, your true-path friends won't be able to find you in the midst of all the noise and commotion.

When you live within your own reality, you will be of real use to the world, since you are the unrepeatable person God sent here to live your life, to think your thoughts, to feel your feelings, and to find your answers. When you move onward into the spirit world, you'll have endless opportunities to be neutral and faceless. While you live in your body, it's best to be your flawed, silly, stupid, majestic, reactive, wonderful human self.

When you find jaggedness or spikiness in your aura, it can also mean that you are trying too hard to go beyond specific "bad" emotions. If so, your aura is having to do all your emotional protection and reaction duties for you. Please re-read the chapter in Part II called *Channelling Your Emotions* and remind yourself that in a healthy quaternity, we have body, mind, spirit, *and* emotions. Emotions are not simply a reaction to thought, or a sign of bodily imbalance. Emotions have a life and an experience and a wisdom that is absolutely integral to balance and wholeness. If you ignore or try to go beyond your emotions, you'll create a body/spirit split again, and you'll soon be back in a dissociated position.

Trust your emotions, channel them, and they will move on peacefully after giving you their indispensable messages. Ignore and denigrate them, and you'll be stuck inside an unhealthy, overly-intellectual life—without the tools you need to process, grow, change, and love.

If your aura is filled with jagged, spiky edges, you will need to review your earlier skills, such as grounding, getting in your head, checking in on your little one, and creating a strongly grounded blanket of Sentries. You will also require frequent Gold Sun healings.

Take some time alone to dance around with your own moods, feelings, and reactions to life. Use your hands to smooth out the edges of your aura boundary, and to close any jagged holes or tears as you massage your own golden energy into your aura.

PULSATIONS: Skittery, jumpy auric pulsations (as opposed to the normal pulsations of the aura, which look like the movements inside a lava lamp) signify a great deal of scattered, excitable energy. When you begin to work with your energy, your aura will go through periods of excitability, which is not anything to be concerned about. They are proof that you are doing your work. Most skittery pulsations will be calmed down during a normal Gold Sun healing.

Pulsations which center around or within a specific area can be a sign of a physical distress or an upcoming injury. Thank these pulsations as you ground them out and perform a Gold Sun healing. Cover the area with a grounded Sentry blanket, and go see your acupuncturist or holistic practitioner.

Pulsations and lightning bolts of energy can also be a sign of drug damage, especially from stimulants, hallucinogens, and cocaine. Once again, drug energy rears its ugly head and shows how completely unhelpful it is in the evolved, conscious care of the body and the energy field.

RIPS or TEARS: Rips in the aura are signs of injuries to our view of ourselves. These injuries can be self-caused, or they can come from our agreement with the detrimental views other people have of us.

As with any opening in the aura boundary, rips are places where our energy can leak out, or other people's energy can sneak in. They need to be mended during a Gold Sun healing, and covered with a blanket of strongly grounded Sentries.

Also, please burn your contracts with the injury, and your view of yourself as a victim of your or anyone else's thought forms. Remember that all thoughts and emotions are bits of energy and attention trapped in an attachment. When we release the attachment, the clean and cleared-out energy is available for us to use in any way we like.

As you mend the rips in your aura, sit inside the room in your head and watch the energy inside the rips fly up to your Gold Sun. See the conflict, or the anger, or the self-hatred burn off as the energy enters your sun. Welcome your lost energy back into your total energy store. Then, do something different with it.

As I said before, almost all auric deviations will be healed in a regular Gold Sun healing, which you should do now if you are currently reading your aura as you are reading this section. It is only when deviations show up repeatedly that they need to be singled out for a special healing.

Remember that your aura has come to an almost complete stop to enable you to see it. While you're sitting and reading its momentary Polaroid, it may already be going on to heal all the deviations you're noticing. Perform your Gold Sun healing and trust that your aura is doing its work—just like you're doing yours—and don't obsess on it. If you pick at it, it will never heal!

ADVANCED AURA DEFINITION

There may be times when your lit-up aura boundary and Sentry won't be enough to keep you separate from certain people or experiences.

In my own case, my aura has a hard time remaining separate and whole in the presence of drug abusers. I had my drug days in my teens, and my aura remembers being damaged by drugs, so it takes work for me to keep it separate from that wavery, blobby, skittery drug energy.

If I don't know that people near me are doing drugs, I tend to suffer the effects of their addictions along with them, only finding out later why I suddenly left my body and had pains in the region of my third *chakra* (which means my psychic immune system was in trouble). I have also found that auras will not separate us from people who express our shadow material. Robert Bly, in his exquisite book, *A Little Book On the Human Shadow*, describes the shadow beautifully.

In a nutshell, Bly says that your shadow encompasses all the true but unaccepted parts of yourself--the ones you ignore and despise and hide carefully in your unconscious. Your shadow can contain selfishness, brutality, and jealousy, certainly, but it can also contain joy, hope, your talents, and your dreams.

The way to identify your particular, individual shadow material is to write down a list of all the things you despise in people. I don't mean general stuff that most people dislike, such as dishonesty, abusiveness, or aggrandized behaviors, but traits you DESPISE, traits that send you right up the wall and out of your mind. Take a look at the list and say hello to your shadow!

Your shadow material contains aspects of your total humanity that you refuse to bring into the light. Each of us has as much human majesty and human ugliness as anyone else, but it's not fashionable to be aware of that here in the west.

We westerners have to be perfect and honorable and high-minded at all times (even though we're not). Our real and not so wonderful detritus gets swept away. Our selfishness, our anger and violence, our lusts and hatreds, our self-adoring moments... all are swept out of sight and out of mind.

This sweeping away of human fallibility and imperfections has the same dissociating effect as the compartmentalization of our molest experience. Without the support of all our energy and all our experiences, we are less grounded and aware; therefore, we become much more susceptible to the very energies or memories we are trying to suppress.

For instance, if you are driven out of your mind by people who talk on and on about nothing at all, and you're so uncomfortable around them that you'd like to jump out of your skin and strangle them into silence, you have not only lost your peace and your aura boundary, but you've come face to face with your own shadow.

If talkativeness were merely *annoying* to you, you would still have your boundaries and you'd still be in control of your thoughts and actions, even if you were somewhat bothered by the blathering. Instead of merely bothering you, the jabbering throws you off your center. This is because talkativeness is an aspect of your wholeness that is at odds with your current self-view.

If you take a look, you will find either that you talk too much, or that you don't say enough in important situations when you really should, because you are *afraid* of talking too much. You may also have overly talkative inner intellectual or emotional aspects, and a complete unwillingness to listen to them. Talkativeness will only drive you insane if it is one of your core issues. Otherwise, it will only be mildly irritating to you.

Your aura will always open up in the face of your shadow material, because it recognizes it as an integral part of you and of your healing, even if you don't. The trick (which I still have to learn each time my shadow material comes careening back to me) is not to resist the person or moment that lights up your shadow, but to engulf the experience and accept the powerful lesson offered.

In his book, Robert Bly suggests that we eat our shadow material, and I've found that to be very healing. When I can, I get away from the person to whom I've lost my boundaries, gather their image in my hands, and eat them! After I eat them, I re-form my aura boundary, and then do a little bit of contract burning and writing and thinking about myself. I've found that a good way to avoid such shadow-in-my-face experiences is to be honest with myself about my hatreds and jealousies in the privacy and safety of my meditation sessions, and to eat my shadow then.

We've already worked with the shadow. Through burning contracts with our molest and our molesters, we separated ourselves from their energy. When we acknowledged our contractual relationship to our molesters and to the spirit of molest, we acknowledged our unconscious collusion, and our shadow. We didn't pretend that we were never in pain, nor did we pretend that we never abused ourselves and others in response to our pain. We accepted the abusive, molesting qualities in ourselves. We took responsibility for that part of the human shadow, and we brought it out into the light so it couldn't torture us any more.

As we learn to channel our emotions and attitudes, we begin to acknowledge our shadow. We don't have to hate our terror or fury, or hide our suicidal feelings deep in our subconscious any more; when we channel their energy through our bodies and auras, they give us vital messages about how to integrate. Our emotions are an essential, utterly useful, and utterly necessary part of our wholeness. If we play the game of make-nice, and ignore our true but often socially unacceptable feelings, our emotions will boil and fester until we are either very ill, very trapped, or very crazy.

We molest survivors know better than anyone that life is imperfect; we know that people are often seriously flawed, and that what is called "negativity" is an integral part of life here on earth. When we can stop splitting off in response to these realities, and instead learn to deal with them by addressing them and halting our own split-inducing chain reaction, our lives will begin to flow and become more liveable.

Molesters become molesters when their totally unintegrated and ignored (and therefore dangerously toxic) shadow material rears its ugly, frightening head. Our denial-happy, emotionally stunted, make-nice culture helps build molesters and criminals, because people simply have no permission to channel their shadow aspects.

We either repress our shadows dangerously, or act them out tragically, and there is no medium in between. Whatever "good" material potential molesters harbor gets less and less strong as more and more of their energies get stuffed into their shadow. Soon, they are simply unable to rein in the repressed material, and it gets acted out on some unprotected person.

Before we split off and consider the sad plight of the molester, let's look at the sort of lives our repressed and shadow-filled molest memories created for us! Though the person who chooses to molests others is clearly society's criminal, we as molest survivors have committed equally serious crimes against ourselves. We have most likely placed ourselves, almost willingly, into the path of real danger again and again in order to be engulfed in the ugly shadow material we repressed. That ugliness has, up until now, felt comfortable, logical, and familiar.

In the case of the molester, the shadow looms and one hurts others. In the case of the victim, the shadow looms and one hurts oneself. Both are violent crimes against humanity. Both are the effects of an unmanaged, shadow-filled psyche, and both are equally molest. We haven't escaped the shadow simply because we aren't out molesting children. If we allow ourselves or others to hurt and devalue us now, we still live in the darkness.

Thus far, we have been learning to separate ourselves from pain by reintegrating our energy bodies. In many cases, we have experienced self-definition and personal safety. By now, though, we have rejoined the not-so-healing world of human and spiritual interaction. Here, we will meet the shadow, but we do not need to be extinguished or harmed by it.

We will always have socially unacceptable, shadowy feelings at just the wrong time. If we go back to our split state, we will repress these feelings, or express and project them onto other people without ever bringing them into the light. When we channel our emotions or burn our contracts, we rededicate these aspects of ourselves and our lives; in doing so, we explore, honor, address, and eat our own shadow.

So, our "bad" aspects help us grow into whole, real, deeply human beings just as surely as our "good" aspects do. When we can own our own shadow material, we become our healing, humorous, and beautifully flawed selves. If we ignore our shadow and try to live only in the light, we usually become frenetically unintegrated.

A runaway healer's chaotic and uncentered life is a perfect example of the kind of trauma that erupts when illness or darkness is constantly swept away, and the lighted half of life is the only one given any credence. The runaway healer's mission: to be hostile to the shadow in all of its forms (and in the light at all times, no matter what) creates unbelievable trauma, illness, and damage, to the runaway healer, and everyone nearby. The lesson? Sit down and eat your shadow.

Be aware: when your aura drops and you lose your centering skills, you could be coming up against your own shadow material, and not just a "bad" person or situation that disrupts people for fun. There are definitely a number of ungrounded people and situations that tend to steal the grounding and boundary systems of people they encounter, but these show up rather infrequently. In most cases of boundary loss, you are most likely coming up against your own shadow. When your aura drops or loses its definition, it's lesson time!

Thank the person or experience that helped you see your shadow, and get back to your center as soon as you can. Reform each of your basic tools, give the person or situation dozens and dozens of gift symbols, place an image in a candy-flavored gift, and eat it. Burn your contracts and channel the emotions that come up in response to the person or situation that caused your boundary loss. Let their unappealing behavior show you, in this safe space, what you need to know about your own shadow.

It is very helpful to choose a color and movement pattern for the specific behavior or emotional state that kicked you out of your center, and to use that color in your aura boundary for a period of days or weeks. For instance, you could choose a swiftly moving yellow, bright red, or green energy to represent talkativeness, a hot orange energy to represent rage, a dark brown, thick-as-molasses energy to represent whiny despair, or a florescent pink energy to represent attention-seeking.

When you channel this previously despised or disowned energy, and your aura sees that you are at least trying to integrate a long-hated or ignored aspect of yourself, it won't need to drop itself the next time you encounter talkativeness, rage, grief, showing-off, or whatever unhinged you in the first place.

Soon, you'll be able to understand and have compassion for the previously despised energy instead of reacting to it violently and sending your whole energy pattern into a tizzy.

Integrating your shadow material is very like integrating your emotions by channelling them. You will find that each piece of your shadow brings you important life skills, just as each repressed and previously hated emotion brought you understanding.

When you channel your fury instead of ignoring or exploding with it, you will find certainty and resolve you didn't have before. When you channel your suicidal feelings instead of repressing or wallowing in them, you will find the rebirth in the death, and you'll be able to start over.

When you channel your shadow instead of stuffing it, or despising it in others, you will have more light available, and you will be able to move on to the next level of awareness. Your aura knows this, and that's why it drops away in response to shadow material. It wants you to notice, and then heal, your deficiency. Thank your aura and do your work.

In instances of periodic boundary haziness or spottiness, which could come from all sorts of illnesses, drug energy, fatigues, and so forth, a Gold

Sun healing will always help your aura to heal and re-integrate itself. Choosing a very vibrant color for your aura boundary will also help a fuzzy or indistinct aura to get back to work.

If you lose your boundaries a great deal of the time, and your aura has a daily problem helping you separate, you may need to go back to the very beginning of aura definition in Part I.

Now that we've covered the whole shadow concept, I'll back off a little and allow that, yes, there are some people who can affect your aura and your grounding without there having to be any shadow-connection between you at all. Psychics call these kinds of people *energy sappers* or *whackers*. Energy sappers are sort of like energy parasites. For whatever reason, they've decided it's easier to ground through other people and borrow their auras than to maintain their own.

It's very hard to identify energy sappers the first time out, because they learn to be energetically sneaky. When you sit to re-center after being whacked, you can usually trace a trail back to them, but it's rare to notice them while they are up to their tricks. They're like mosquitoes.

Energy sappers are either very ungrounded and flaky, or very ungrounded and controlling. The flaky sappers like to be out of their bodies and don't want to do the work it would take to get in, so they'll often ground through your first *chakra* to keep their bodies going. They run a little cord from their own first *chakra* into yours, and ground along with you. Your grounding cord and your *chakra* will usually feel sort of sickly, and you might drop your cord and not want to create a new one. Your aura will soon get wobbly without grounding, and voila! You're uncentered!

Controlling sappers are sometimes in their bodies, but they don't want anyone else to be; they'll either ground through you with a thick controlling cord, or whack your aura so you'll be uncentered and therefore controllable. Usually, your third *chakra* will alert you with a stomach-ache when controlling sappers are around, but sometimes your *chakra* system will become uncentered too, and you won't be aware of the sapping until your next meditation.

Your energy can also be sapped by jobs, buildings, or experiences (being in a crowd, riding the bus, or anything else that throws you out of center). If this happens to you frequently, it is a sign that you are very sensitive to your surroundings. This is wonderful and awful: wonderful, because you are becoming a very attuned organism; and awful because there are a lot of energies out there you'd probably like to be able to ignore. If you are very sensitive and susceptible to your surroundings, use the strengthening and separating skills outlined below, but also take a look at your situation.

Being seriously affected by something, to the extent that you lose your grounding and centering abilities, is a warning. If you are certain that an ungrounding situation or experience is not an expression of your shadow, then it's clearly damaging to you as an individual organism.

Just as I would not counsel you to seek out or befriend chronic energy sappers, I would also not suggest that you stay in a job or situation that saps your strength and hinders your growth as a spirit. When an experience de-centers you for no apparent reason, and none of the psychic strengthening work you do helps, it means you need to get out of there!

If sappers make you feel angry, that's great! Anger is all about boundaries. You'll have a very easy time blowing sappers to kingdom come and re-forming your aura, grounding cord, and Sentry with the powerful energy anger brings. If sappers make you tired, that's not so good, but following the steps below should help in either case.

THE AURA STOMP

First, get all your basic tools up and running again and do as much separation, image destruction, and contract burning with the sapping person or situation as you can. Surround your aura from top to bottom with hundreds of thorny, grounded Sentry roses, and clean out any sapping energy cords or footholds in your first *chakra* with Gold Sun energy. I like to make my first *chakra* and my grounding cord very slippery and oily so nothing can grab hold and stick to them.

When you encounter a sapping person or situation, brighten your aura boundary, and create an outer aura curtain in a deeper, more intense color. See this darker aura boundary coming down around your aura like a garage door, and let it hit the ground with an audible clang. Make sure the energy sapper is near enough to hear the clang (intuitively, of course), and don't be afraid to clang down a few more curtains if they try anything funny. I call this The Aura Stomp.

Sappers are sneaky, which means they're scared. Even if they're bullies, they're still scared. The Aura Stomp draws the line in the sand. When you've got powerful grounding, aura definition, hundreds of thorny, grounded Sentries, and the ability to move your aura at will, you're nobody's ninety-eight pound weakling.

I find that I rarely have to do The Aura Stomp twice in a row, because I become very uninteresting to energy sappers when I am clearly more capable than they. They don't like hard work, so they leave me alone and go on to some other poor soul.

I'm not sure what to do about people I've identified as energy sappers, because I don't want to just send them out to bother others. The problem is that I've only rarely been able to get a chronic sapper to ground themselves and stop sapping. It's like an addiction, and you can't assist or interfere with an addiction unless the addict wants your help. Perhaps by destroying their image and modeling responsible spiritual communication, I am planting a seed that will one day help sappers in their inner growth. I hope so.

If your sapper or sapping situation does not respond to any of your healing work, consider that you may simply be in the wrong place or relationship.

Often, people and situations vibrate at disparate frequencies. Sometimes a lover or a friend will naturally throw you out of whack because their energy is too different from yours, and sometimes a job or situation will be completely unsuitable for your individual needs.

I knew of a psychic who had a strange offshoot of his practice, which was to match people up as sexual partners when he saw that their energy was similar. It didn't matter if the people were married to others, homosexual or heterosexual in orientation, or completely unsuitable for one another in terms of age, language, or location.

This psychic's theory was that sexual contact, because it brought another's energy directly into the aura and body, needed to be between people whose energy vibrated at a similar frequency. Apparently, sex between similar people could heal--while sex between dissimilar people created illness, regardless of any other facet of the relationship.

I don't know if he ever correlated his results, but the implications are riveting. What if certain people's sexual energy heals you because it is like yours, or hurts you because your body can't process its vibrational frequency? It could explain why we are drawn to sexual partners who are completely wrong for us socially, or why otherwise perfect relationships stop working for no reason. As you fine tune your awareness, keep this in mind.

In reference to jobs or situations that just don't work, I had an interesting experience. While working at a radio station, right under the tower and next to the transmitter, I couldn't stay centered at all. I was an emotional, physical, intellectual, and spiritual wreck most of the week, but fine on the weekends. After looking at every possible reason for my condition and blaming as many people as I could, I finally got the big picture.

It turns out that I am very sensitive to electrical energy fields, whether they are from electronic machinery, or living people. The energetic sensitivity which allows me to see and feel auras and *chakras* also picks up the vibrations and frequencies in electromagnetic fields.

It took me more than two years to figure this out and quit my job, but now I'm very careful about being around too many electronic devices at one time. Though the information out now about the dangers of electromagnetic fields is generally downplayed as reactionary, I know I can't be around too many electrical or electronic devices and remain healthy.

The most excellent and annoying part of healing spiritual wounds is that the healing requires you to live in a more conscious and self-respecting way. Once you are awake, your aura will call out for more consciousness, which can often feel like less freedom if you are in a particularly reactionary mood at the time. I say, head toward consciousness anyway, even though becoming yourself in this world is often a tremendous ordeal. Heck, it's also a tremendous ordeal to become the shift manager at McDonald's. Everything takes hard work and courage, but the smart people concentrate their energy where it will do the most good. Like, in their own lives.

SPECIAL ADVANCED HEALING: THE AURIC PAIN RELIEVER

Since you've been communicating with your aura, you may have found this healing technique, or something very much like it, on your own.

Pain and disease can be attributed to any number of logical causes, but it can also be a sign of trapped or sluggish energy. Many emotions can become trapped in the body, and their energy can transform into migraines and ulcers, psychiatric disturbances, back pains and stiffness, and even hysterical paralysis, deafness, or blindness.

If you have been working with an illness or imbalance without success, your body may be trying to tell you something about how you manage your energy and your emotions. If your body simply will not release an illness or disturbance, it may not be asking for relief as much as awareness.

As you become more centered and aware in this Garden process, your body will become more aware as well. This may not be completely comfortable, because aware bodies don't like their symptoms to be suppressed. The old pain-reliever, cough-suppressant routine will suddenly stop working for you. When your body sees that you are honoring your mind, your spirit, and your emotions in non-suppressive ways, it will expect the same treatment.

A body that will not hide its pain and difficulty would have been an absolute living nightmare in our pre-Garden existence. In our current lives, we have a set of skills to help our bodies heal. As long as we stay inside our bodies and remember our skills, we will be able to process their issues and examine the situations that require assistance.

Here's a technique for examining long-standing or stubborn pains and illnesses: after you have performed an aura healing in your regular centering and meditation session, concentrate on the disturbed area of your body, but keep your awareness inside the room in your head as you do. Staying in your head will allow you to more fully decipher the information coming from within your illness or discomfort--whereas jumping into the middle of the troubled area could create too much confusion at first.

See your painful area heating up or becoming lit up with its own energy, and imagine this energy radiating out from within your body and moving into your clean and healthy aura.

For instance: if you have a chronically sore elbow, see the energy of the soreness radiate out in any direction that feels right. If any internal organs hurt or are not functioning properly, see the energy of the pain or the dysfunction radiating out through the front, the back, or the sides of your torso and into your aura.

Now, as the energy moves out into your aura, notice its color, its movement, and its general quality. Does it feel like any emotion you have channelled, or is it totally unfamiliar? Does it remind you of old feelings, or does it remind you of another person's attitudes? What is this energy your body has been holding onto?

If you can, gather the energy into an area in front of you, and ask it what it wants, or what it has been trying to show you. The answer may astonish you. Honor it.

When you have received some sort of idea or communication from this energy, create an aura grounding vacuum, and bless this energy before you ground it out of your aura. This energy can be one of your greatest teachers.

When you are through (you may want to focus on more than one difficulty. Go ahead!), perform a Gold Sun healing for your body and your aura. Your newly cleansed energy can now be called back and rededicated. Make sure you bend over and touch the floor when you are done, so your body knows it has choices about how much golden energy it wants right now.

Bless your aura, and keep an eye on it throughout your day. A healthy and protected aura can help you to understand the energies in your milieu, certainly. It can also help you to understand the energies inside your body by providing a safe place to bring them into your conscious awareness and control. Protect your aura and honor its communications. If you do, it will protect and honor you.

PART III

ADVANCED MEDITATION & HEALING

ADVANCED IMAGING

We've already used gift images in a number of spiritual communications, but there are also ways to use gifts to heal and cleanse specific areas of our bodies.

We'll start off with a special healing for the first-*chakra* area, for those of you who are having trouble grounding and were sent here from Part I. It would be a good idea to read through the chapter called *Gifts From Your Garden* before you start, though, so you'll understand the function of these energy tools and have your basic questions answered.

THE SPECIAL HEALING FOR THE FIRST *CHAKRA*

When our bodies are in psychic or physical trouble, we can use special grounding cords to drain trapped energy and heal ourselves. However, when the trouble is that we *can't* ground, we need a special gift symbol to come to the rescue.

Please start this healing by sitting in a quiet room in a straight-backed chair, with both feet on the ground and both hands uncrossed and upturned on your knees. Separate your legs as much as you can, because we'll be working between them. Your pelvic area should be relaxed and open. If you can get into the room in your head, or if you can manage any other, later meditation skills such a defining your aura or putting up your Sentry, please do so now.

When you are as centered as you can be right now, imagine a large, healthy plant or flower right under your chair, with its leaves or petals open and facing upwards towards your genitals. See my illustrations on the next page for a clear understanding.

If you know where your first *chakra* is, place the very center of the greenery under it, otherwise, point the center of the plant or flower directly between your pubic bone and your anus.

Keep your gift symbol about four to ten inches away from your body, and make it large enough for you to see it easily. Ground the center of your gift with a golden cord (I know *you* have trouble grounding, but this gift doesn't) which travels down the center of the plant and into the center of the planet.

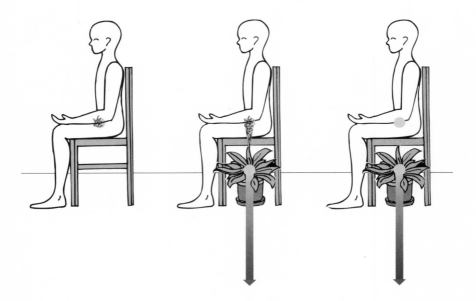

Now, imagine a vacuum in the center of the flower, and let it draw energy out of your genitals and pelvis. You should feel a gentle, releasing tug, as your first-*chakra* area pulses energy downwards and onto the leaves of your gift.

Know that your gift symbol loves to accept any and all energy from you, no matter what. If the energy is positive or neutral, your symbol wants to have it; if the energy is filled with confusion and pain, your gift symbol wants that too.

See your energy as fertilizer, and know that everything that comes out of you makes this healing plant stronger, healthier, and happier. You may even see your healing symbol growing larger or more colorful as it receives all the energy coming from your body. Good.

Stay in your head and let the stuck energy from your genitals and pelvis move out of your body and down into your gift's grounding vacuum for as long as you like.

You can watch the departing energy from the room in your head, and try to pick out colors, faces, memories, or specific emotions from within the flow, or you can relax and let the energy go without having to study it. Know that your gift is accepting and grounding out all the old muck stored in your pelvis. If you've been out of your body and ungrounded for a long time, you may want to continue this healing for an extended period of time. That's fine.

You'll know when you're done (for now) when you feel a sense of release, warmth, and comfort in your pelvis. At this time, you can let your gift's grounding cord vacuum itself away. See your gift collapsing into its own cord and falling towards the center of the planet. Thank your gift symbol as you watch it go.

Now, stay in your head and try to ground from your first *chakra*. Imagine a cord of golden energy anchoring to your *chakra* and travelling down through your perineum, and through your chair. Imagine your cord travelling downward, through the floor, down through the foundation of your building, down through the layers of the earth, and on down to the center of the planet.

Grounding should be much easier after you clear out with your gift symbol; the gift is actually a grounding cord in itself. When you use tools as grounding intermediaries, you are grounding! It doesn't matter if you ground through a plant or flower, it only matters that you ground. If you can ground through a gift image, but you still can't ground in the usual way, forget the usual way and ground through your gift.

Please create a new gift symbol under your chair, and move it upwards into your first *chakra* if you can. If you can't get your gift symbol into your body, please place it no more than five inches below your genitals--this will work just fine for now.

After a few days of grounding with this symbolic assistance, you should be able to easily move the gift symbol into your body and attach its gold grounding cord directly to your first *chakra*. At this point, you can let go of your gift symbol, because you are now grounding for yourself. If you like your gift, keep it. You don't need this magic feather anymore, but it won't hurt you to hold on to it.

As we learned in Part II of this book, sexual assault wreaks havoc in grounding abilities. Oftentimes, our molester's energy still lives in our ungrounded body. Grounding can draw the foreign sexual energy out of our bodies—but sometimes, we refuse to release the energy because we still have powerful contractual obligations to our molester. Please see the chapter in Part II called *Burning Contracts* for an in-depth look at relationship contracts and agreements that can get in the way of your grounding and your healing.

With this special gift healing, you can place a gentle and non-threatening energy tool into the foreign energy that interferes with your first *chakra* and its ability to ground. This neutral healing symbol can drain foreign energy away, quickly and quietly.

The old contractual rituals and stereotypical response systems won't be able to identify your healing symbol or its gold grounding cord until it's too late. Before any contractual alarm is sounded, the old abusive energy will be dislodged from inside your body and your *chakra*. Once it is dislodged, you can re-inhabit your previously ungrounded and unknowable areas. You can start to clean house, burn contracts, destroy images, and channel any emotions that come up.

This next special gift healing can be used on any part of the energy body or physical body. These grounding gifts can drain excess energy from the aura, any *chakra*, or any fatigued and overwrought area of the body. Try this next gift healing when you are overstimulated and headed towards a frontal-lobe headache.

THE GIFT FACIAL

When we meet or interact with people, the bulk of their attention is generally focused on our face and eyes. If their attention is there, their energy will most likely be there too. Sometimes, our face can be clogged with so much of other people's energy that we feel old and wizened before our time. Too much external energy and attention on our faces can even feel like a sinus headache. Try this gift facial at the end of a public-relations filled week, or anytime you feel yourself squinting or clenching your teeth with stress and fatigue:

Sit in a grounded, aura-defined body, and look out from inside the room in your head at a large, soft-leafed plant or flower. Place this image inside your aura, and directly in front of your face. This gift symbol should be a little bit larger than your head, and close enough to you so that you can see the veins and dew on its leaves or petals. This gift symbol should be large--cabbage-sized--so that all you can see before you is the gift itself.

Ground the center of this gift with a gold grounding cord. See this cord moving down through the plant's stem and roots, on downward to the center of the planet. Don't follow this grounding cord. Direct the cord from inside your head, and know that it will do what you ask it to.

Turn this gift symbol's grounding cord into a vacuum, and let it pull blocked and foreign energy off of your face. You may feel the pull in your eyes, your jaw, your teeth, your cheekbones—even in the back of your head or your neck. Let the energy go.

See your gift symbol becoming stronger and healthier as it grounds the old energy out of your face. See this clogged, foreign energy as fertilizer for your plant. Know that all departing energy will be cleansed and returned to its owner (or to you the next time you perform a Gold Sun healing). Let it go.

Continue with this gift facial for as long as you like, and be aware of how much energy comes off of you. If you feel tremendously lighter afterwards, you need to take a look at your Sentry.

Is your Sentry normally in front of your face, or do you move it aside when you interact with people, almost as if it's an oversized centerpiece? Don't!

Keep the entire flower part of your Sentry directly in front of your face. If a lot of energy came off of you in this healing, your Sentry needs to be stronger, because too much of other people's energy is being deposited on your face.

If you are in a people-intensive job, or a life situation where much energy is directed at you, you'll need to adjust your tools accordingly. I would suggest a Sentry blanket instead of just one Sentry; a Phone, Door or Window Gift (the next topic); and a steady supply of ungrounded hello gifts at your disposal.

If you are prepared to deal with a barrage of people, you won't be affected by all their energy. If you're not prepared, your healing and meditation work will be harder, because you'll be full of trivial bits of other people's attentions, needs, demands, and energy.

You can be more effective as a receptionist, retail clerk, or seminar leader when you are in charge of your aura. It doesn't make you colder, less aware, or less humane to separate from people. It helps you to live as an individual within your own life, your own lessons, and your own karmic pattern. What could be more effective?

THE DOOR, PHONE, OR WINDOW GIFT

Door, Phone, or Window gifts are a special kind of ungrounded hello gift we send to greet people *before* they reach us. The difference between these gifts and regular hello gifts is that Door, Phone, or Window gifts are placed in areas where we can't always see who is coming.

When you work with the public face-to-face or over the phone, you really can't prepare for all the differing attitudes, relationships, or difficulties that might come up. Placing a large number of ungrounded Door, Phone, or Window gifts at the area of initial contact can help calm people down as they come into your sphere of influence.

The use of these public relations gifts will make your personal Sentry's task much easier. Your Sentry won't have so much work to do to protect you, because people already will have received a bit of free love and beauty before they actually get to you and your aura.

Door, Phone, and Window gifts are placed liberally and freely at the entrance to your sphere, whatever that is. If people enter your workspace through a door or an opening in a cubicle, you will place at least a hundred ungrounded gift symbols at the door or opening every morning.

If people contact you through the phone, intercom, or computer modem, you will place another hundred ungrounded gifts inside each machine. Envision one or more of your gifts travelling across the transmission cable directly in front of your standard typed or vocal greeting (of course gift symbols can travel through transmission cables; they're made of energy!).

If you work behind a sliding window, such as one in a doctor's office, it would be a good idea to place another hundred or so ungrounded gift symbols just outside the window, in addition to those you have placed at the doorway. I've never seen an office with a sliding window that wasn't filled with stress; it's a good idea to plan ahead for that stress and provide as many Door and Window gifts as you can.

Using these specifically placed hello gifts can help to make your work place as safe as your home. They will also provide excellent spiritual communication to anyone who is fortunate enough to come into contact with you.

THE NEGATIVITY-EATING GIFT

This negativity-eating gift symbol is a fun little friend to have; it grows and thrives on other people's intense and negative energy. The negativity-eating gift especially loves it when other people try to project their shadow material (which begins with any phrase that sounds like, "Do you know what your problem is?") in order to control you through fear or shame.

Whenever you find yourself in a place where negative attention is being focused (at a job interview, in court, when the police pull you over, when someone says, "You know what your problem is?"), you can immediately create a gift symbol that absolutely thrives on negativity!

While your regular Sentry and your aura boundary deal with keeping you separate, your negativity-eating gift will bop around your aura, eating up the human fertilizer that makes you so uncomfortable and it so happy. When this negativity-eating gift gets big and full, you simply give it to the person whose energy helped create it, and you'll both experience release and healing.

Here's how to do it: create a medium-sized, *ungrounded* gift plant or flower somewhere inside the front of your lit-up, protected aura, and dedicate it to any negative or threatening person you encounter. This gift is ungrounded because it will be given away.

Give the plant or flower a face with teeth that like to gobble up energy, and the ability to move so that it can zip around eating any energy that gets past your Sentry.

I usually place my ungrounded negativity-eating plant somewhere between my eyes and my heart. Sometimes it's on my lapel and sometimes it's directly in front of me, but it is always able to move around like a little Pac Man, searching for delicious bits of projected energy. I make it into a thorny fist-sized flower with a silly, hungry face and pointed teeth, like the man-eating plant Audrey in the movie *Little Shop of Horrors*.

As my negativity-eating plant seeks out and eats energy, it grows bigger and healthier, grinning all the while. When it eats enough energy to grow to the size of a cabbage, I send it to the person whose energy it was eating.

Sometimes, my plant grows that big right away, before the negative encounter has even begun! No big deal. I send the gift symbol to the person who helped it grow so big, make another negativity-eating plant, and start again. I've got a million plants and flowers in my Garden.

If there is more than one person in the negative encounter, I make a negativity-eating gift symbol for each one, and differentiate the colors a little. The easiest way to keep them straight is to place the gifts in the same physical order as the people themselves. You can also attach a little picture of each person to the back of their particular gift. Once dedicated, each specific negativity-eating plant or flower will take care of their own person's energy. All we have to do is give each person's gifts to them when we're done.

When the negativity-eating symbol has eaten its fill, and we give it away, we have the chance to sit back and see that we are separate from other people's relating styles. Added to that, though, is that the person who fed the plant or flower gets an intuitive look at how much energy they use in being threatening, unkind, and controlling.

Many times, the receipt of this gift symbol will shock such people terribly, because they rarely see themselves as irritating forces in the universe. They think they're dominating, unwaveringly honest and direct, or trying to take care of their or their corporations' interests in the face of a world filled with crooks and liars. When their silly gift comes at them, fat and happy and grinning, absolutely stuffed with their own truculence, they have to take a look at what they're doing in the world. Sometimes the results are as funny as the negativity-eating plant itself.

A friend of mine used a negativity-eating bird-of-paradise on a motorcycle cop who pulled her over by mistake (he thought her license plate had expired, but it hadn't), and then hung around looking for reasons to have done so.

The police officer started checking her lights, her turn signals, her insurance certificate, and whatever else he could find. Halfway through his inspection, my friend remembered her skills and created a negativity-eating flower for him.

This flower got so big so fast that she had to give it to him almost immediately. Apparently, the policeman stopped talking in mid-sentence, turned on his heel, got on his bike, and left her standing by her car, stunned!

Because of this immediate and startling result, my friend worried that she had somehow manipulated the police officer into action. In truth, the simple return of his energy snapped him back into shape. He couldn't speak to her rationally and apologize, because what affected him did not come from the rational world. He was aware enough to realize he had made a fool of himself, but not aware enough to talk about it. Leaving was all he could manage at that moment.

Don't criticize yourself if you have to use many of these gifts at first-- your Sentry and aura boundary may not be able to keep certain types of energy out of your aura. Also, don't be worried if all of your negativity-eating gifts grow very large very quickly.

Take the hint and re-create your protective boundary symbols in stronger, more vibrant colors, and make sure your Sentry rose has a good number of large, pointy thorns. But, don't be afraid to support your normal boundary tools with the use of your negativity-eating plants and flowers. They are very good gifts for all occasions.

If your negativity-eating gift doesn't get very big, and there's still a lot of tension in the room, it means that your regular Sentry and aura boundary are keeping you separate on their own. Fabulous! When it's time to go, give the tense person their little gift anyway. It couldn't hurt.

THE VELCRO WAND

This Velcro wand image is a good tool to use inside your aura when you feel scattered and full of confusing or unhealthy energy. When I feel this way, I get a buzzing front-of-the-head headache and a feeling of eyestrain, along with a general clumsiness and muscle tension, and a sense that I don't have enough time to get everything done.

The Velcro wand helps me to remove scattered energy in my aura when I don't have time to do a full Gold Sun aura cleansing. It's a good quick-fix until I can sit and meditate again.

Here's how to use a Velcro wand: create a large, not-too-thorny grounded flower or stalk (cattails are perfect) inside your aura. Envision the flower or stalk as being covered with the sticky portion of a Velcro fastener, the side that snags onto everything.

Hold this plant by its stem in your hand as you move it all throughout your aura, front and back, top and bottom. See your Velcro wand picking up all of the energy lint in your aura until it is quite full of energy. When your wand is full, let it drop down its own grounding cord, and you're done!

If one Velcro wand doesn't do the trick, create another and repeat the process until you feel clearer and more relaxed. You won't run out of gift symbols. Your Garden guarantees you an unlimited supply. Remember to use your Gold Sun healing when you have the time.

THE SENTRY BLANKET

We've already talked about Sentry blankets throughout the book, but they are so useful that it is good to go over them again.

Sentry blankets can be used in their *grounded* form as a very strong Sentry system around the entire aura. With a grounded Sentry blanket on guard, there is no place at all where people can get through to your aura or your body.

People coming at you with the intention to disturb, harm, sap, or control you will be met at every possible entrance with hundreds of thorn-filled, grounded roses (you can also throw in other favorite flowers, plants, or trees if you like). The pest's energy will be accepted, honored, and grounded; your aura will be protected; and the pest will be calmed and neutralized simply by having their energy accepted by *something*.

As I said before, everyone is intuitive, and everyone communicates on an intuitive level, whether they are aware of it or not. If some aspect of you acknowledges, accepts, and responsibly grounds the communications of people around you, the people will notice it on some level. It will have a healing effect. By honoring spiritual communication, you will make people's lives as spirits on this planet more real, which is a tremendous healing all by itself.

With the use of Sentries and Sentry blankets, that healing spiritual acknowledgement will occur *outside* of your personal auric field. You'll protect your reality while spiritual contact is happening, and you'll teach others about conscious, responsible spiritual communication.

By placing a rose-and-gift-filled, protective facsimile of ourselves outside of our auras with the express job of greeting others and keeping our personal territory sacred, we are not retreating from the world. On the contrary, we're right out there, offering an intuitive ear, a lesson in grounding and separation, and a whole lot of consideration for all the other beings on this planet.

Sentry blankets are also extremely useful for early Garden students who have spent years outside of their bodies, because it seals them within their own protective, spiritual, loving energy.

Usually, assault survivors spend decades searching for exterior security in relationships, appearances, finances, or families, but security is never there. It is always inside them, and the use of the Sentry--especially the Sentry blanket--gives them a palpable, visual connection to their true safety and security.

With the use of Sentry blankets, we can begin to create the security we've been searching for *inside* of us, instead of wasting futile years trying to find it in intrinsically transitory relationships or situations.

In their *ungrounded* form, hello-gift blankets are also excellent placeholders for any grounded areas you create in other people's spheres. When your office or room or cubicle is grounded, it may attract people who either need grounding, or want you to stop grounding—you won't have any privacy. Placing a blanket of free, ungrounded gift symbols at the edges of your defined area will give people a chance to see your life and energy needs as separate from theirs.

People will come towards your area to find out what you're doing, or to stop you from taking control of your life, but they'll go away with the free love and attention your hello gifts always give. Your gifts will help you maintain your privacy, while providing the people around you with healing spiritual contact at the same time.

Remember to refresh your grounded and ungrounded blankets daily. If you sensed that they were necessary for your safety, you are probably in a situation that is fatiguing for you and your normal Sentry. Give your symbols lots of love and support, and replenish them frequently.

There is a not-so-subtle relationship between victim and perpetrator; it's often a dance whose steps are contractual in nature. If we know we've gotten into a stereotypical pattern where we're easily victimized, we can burn our contracts.

This separation process will protect us, certainly, but it will also protect our dance partners from our need to have exterior villains. After that, our grounded or ungrounded Sentry blankets protect our territory and theirs by transmitting love and strength to our former tormentors.

When a certain level of spiritual consciousness and ability is achieved, it is no longer acceptable to play the tired old victim role. It becomes our imperative to protect others from taking on the role of tormentor in our lives. Our need for dissociation and exterior chaos were survival quirks. We're not in survival anymore.

Feel free to create new and novel uses for your gift symbols. They are, after all, symbols of your ability to love and heal and protect your reality, which is as individual as you are. I have friends who use travelling gift images to find parking spaces downtown, or great clothes in thrift shops, and some who use reading roses to get a look at jobs or love relationships. These are perfectly acceptable examples of lighter uses of spiritual communication techniques.

Whatever you feel like doing with your gift symbols is what you should do--as long as you stay in your body, respect the privacy of others, pay attention to the rules of grounding and responsible spiritual communication, and maintain your ethics.

Remember, always ground the symbols you use in your aura and your body, but *do not ground the gift symbols you provide for others*. You must be able to hold on to your personal healing symbols (which is why you ground and anchor them), and you must be certain that your spiritual communications are neutral and responsible (which is why you don't ground or anchor the symbols you send to others).

You must never infer that spiritual healing and communication come directly from you, which is what would happen if you grounded the symbols you sent to others.

Beyond that, have fun creating and destroying gifts and images, and learning how easy it is to communicate spiritually when you communicate responsibly, and with love. People really do want to live in peace and happiness, and if you can apply the lessons and spiritual concern your gift symbols offer, both you and they will tend to remember that.

THE TROUBLESHOOTING GUIDE

THE TROUBLESHOOTING GUIDE

It's exciting to become immersed in a self-help book's ideologies, but awful to become stuck in the midst of a technique or a diet suggestion. Usually, you can't contact the author for any help (though they might send you a newsletter or reorder form), so it's like being under a doctor's care without ever being able to talk to the doctor. Not good.

I thought a long time about writing a book with so many energy techniques in it. I know from my own experience as a healer that many people will lightly skim over a new set of theories or techniques and try them without much thought.

I have healed dozens of people who astral travelled but couldn't get all the way back into their bodies, and I have turned off numerous *kundalini* rushes in first *chakras* whose owners couldn't center long enough to do it themselves.

It's not difficult to heal these people (unless they have been out-of-body for an extended time and are stuck in a reactive, multi-layered survival mode), but, I do think the airy-fairy, unexamined attitudes and expectations that are found in many self-help books tend to create more questions than they can possibly answer.

Either that, or the books are so certain and unbending in their dogma that many readers neglect to ask enough questions before they embark on a new regime. I wanted, with this book, to teach energy work in a responsible and logically-centered way.

My solution is three-fold. First, I offer this alphabetized Troubleshooting Guide, similar to one you'd find in a computer or electronics manual. I've included every beginner's reaction, difficulty, and mistake that I've seen in my twenty-six years of study, and even a few things that are definitely out of the spiritual beginner's category. I want you to be able to thumb through this portion of the book and find concrete help if you get stuck.

Second, I include an order form for the companion book to this one, FURTHER INTO THE GARDEN: *Discovering Your Chakras*. A description of that book--and its intended reader--is on the back page.

My third solution is to include a way to contact me if you experience some puzzling thing I didn't think of, or if your awareness levels start taking you into areas I haven't covered.

If you need more help than you can find in the Troubleshooting Guide, please write, and we will work something out together. I promise not to send you an autographed photo, a newsletter, or a list of promotional items you can buy. Thank you.

Karla McLaren
c/o Laughing Tree Press
Post Office Box 1155
Columbia, CA 95310-1155

ANGER: Anger is a sign that boundaries have been crossed without permission. Though this may also bring up fear, sadness, depression, or diminishment, it is anger that both signals the injury and creates new boundaries after any damaging incident.

Because of this usual layer of emotion right under anger, anger is often misrepresented as a second-hand emotion, which leads people to see it as unimportant or counterfeit. This is a mistake. Anger is just as important as sadness, fear, joy, or desire. It is a real and irreplaceable emotional state that offers protection and requires action. For an overview of the usefulness of anger in concise spiritual communication, please see the chapter called *Anger and Forgiveness*.

Special topic: If you are currently experiencing uncontrollable anger, rage, or fury, please see the chapter called *Channelling Your Emotions*.

ANXIETY: I see anxiety as fear of the unknown. As with any other emotion, anxiety holds a specific place in healing.

Often, the only clue an otherwise aware person will have that anything is at all wrong will be a gnawing anxiety. There will be fear of going out or making movement, fear of natural disasters or attack, severe reactions to certain stimuli, or a generalized dread of people.

Dealing with anxiety from a psycho-rational viewpoint can help, because it can bring the shadowy causes of anxiety out into the open. Talk-and-desensitization therapy for specific anxiety-causing events makes the anxiety real, and therefore curable; however, desensitizing individuals symptomatically can be too much of a quick-fix. It can over-emphasize the fear of heights or going outside, but fail to address the underlying imbalance that brought the anxious symptoms to consciousness.

When channelled in the body and throughout the energy tools, anxiety becomes very clear, concise, and useful; its action-oriented, protective energy helps create real solutions and real change. Please see FEAR, PANIC ATTACKS, and TERROR, below, and the chapter called *Channelling Your Emotions* for help in working with your own anxiety.

AURA: An area around any living organism, best described as the energetic territory, or spiritual skin. The aura is often seen as a halo or aureole of colored energy emanating from the body. The aura is a protective energetic boundary; auric damage affects the entire organism.

For general information on the aura, please see the chapter called *Defining Your Personal Territory*. For an in-depth look at auric reading and healing techniques, see the chapter called *Advanced Aura Reading and Definition*.

AURA COLORS: People with the psychic talent of clairvoyance can see colors in auras with the help of their sixth *chakras*. Though such colors can have specific meanings, the meanings usually vary from individual to individual. In addition, auras change colors in response to spiritual communication, health issues, emotional states, and thought processes—so any color seen could be expected to change within seconds.

General color interpretations can be found in the chapter called *Advanced Aura Reading and Definition*, but a much more useful gauge of auric health will be gleaned through its size, shape, and condition. These aura reading categories are covered in the same chapter.

AURA HEALING: Auras can easily be healed with meditation techniques taught in this book. Simple self-definition of the aura as taught in *Defining Your Personal Territory* is a healing in and of itself, but for a more advanced auric healing, please see the chapter called *Advanced Aura Reading and Definition*.

AURA PROBLEMS: Chronic and serious aura damage or insufficiency is usually caused by damage from the environment, such as abusive and unhealthy living or working situations. Though aura problems can be disconcerting, they are both instructive and imminently fixable. If the aura is aware enough to break down in response to exterior stressors, it is on its way to a new life, which it will seek out by alerting its owner to what does and doesn't feel good. Please read the chapters called *Defining Your Personal Territory*, and *Advanced Aura Reading and Definition*.
A warning: Auras can also break down if the body is heading towards a serious illness, or in response to drug and alcohol abuse. Stop the drug abuse yesterday, and please see your doctor/healer if your aura is breaking down in the areas around your torso.

AURA READING: Auras contain and process a tremendous amount of information, much of which can be accessed during a fairly simple meditation/reading session outlined in the chapter called *Advanced Aura Reading and Definition*.

AURA STOMP: An advanced technique to re-establish the aura boundary during conflicts, or when one is in contact with unaware people who try to drain energy. The Aura Stomp is outlined in the chapter called *Advanced Aura Reading and Definition*.

AURA VACUUM: A grounding exercise to cleanse and redefine an injured or indistinct aura. Please see the chapter called *Defining Your Personal Territory*.

BURNING CONTRACTS: When people enter into relationships, they often set up a series of postures, behaviors, actions, and reactions that allow the relationships to control their lives. When such relationships and relating styles can be brought into conscious awareness, and can be seen as *contracts*, they can be brought into the light and amended--or destroyed. Burning these contracts helps bring people into present time; it releases the energy that keeps them trapped in old behavior patterns. This is especially helpful in removing behaviors learned during molest incidents. Please see the chapter called *Burning Contracts*.

CHAKRAS: *Chakras* are a series of energy centers inside and outside of the physical body; they can be considered the energetic glands or organs-- whereas the aura can be considered the energetic or spiritual skin. Each *chakra* represents a different aspect of the entire being, and each can be read, healed, grounded, and brought into present-time awareness.

This book lightly explores two *chakras* (the first and the eighth), but for a deeper look at the entire *chakra* system, please see the back page for a description of *The Garden's* companion book, FURTHER INTO THE GARDEN: *Discovering Your Chakras*.

CHANNELLING THE EMOTIONS: Though ignored, demeaned, and devalued, emotions are actually valuable messages from the deep wisdom of the soul. When an inescapable emotional state is reached, channelling the emotion through the body, aura, and grounding cord can bring absolute clarity and healing. Please see the chapters called *Channelling Your Emotions*, and *Anger and Forgiveness*.

CLAIRAUDIENCE: The ability to hear spiritual vibrations through the fifth, or throat *chakra*. Often, the clairaudient hearing of voices is mis- diagnosed as a symptom of schizophrenia. Please see EARS and RINGING IN THE EARS, below.

CLAIRSENTIENCE: The ability to receive spiritual vibrations empathically, through the second *chakra*, which is located just below the navel.

CLAIRVOYANCE: The ability to see spiritual vibrations through the sixth *chakra*, or third eye. Please see VISIONS, below.

COLORS: Colors are often valuable tools in spiritual readings and healings, but their meanings are very subjective. I offer you this general overview of what colors may mean; however, personal definitions are always more valuable than any list made up by a complete stranger.

COLORS: *continued.*

> PINK: Healing humor, protection from abuse, indecision.
> RED: The physical body, power, anger, sexuality.
> ORANGE: The emotions, the muscles, fury, sensuality, healing.
> YELLOW: Intellect, immunity and protection, impatience, fear.
> GREEN: Love, transformation, healing, frustration, loss.
> BLUE: Communication, spiritual knowledge, mourning, separation.
> INDIGO: Spiritual power, telepathy, victimization.
> PURPLE/VIOLET: Spiritual certainty, release, religious confusion.
> BROWN: Earth energy, grounding ability, past-time issues.
> BLACK: Finality, death, rebirth, dissociation, delay.
> WHITE: Spirit guide presence, purity, shock, erasure.
> SILVER: Spirit-world information, ungrounded-ness, uncertainty.
> GOLD: Neutrality, present-time awareness, transformative illness.

COMMUNICATION PROBLEMS: Good communication is a natural part of workable relationships, but communication skills can break down when relationship contracts get in the way (see the chapter called *Burning Contracts*). Often, relationship contracts are unconsciously created to ensure safety and familiarity for all participants. When growth occurs, contracts are usually not re-written, and the growth is thwarted. Soon, the relationship deadens, due to an adherence to old rules and bylaws that do not apply to present-time growth, issues, or needs.

In burning contracts, we learn to bring out, examine, and release all stuck, contract-bound relationship energies. When we are free of contracts, we can be awake, aware, and healthy in each of our relationships, no matter how they made us feel or behave in the past. For support in burning contracts, it is helpful to use the many separation techniques outlined in the chapters on Imaging in Parts I and III.

CONTRACTS: See BURNING CONTRACTS, above, or the chapter called *Burning Contracts.*

CROWN *CHAKRA*: Another name for the seventh *chakra*, which is an energy center located just above the head. The seventh *chakra* is the center of the physical body's connection to prayer, purely spiritual information, spirit guides, and God.

CRYING: Sadness is a wonderful way to add the tempering influence of water back into an arid system. Sadness allows the body to relax into itself after a period of rigidity or self-sacrifice. Sometimes, though, sadness and crying become unmanageable, which is a sign of imbalance

CRYING: *continued.*
throughout the system, and a call for an emotional channelling session. Please see SADNESS and DESPAIR, below, and the chapter called *Channelling Your Emotions.*

DEPRESSION: Depressions are funny things. I don't even know if I could call them emotions, because they either mask all feeling, or trap people in a constantly repeating emotion that doesn't ever go anywhere. It is very hard to remember to channel your emotions during a depression, because the depression sucks all your energy away, leaving you very uninterested in work or effort of any kind. *This is a clue.*

When your energy is tied up in old attachments--in the past, in old injuries, and old relationships--you won't be fully awake or aware. You won't be as capable, or as clear. Your Gold Sun won't be very warm and shiny, because your energy will be someplace else. Depressions are your body's way of telling you this.

Please remember to see depressions as vital warning signs: your energy is leaking away, and *you are not calling it back.* Your body is evolved enough to stop all your forward movement at such times. Why? Because your energy is stuck in a painful relationship, or a painful past-time event, and your body knows that no real forward movement is possible—so why should it pretend that all is well?

Thank your body and your emotions for their refusal to lie to you. Get grounded, and seek out the painful contracts you've forged with old, unworkable energies. Drain your aura and your body, burn your contracts with your despairing or enraging memories, explode your images of your past injuries, fill yourself up with your healing, present-time, Gold Sun energy, and get on with the work of living—and healing—in the present.

If these steps do not relieve your depression, and you still have no energy, please seek out a Bach Flower Remedy practitioner and ask for the remedies Mustard, Gorse, Sweet Chestnut, or Wild Rose. Often, a body experiencing depression will need bolstering before one can get back in and resume the work of cleansing and healing.

When your depression has cleared, please revisit the skills of aura definition, contract burning, and image destroying. See DESPAIR and SUICIDAL URGES, and the chapter called *Channelling Your Emotions.*

DESPAIR: Despair and despondency are signs of a long-ignored sadness that has become an unworkably prevalent emotional state. Any deep, unrelenting emotion is a call for awareness, and each emotion has a specific and almost magical healing property tucked inside it.

DESPAIR: *continued.*
Through channelling despair in the body like any other energy, we can finally see what it has been trying to tell us. See GRIEF, SADNESS, and SUICIDAL URGES, below, and the chapter called *Channelling Your Emotions.*

DISORIENTATION: Disoriented forgetfulness is usually a sign of being out of the body. Grounding and working through the beginning meditative processes in Part I will help to heal the body/spirit splits that can lead to disorientation. It is also a good idea to read the sections on KUNDALINI and KUNDALINI HEALING, below.
Special topic: If you are in your body and you are still disoriented, the room in your head may be too high. This would center your room directly behind your clairvoyant, vision-receiving sixth *chakra* (which is in the center of your forehead). Please destroy your room and create a new one, but this time anchor it below your eyes so that its ceiling is no higher than your eyebrows. This should help to center and ground you.

DIZZINESS: Dizziness can signal all sorts of medical imbalances that should be looked into; however, dizziness can also stem from being ungrounded, out of the body, and out of the room in the center of the head. Please read the chapters called *A Room of Your Own* and *Getting Grounded*, and the sections on KUNDALINI and KUNDALINI HEALING, below.

EARS: The ears are psychically connected to the clairaudient fifth *chakra*, and can sometimes pick up audible spiritual transmissions. These transmissions can take the form of ringing or tinnitus, chronic ear infections, a constant need to pop and clear the ears, or hearing voices. The psychic skill of clairaudience (hearing voices) is a difficult one to possess, and since it is one of the leading symptoms of schizophrenia, it is also a difficult one to share with health professionals.
   Without competent help or useful information, many clairaudients begin to perceive the voices they hear as directive—as if the information from the voices is their own, or God's, and should be acted upon. If an untrained clairaudient hooks up with unbalanced people or beings, and believes the perceived information to be an aspect of their own personality, chaos usually ensues. All clairaudients require psychic training, specifically in regard to separation and protection techniques. This book can be used by clairaudients to center and separate from disturbing or uncontrolled psychic receptions. Nearly everything in Parts I and III applies to clairaudients, as does RINGING IN THE EARS and INSANITY, below, and the chapter called *Burning Contracts.*

EMOTIONS: Emotions carry messages from the emotional body to the physical, mental, and spiritual bodies. Each emotion has its own purpose, voice, and character, along with specific healing information that can easily be accessed. The trick is not to express emotions all over the exterior world, or lock them away and ignore them as they fester, but to use them as healing energies. Please see the chapter called *Channelling Your Emotions*.

EXHILARATION: Though celebrated the world over as the emotion of choice, unending exhilaration brings as much trouble and imbalance as unending sadness, anger, fear, or grief. Exhilaration is especially damaging if it is courted and seduced into existence, and then imprisoned by people who want only to see the bright, up, happy, and good side of life. Sadness is ignored, fear is explained away, anger is shamed, and grief is repressed while all of the life is strangled out of the exhilaration.

In essence, the exhilaration is used as a drug--so that real life and true emotions can be skimmed over. Imbalances in any emotion bring about turmoil, but the dramas of exhilaration-mongers are often the most tragic, because they usually involve large groups of people.

Exhilarated, endlessly joyful people often draw many followers. They live an overwhelmingly seductive lie that says one can be happy and joyful at all times, as if that one emotion were enough. Then, when difficulties inevitably arise and personalities clash, and money gets tight, the group of happiness-addicts often cannibalize each other.

Happy-addicts have no idea about how to have or channel their "bad" emotions. The anger becomes unconscious, sneaky, passive-aggressive rage; the fear becomes anxiety and paranoia; the sadness becomes unmanageable depression and sleep disorders; and the grief seeks the death of the group—or of the exhilaration guru.

Like any real emotion, exhilaration has its honorable place in the pantheon of feelings. The trick is to see exhilaration as a part of the whole, and to accept it for what it is when it comes forward. Exhilaration has the vital role of letting people know that they have just completed a crucial (and often wrenching) series of learning experiences. If such a naturally joyous person tries to stay in his exhilaration, he will not have the emotional arsenal to enable him to go on to the next set of difficult and emotionally involved lessons.

Joy and exhilaration give people a moment to see themselves as wonderful, powerful, and at one with the universe. Then, they have to move on and get back to the real work that will lead inevitably back to the real joy. Healthy joy is meant to be as fleeting as healthy anger, grief, fear,

EXHILARATION: *continued.*
or any other emotional state. It was never meant to be imprisoned and used to gain prestige in an emotionally stunted world. Please see the chapters called *Anger and Forgiveness* and *Channelling Your Emotions.*

FEAR: All forms of fear are protective mechanisms that should never be ignored. Without fear, people would not survive. They would have no sense of self-preservation whatsoever. Fear, like any other emotion, contains vital information when it is simply allowed to be itself. Fear should neither be ignored nor pandered to, but channelled appropriately. Please see TERROR and PANIC ATTACKS, below, and the chapter called *Channelling Your Emotions.*

FURY: Fury is anger with fire, or anger getting an assist from the powerful energy of the first *chakra.* If used in the emotional work described in *Channelling Your Emotions,* fury can be extremely useful in creating real separations from old relationships and restrictive energy patterns. However, fury also signals a boundary violation that is life-threatening, and a generalized inability to protect the body or the energy field. As such, the living environment of a furious person needs to be looked at very carefully. It may have been time to leave such an environment a very long time ago.

Uncontrollable bouts of fury can also stem from organic causes and brain-chemical imbalances, so a visit to an acupuncturist, homeopath, or other energy-aware physician would be well-advised.

GOLD SUN: This is the eighth *chakra:* the symbol used to depict the unlimited amount of energy available to each person on the planet. The Gold Sun is used to re-dedicate one's energy after a healing, to bring the body and all the energy tools into conscious, present-time awareness, and to heal the body. Please see the chapter called *The Gold Sun Healing.*

GOLD SUN HEALING: Please see the chapter of the same name.

GRIEF: Grief is a beautiful, languid, and poetic emotion that helps us feel human. Spirit has no grief, because it sees no death and no loss. Spirit sees the continuum of all energy and all beings. Body, on the other hand, knows of loss. Humans experience death and sorrow; they can no longer touch or speak to the dead, yet they can still feel the embrace of a lost lover, or hear the laughter of a dead child. Bodies miss lost limbs and remember pain. Bodies live here, on the planet, and they experience the reality of injury, loss, separation, and death every day.

GRIEF: *continued.*

Grief is natural to a body, and channelling grief helps the body to mourn real injury and real loss. Spirit can't really understand grief, and the intellect likes to whisk it away in a whorl of explanations, but bodies know grief. Channelling grief--and honoring the reality of the body and the emotions--will help the intellect and the spirit integrate and mature. Please see SADNESS, below, and the chapter called *Channelling Your Emotions.*

GROUNDING: An energy technique that helps to center the spirit in the body by centering the body on the planet. Please see the chapters in Parts I and III on Grounding.

GROUNDING PROBLEMS: Difficulties in grounding are common in survivors of childhood sexual assault. Topics covered throughout this book aim to address the many possible reasons, and offer many possible solutions. Please see the chapters in Parts I and III on Grounding, plus the chapter on *Burning Contracts* and the special healing for the first *chakra* area in the chapter called *Advanced Imaging.*

GROUNDING RULES: Grounding is a primary step in this spiritual growth process, and with growth comes responsibility. Please see the sections on specific grounding rules in the chapters in Parts I and III on Grounding.

GROUNDING VACUUM: Grounding cords used for centering can be turned into energy vacuums used for cleansing. Grounding vacuums are discussed in the chapters in Parts I and III on Auras and Grounding.

HATRED: Hatred, or a complete aversion to a person, place, or situation is a sign of a chronic lack of clear boundaries, the presence of unintegrated shadow material, and possibly of life-threatening boundary violations. Hatred, like any fiery emotion, is difficult to repress or express in any rational way; however, when hatred is channelled and used in energy separations (such as destroying images or burning contracts), it offers tremendous strength, certainty, and resolve. Please do not express hatred in the world, or turn it on yourself; instead, see ANGER, above, and read the chapters called *Anger and Forgiveness*, and *Channelling Your Emotions.*

HEADACHES: Beyond all the physical reasons such as illness, hunger, electrolyte and chemical imbalances, or tumors, headaches can mean you're ungrounded and out of your body (see the chapter called *Getting Grounded*, and KUNDALINI, below). Headaches can also mean you're not in the room in your head (see the chapter called *A Room of Your Own*).

HEARING PROBLEMS: See EARS and CLAIRAUDIENCE, above.

INSANITY: Beyond the more mundane, chemical-imbalance-induced model of psychiatric disorder is the concept of spiritual imbalance. Psychiatric treatment modes do not even consider the possibility of clairaudience in schizophrenics, trance-mediumship and *kundalini* problems in aphasics and seizure-prone individuals, and second/third *chakra* breakdown in depressives.

One thing is certain: drug modalities and institutionalization have never proved worthy of the inexplicably hallowed place they hold in treatment of the disordered.

In my own bout with teenage depression and borderline schizophrenia, I found a wheat allergy, a severe niacin deficiency, an over-receptive fifth *chakra*, and a complete lack of grounding to be causal factors. When addressed intuitively, my symptoms subsided. I was able to heal in months two mental illnesses that essentially destroy entire lives in the western medical model.

Though psychiatric drugs may help patients to relieve symptoms enough to deal with their underlying imbalance, drug therapy is often seen as a curative rather than supportive measure. Many drug-therapy support groups exist to provide succinct disease identification and techniques for the alleviation of drug side effects, instead of uncovering the real issues that led to the psychiatric illness in the first place.

This is part of the legacy of western medicine, which is to find perfectly beautiful and properly spelled names for diseases without ever looking at the breakdown in life force that cause them. Holistic mind/body awareness is making inroads into modern medicine, but the spiritual/emotional aspects of disease are still a non-issue.

Don't misunderstand me: naming an illness is important, and western medicine triumphs in that regard, but after a while, being the bi-polar depressive in ward two, or the myocardial infarction on the table is limiting to the spirit. Knowing the name of a disease and treating its specific symptoms is only a first step in the journey, not the be-all and end-all of healing.

There are no simple cures for psychiatric disorders. Nutritional imbalances and psychic injuries, though, should always be explored in each case. In addition, teaching a psychiatrically disturbed person to ground, center, meditate, and heal their aura will be invaluable. I have never, ever healed an emotionally disturbed person without finding a seriously disordered energy body. Whatever the causal factors are in terms

INSANITY: *continued.*

of childhood memories or other trauma, the symptoms of mental-spiritual disturbances respond far better to nutritional and spiritual intervention than they ever will to drug therapies and institutionalization. Plus, once the symptoms have calmed down a bit, correct body care and competent spiritual grounding will help the person to more easily explore and heal whatever it was that caused them to leave the "normal" world in the first place. Drugs and institutional care cannot offer this same support.

Drugs and institutionalization also cannot offer--or touch--the idea of madness-as-spiritual-opening, which is nearly always the case. Such incredible energies; such fantastical visions; such violent motion--it's all seen as disarray and disease. What a fatal mistake.

My suggestion for emotional disorders in regard to this book is to go through it in its entirety, mentally replacing the term "childhood sexual assault" with whatever trauma seems to have caused the current imbalance. The work of revisiting the core split-inducer, and rebuilding the central foundation of the self--this is the essential work of all spiritual journeys.

I also recommend spending extra time and energy in Part III of the book, especially on the aura work and the auxiliary grounding techniques.

INSOMNIA: When a child can't or won't sleep, it is usually because she fears missing out on something. It is the same with adults. Sleeplessness that is not caused by health or environmental disturbances generally stems from a gnawing lack of completeness or closure in situations or relationships. The body can't relax and let go because the day isn't really finished. In instances of sleeplessness, it is always good to ask, "What is still undone?" as you ground and get centered. The issue will usually pop right up, and the techniques of image-releasing and contract burning will discharge energy from the issue.

In some cases, your sleeplessness may stem from a childhood memory of assault at night or in your bed. If this is so, please perform a number of rescues and be available to channel any emotions that come up (such as FURY, or TERROR). Please see SLEEPLESSNESS, below, and the chapters on *Destroying Images* and *Burning Contracts.*

Special topic: If your insomnia is of long duration, and you are edgy, uncentered and ungrounded after a spiritual experience, you may have blasting *kundalini* energy that needs to be brought back into your first *chakra.* Please see the KUNDALINI HEALING, below.

JOY: See EXHILARATION, above.

KUNDALINI: This is the Sanskrit word for the energy of the first *chakra*, which is a fiery red energy that sometimes blasts itself upwards into the other *chakras* during meditation, or in situations of immediate threat. Many spiritual practices encourage and manipulate these *kundalini* blasts, but if students are not advanced and centered, there can be difficulties. Please see the KUNDALINI HEALING, below.

KUNDALINI HEALING: When the energy of the first *chakra* blasts upwards, it does so to clean out the other *chakras* momentarily, or to lend power to the body in situations of immediate threat. *Kundalini* energy is the energy behind the fight-or-flight reaction, and the energy that allows 110-pound mothers to lift cars, trucks, or heavy machinery off of their children. It's powerful. *Kundalini* energy is also very damaging if it is left blasting for too long.

In many cases, molest victims will create disturbances in their grounding and *kundalini* energy by leaving their bodies frequently, and by using anger and rage inappropriately, both of which can detach the grounding cord and blast the *kundalini* upwards. This is often the only defense such victims have against brutality, or against people who come too close. The healing that follows will be useful in such cases, but the fundamental work in Parts I and II of this book should be mastered as well.

Too much *kundalini* can blast out the entire *chakra* system, burn holes in the aura, and shoot a person out of his body. If too much *kundalini* is in place for too long, the body may even be damaged.

Symptoms include dizziness and lack of appetite, insomnia, waking dreams or visions, photophobia, skin rashes, and tics and twitches that resemble St. Vitus' Dance. For specific help in calming a blasting *kundalini*, here is the **Blue Moon Healing**:

Caveat: I am not presupposing a knowledge of any technique in this book as we go into this healing. I strongly suggest going back to the very beginning if you haven't any experience of grounding, getting in your head, or defining your aura. Without these basic tools, you may not be able to keep your first *chakra* (or yourself) safe from *kundalini* rushes.

Sit in a straight-backed chair with your feet uncrossed and flat on the ground, and your hands uncrossed and upturned on your knees. Breathe normally and keep your eyes open. This will help to keep you centered in the present, whereas closing your eyes could make you feel a little dizzy.

KUNDALINI HEALING: *continued.*

Try to envision or get a feeling for the energy in your body and aura right now. It may be hot and fast-moving. It may have a red-orange color or a ringing sound. You may even be able to feel the energy as a blast of heat or fire. This is your first-*chakra* energy, or your *kundalini*.

Now, imagine a cool blue moon about a foot or two above your head. See its color and texture, feel its calm coolness, and attune yourself with its gentle, relaxing energy. Allow it to transmit its peacefulness to you as it bathes you in quiet blue moonlight.

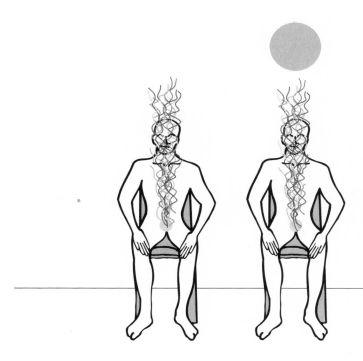

Envision your *kundalini* fire as a column that originates in your genitals and blasts up in a straight line through the center of your body and out the top of your head. The energy coming out of your head may be a flame, a snake ready to strike, or a flame-thrower. It may even look like fireworks. Sit as calmly as you can, while your blue moon shines above you.

KUNDALINI HEALING: *continued.*

When you can easily sense or envision the *kundalini* shaft and the blue moon (remember, these are both made up of your own energy, which means you are in charge of how they look and what they do), allow the blue moon to shine a shaft of light downwards, directly into the fire coming out of the top of your head. See or feel the shaft of blue light cooling and calming the fire, and pushing the fire before itself and back down into your body.

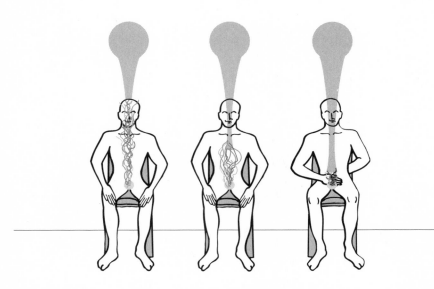

Feel the blue moon energy pushing the *kundalini* fire down into your head, down under your eyes, down into your jaw and throat, and down into your chest. Feel the calm coolness that has replaced the heat above your chest. Keep the blue energy moving, down through your sternum, and let it push the *kundalini* fire down under your solar plexus, down under your navel, and on down to your pubic bone. Feel the coolness in your body as the red-orange fire recedes.

Now, with the blue moon still shining down in a shaft, center the *kundalini* fire in your first *chakra* (a circular area of three-to-five inches in diameter, in the low-center of the vagina in women, and just above the testicles in men). Place your right hand on top of your pubic bone and your left hand at the base of your coccyx, and massage downwards as you envision holding the fiery energy in place with your hands. Watch as the energy begins to center itself and swirl inside your first *chakra*.

KUNDALINI HEALING: *continued.*

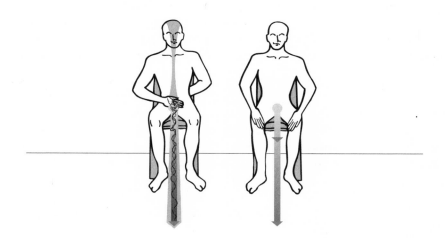

Ground yourself by allowing some of this fiery first-*chakra* energy to travel downwards to the center of the planet in a solid red-orange cord. Grounding will help to anchor your *kundalini* energy in your first *chakra* by providing real work and specific instructions for your once-blasting *kundalini* energy. Luckily, your first *chakra* energy will do anything you ask it to. All you have to do is communicate with it clearly. Once it knows what you want, your *kundalini* energy will settle in and stop blasting itself through your upper *chakras.*

Thank your blue moon and let it disappear. Allow the shaft of blue energy in your body to exit through your new first-*chakra* grounding cord. Grounding out this cool energy will further help to keep your first *chakra* calmed and centered.

Your work after a *kundalini* healing will be to maintain a constant awareness of your first *chakra*, and to bring healing and balance to your energy system as a whole. Please work through Part I of this book in its entirety, and consider looking into *The Garden's* companion book on the *chakras* (see back page for details). Stay grounded and in your head, please.

LIGHTHEADEDNESS: See DISORIENTATION and/or DIZZINESS, above.

PAIN: Pain is the body's way of signalling imbalance. Pain requires awareness and assistance if its message is to be deciphered. Running from,

PAIN: *continued.*

drugging, or ignoring pain heightens it, and can set the stage for serious illness. As pain is a message from the body, those with past spirit/body splits would do well to listen. Grounding the painful area is an excellent way to release the message within the discomfort. Please see the chapter called *Getting Grounded* for a specific pain-relieving exercise, and also see the special auric healing technique for chronic pain in the chapter called *Advanced Aura Reading and Definition.*

PANIC ATTACKS: Panic attacks are fear messages from deep within the subconscious--messages that have been suppressed or ignored for years or even decades. These fear energies are still quite usable--if somewhat urgently so, in emotional channelling sessions. Please see FEAR and TERROR, and the chapter called *Channelling Your Emotions.*

Panic attacks can cause (or stem from) organic imbalances, so a trip to the acupuncturist or homeopath would be well-advised. Also, the Bach Flower remedies Rock Rose, Aspen, Cherry Plum, or Rescue Remedy will help to balance and heal you.

RAGE: Rage is anger with *kundalini* fire attached. It is not going to let anyone tell it what to do, where to go, how to feel, or how to live. Rage is a wonderful healing energy when channelled into separation work, but a pretty nasty energy when dumped onto others or repressed. Repressed rage often turns into suicidal feelings (see SUICIDAL URGES, below), but even then, it can still be channelled and used in healing and self-awareness. Please see ANGER and FURY, above, and the chapters *Anger and Forgiveness* and *Channelling Your Emotions.*

REPRODUCTIVE DISEASE: Imbalances of the reproductive organs are common in survivors of childhood sexual assault, as are lower back problems, colon and bowel disturbances, and digestive tract diseases. With our understanding of the energy transfer that occurs during sexual contact, we can begin to see that the foreign energy of the assault experience often lodges itself inside our bodies, where it can cause not only spiritual pain, but physical pain as well. Techniques throughout this book offer relief from trapped, abusive energies. Please see all the chapters on grounding, the aura, and the destruction of images.

RINGING IN THE EARS: Ringing or tinnitus can have physical origins such as electrical imbalances or misplaced vertebra. Ringing can even be caused by metal dental fillings that receive radio or television transmissions; however, ringing in the ears can be a sign that spiritual

RINGING IN THE EARS: *continued.*
communication is being received and translated by the fifth, or throat *chakra*. Please see EARS and CLAIRAUDIENCE, above.

ROOM IN THE HEAD: A meditative sanctuary created right behind the eyes, specifically for people who have maintained a long-standing spirit/body split. Please see the chapter called *A Room of Your Own.*

If staying in the room in your head is difficult, please make sure it is centered below your sixth *chakra* (see DISORIENTATION and DIZZINESS, above). Also, see that your Sentry and aura boundary systems are strong enough to allow you some spiritual privacy (see the chapter called *Defining Your Personal Territory,* and the chapters on Imaging).

SADNESS: Sadness is a beautiful watery energy that can bring stability to an overwrought emotional body. Sadness asks us to slow down, feel the losses of life, and mourn them properly; however, sadness can become chronic when it is ignored or suppressed. Please see CRYING and DESPAIR, above, and the chapter called *Channelling Your Emotions.*

SCHIZOPHRENIA: An incurable psychiatric disorder in the western medical model, often linked to the misunderstood fifth-*chakra* ability of clairaudience, or hearing voices.

Uncontrolled clairaudience is curable through the spiritual healing techniques taught throughout this book--especially grounding, creating a room in the head, and burning contracts. Please see EARS and INSANITY, above.

SLEEPLESSNESS: After all the physical causes are examined and discarded, sleeplessness can be seen as an unwillingness to doze off while things are undone and issues are unresolved. Sleeplessness can be seen as a good thing if it signals a heightened awareness that will not allow one to go unconscious any longer; however, a sleepless body needs help.

Please see INSOMNIA, above, and all the chapters on Images. The destruction of images can help to release and heal unfinished and unsettling energy from relationships and situations, as can the burning of relationship contracts. Please see the chapter called *Burning Contracts.*

SPACINESS: A sign of imbalance in grounding, or in the *chakra* system. Please see DISORIENTATION and DIZZINESS, above.

STOMACH PAIN: Fleeting stomach pain can often be a signal from your aura about unhealthy energy in your area. Often, a beefed-up aura boundary and a stronger Sentry are called for when your body becomes

STOMACH PAIN: *continued.*
involved in your spiritual defense mechanisms. If your stomach distress is of a very long duration, and includes hiatus hernias, ulcers, or colon and bowel distress, you may have a chronic case of poor auric protection.

Please pay specific attention to the Sentry and aura work throughout this book, and check in on the chapters called *Advanced Aura Definition* and *Advanced Imaging*. Chronic stomach pain can also be a sign of a damaged third *chakra*. This topic is covered fully in *The Garden's* companion book on the *chakras* (see back page for details).

SUICIDAL URGES: Often a sign of repressed anger, rage, and fury, suicidal urges have a power that can easily overwhelm their owner—not to mention their owner's friends, family, support group, or therapist (no kidding!); however, when they can be re-dedicated and channelled, suicidal urges can bring complete certainty to long-standing emotional confusions, or muddled and obscure relationships. Suicidal urges can also be channelled into swift and decisive action in situations where one might otherwise be paralyzed by indecision.

The energy of suicide requires a death, *but not the death of the central being!* Suicidal feelings say, "Give me liberty, or give me death!" If you ask your suicidal urge what you should kill, it will tell you specifically: "This weakness, this relationship, these flashbacks, this poverty, this feeling of worthlessness, this discomfort in the world, this depression, this situation...." It will tell you what part of your life is unlivable, and if you let it, your suicidal urge will help you kill off the life aspect that is tormenting you. In essence, you can channel your suicidal feelings into your image destroying, your contract burning, and your separation processes. Your suicidal energy will help you liberate yourself on an energy level--and this inner liberation will help you become free in the world.

This is a repetition of the information in the chapter on emotional channelling, but it bears repeating if you have come to this topic in terror of your own suicidal urges: nothing exists in your life or your psyche unless it is meant to be there. All parts of you have healing attributes *and* destructive attributes. Each illness, wellness, triumph, and catastrophe have their place in your wholeness; each will move you along in consciousness if you will only be aware of their message, and of the necessity of their presence. Everything in your psyche has been placed there specifically, by you, or by your choices in life. Every part of you is a double-edged sword that can protect and heal you, or slice you to bits. Suicidal urges are no exception to this rule.

SUICIDAL URGES: *continued.*

Suicidal urges are a semi-regular and even daily occurrence for many survivors of childhood trauma. This means they are necessary to survivors of childhood trauma. Why? Because sometimes, suicidal feelings are the only ones that offer any hope of escape at all--they can be very comforting in that way. They offer an end to the drama, and the possibility of a rest; however, we know that expressing suicidal urges will end our lives, while repressing them will drive us out of our minds and our bodies. But, as with the channelling of any other strong emotional state, the channelling of suicidal urges can bring about remarkable healing changes, and along with them, a cessation of uncontrollable suicidal mood swings. When suicidal urges are neither expressed nor repressed, but *channelled* instead, their exquisite arsenal can be used to help us kill off old, unworkable aspects of our lives.

The current model of talking the suicidal urge away with beautiful tales of the inherent meaning of life--or drugging it to sleep--does not in any way address its reality. Suicidal urges require *death*, and often violent death at that. All the sweetness and light in the world are a total lie to the suicidal urge; peppiness only serves to degrade and ignore the brilliant, integral message of the urge.

Suicide says it will have freedom or cease to exist. It is that serious about the issues it has come to address. Suicide does not ask for lithium or Prozac, nor does it want to be lulled by pretty songs. *It wants to kill.* If we use its energy to blast images to smithereens, and torch contracts in huge pyres, it will have its kill, and it will abate as it is meant to.

In a healthy system, emotions are fleeting. They come, they speak, they conquer the issue, and they go. Even suicidal urges, if properly channelled, will go away until another death is required (if you maintain emotional awareness, such requirements tend to arise less frequently).

In our society, though, emotions are tragically misunderstood. We label each emotion as positive or negative. We strangle all the life out of the positive ones by trying to have them at all times, no matter what is happening in our lives. We stuff and ignore the negative ones, or bury them in a pile of pseudo-spiritual psychobabble, and we go quietly insane in the process. Then we wonder why we can't make decisions, why our lives have no meaning, and why we feel completely powerless— disconnected from our body *and* our spirit.

Let's go over this one again: true wellness is *wholeness*, not perfection. True wellness includes the body and all its wisdom, the mind and all its data, the spirit and all its information, and the emotions and all their

SUICIDAL URGES: *continued.*

messages. Balance comes when all four parts of the quaternity are working together. It's not easy to balance mind, spirit, body, and emotion; it's imperative.

Please, if you have experienced suicidal urges in your life, go back and re-read the chapters called *Anger and Forgiveness* and *Channelling Your Emotions*, but remember that calling up any emotion to practice channelling is counterfeit.

If you are feeling suicidal right now, your emotions are signalling that it is time for you to channel. If you are just reading this topic for fun, and you are not currently experiencing suicidal urges, DO NOT CHANNEL THEM! If you're alive in today's culture, you already have too much practice in playing with, devaluing, and faking your emotions. Don't do it now. Your emotions have had enough of that nonsense.

As with other deep emotional states, suicidal urges may call for a balancing Bach Flower Remedy. I've had excellent and long-lasting results with the remedies Cherry Plum, Gorse, Mustard, Sweet Chestnut, Star of Bethlehem, and Walnut.

TERROR: Terror is fear gone wild, and a sign that normal levels of fear have been long-ignored and belittled. This hot, intense, get-me-the-hell-out-of-here energy signals a tremendous life-threatening danger in the inner or outer environment. As such, terror must be dealt with immediately, and not coddled or reasoned back into shallower, more manageable levels of fear and trepidation.

As with any strong emotion, an underlying physical imbalance may be at cause. A trip to the acupuncturist is well-advised; however, channelling the emotion of terror will often light up the root cause more effectively. Please see ANXIETY, FEAR, and PANIC ATTACKS, above, and the chapter called *Channelling Your Emotions.*

THIRD EYE: Also known as the sixth *chakra*, the third eye is the energy center of clairvoyance and discernment. Please see VISIONS, below.

THROAT *CHAKRA*: Also known as the fifth *chakra*, the throat is the energy center of communication, clairaudience, commitment, and the ability to change. Please see EARS and RINGING IN THE EARS, above.

VICTIMIZATION: This is the powerful and societally approved idea that if something bad happens to you, you will be scarred, damaged, and crippled for the rest of your natural life. The realization of victimization must come up in any real healing journey, but it is simply one step in a

VICTIMIZATION: *continued.*

longer and more important series of realizations. Please see the chapters called *A Room of Your Own, Defining Your Personal Territory,* and *Anger and Forgiveness.*

VISIONS: Visions are signs of activity in your sixth *chakra,* or third eye. If the visions are reasonably connected to your life, enjoy them. If they are unconnected and confusing or disturbing, please read on: if you have created a room in your head, and the visions started soon after, you have probably placed your room too high. If so, you are sitting behind your clairvoyant, vision-receiving sixth *chakra* (which is in the center of your forehead), instead of behind your eyes. Please destroy your room and create a new one with the ceiling no higher than your eyebrows.

WEEPINESS: See CRYING, DESPAIR, and SADNESS, above.

SUGGESTED FURTHER READING

HEALTH SUPPORT

Mechthild Scheffer. *Bach Flower Therapy: Theory and Practice*. Rochester, Vermont: Healing Arts Press, 1988.

Caroline Myss. *Why People Don't Heal*. Audiotape: Sounds True, 1994. Boulder, CO. (800) 333-9185.

Barry Sears & Bill Lawren. *Enter the Zone*. New York: Regan Books, 1995.

SPIRITUAL GUIDANCE

R.L. Wing. *The I Ching Workbook*. New York: Doubleday, 1979.

Shakti Gawain. *The Path of Transformation*. Mill Valley, CA: Nataraj, 1993.

PSYCHOLOGICAL SUPPORT

Lewis Engel & Tom Ferguson. *Hidden Guilt*. New York: Pocket Books, 1990.

Susan Jeffers. *Feel the Fear and Do it Anyway*. New York: Harcourt Brace, 1987.

Robert Johnson. *He: Understanding Masculine Psychology* and *She: Understanding Feminine Psychology*. New York: Harper Perennial, 1977 (both titles).

James Hillman & Michael Ventura. *We've Had a Hundred Years of Psychotherapy, and the World's Getting Worse*. San Francisco: Harper, 1992.

James Hillman. *The Soul's Code: In Search of Character & Calling*. New York: Random, 1996.

MYTHOLOGICAL UNDERSTANDING

Robert Bly. *A Little Book on the Human Shadow*. San Francisco: Harper, 1988.

Robert Bly. *Iron John*. New York: Vintage Books, 1990.

Robert Bly. *The Sibling Society*. New York: Addison-Wesley, 1996.

Michael Meade. *Men and the Water of Life*. San Francisco: Harper, 1993.

Clarissa Pinkola Estes. *Women Who Run With the Wolves*. New York: Ballantine, 1992.

Karla McLaren has studied spiritual healing for twenty-six years, and written professionally for eighteen. Never a party psychic, Karla has centered her practice on survivors of dissociative trauma, and on the spiritual aspects of mental-emotional (as opposed to physical) illness. Karla lives with her excellent husband and gargantuan son in the foothills of the Sierra Nevada mountains, where she tutors dyslexics and leads an *a cappella* soul/gospel choir.

ACKNOWLEDGEMENTS

I'm glad I've written four more books; eventually, I'll be able to thank everyone I've ever met. I am grateful to my husband Ron for making this work imperative; to my husband Eric for making it seem possible; and to my husband and best friend Tino for making it such fun. Much gratitude to Mic and Kath for offering help three years ago, and not being surprised at the lapse between offer and acceptance. Thank you Sarah Stone, Kimberly Haskell, Jan Weisberg, Ken Carper, Pennie Austin, Cindy Brewer, Mic Harper, Kara Hubbard, Tony Smith, Betty Holder, Anita Mukai, Robert Madsen, Jennifer Hubbard, and Christian Damek. Artful thanks to Ann Koziol for the exquisite cover painting; to Kath Christensen for guiding artistic wisdom; and to Suzan Still for insightful editing.

For my early spiritual training, thank you Marshall, Quinta, Brocke, and Kyia Lever, and thank you Lewis Bostwick. To the writers of all the books on my suggested reading list: thank you for your work. You made much-needed healing affordable, and you, unknowingly, supported me in the work I needed to do. Your words were and are magic, your books are my companions, and your thoughts set me free. Thank you.

To my molester: I wish I had been handed a more palatable mission, but the fact is, your twisted initiation pulled my spirit out of this life and kept most of me out of my family, out of the horror of public school and adolescence, and out of the abuses I once considered normal. In my Garden, I found a split-off spirit who had never been amended by the inanities of day-to-day living. Once I was back together, I had the almost untouched energy, wisdom, and spiritual certainty of a child--along with the knowledge, experience, and endurance of an adult who'd seen just about everything. This was the gift inside the chaos and terror.

You and I, we were once a part of the same energy. I'm free now, but the business of freedom is freeing others. I pray that you can, in this life or the next, free yourself from the self-made dungeon of the perpetrator. Your ability to bring about deep change, and your understanding of the depth of loneliness and need in others is vital in a world as troubled and unconscious as ours. The trick now is to cleanse and redirect your energy; the trick is to turn yourself around. That's why you're alive; that's why we're all alive. You made some bad-crazy decisions, and you hurt many children unnecessarily, but you can make amends, stop your repugnant behaviors, and become a functional member of the human race. My prayers are forever with you.

DID YOU BORROW THIS BOOK?

You can purchase your own copy directly from Laughing Tree Press. Please send a check or money order for $13.00 ($11.00 plus $2.00 postage). California residents, please send a total of $13.80 to account for sales tax. Address your order to:

Laughing Tree Press
Post Office Box 1155
Columbia, CA 95310-1155
(209) 533-1127

A discount of $1.50 per book is available on retail bulk orders of five or more copies.

DO YOU WANT TO GO FURTHER?

This book has a companion volume for those of you who would like to go further into the spiritual aspects of childhood sexual assault.

FURTHER INTO THE GARDEN: *Discovering Your Chakras* looks at the subtler energetic world of the *chakras* in detail, through the eight central *chakras*, and through the *chakras* of the hands and the feet.

Though this *chakra* work is invaluable in many cases, it is not necessary work for everyone, thank goodness. If you would like to delve more deeply into spiritual study, or if your molest journey has included severe post-traumatic emotional imbalance, systemic or auto-immune illness, or reproductive disease, you may find this book of great value.

FURTHER INTO THE GARDEN will not be available in bookstores, because it is not a stand-alone book. It assumes a facility with all the energy work you learned in REBUILDING THE GARDEN, and takes off from there. It is meant only for readers of this first book. Also, in order to keep costs down, it has been packaged in a simpler format.

If you would like to order FURTHER INTO THE GARDEN: *Discovering Your Chakras,* it will be available in October, 1997. Please send a check or money order for $9.00 ($7.00 plus $2.00 postage). California residents, please send a total of $9.50 to account for sales tax. Address your order to:

Laughing Tree Press
Post Office Box 1155
Columbia, CA 95310-1155

If you would like a synopsis or more information before ordering, please send a stamped, self-addressed envelope to the same address.